The
JEALOUS POTTER

Maya. *Codex de Dresde,* p. 74.

CLAUDE LÉVI-STRAUSS

The
JEALOUS POTTER

Translated by Bénédicte Chorier

The University of Chicago Press
Chicago and London

Claude Lévi-Strauss is professor emeritus at the Collège de France. His previous books published in translation by the University of Chicago Press include *The Savage Mind*; *Structural Anthropology*, volume 2; *The Raw and the Cooked*; and *From Honey to Ashes*.

The University of Chicago Press, Chicago 60637
The University of Chicago Press, Ltd., London

© 1988 by The University of Chicago
All rights reserved. Published 1988
Printed in the United States of America

97 96 95 94 93 92 91 90 89 88   5 4 3 2 1

This book was originally published in Paris under the title *La potière jalouse,*
© Librairie Plon, 1985.

Library of Congress Cataloging-in-Publication Data

Lévi-Strauss, Claude.
  [Potière jalouse. English]
  The jealous potter / Claude Lévi-Strauss : translated by Bénédicte
Chorier.
      p.   cm.
  Translation of: La potière jalouse.
  Bibliography: p.
  ISBN 0-226-47480-1.   ISBN 0-226-47482-8 (pbk.)
  1. Indians—Religion and mythology.   2. Pottery—Mythology.
3. Indians—Folklore.   4. Psychoanalysis and folklore.
5. Mythology—Psychological aspects.   6. Tales—Structural analysis.
I. Title.
E59.R38L63   1988
398.2'08997—dc19   87-30076
                                                    CIP

Contents

*

Contents

Contents

The
JEALOUS POTTER

*

For the race of men was living upon the earth free from evils, troublesome toil, and painful disease, which bring death to men. But the woman, removing the great lid of the jar with her hands, scattered them, and brought about baneful sorrows for men.

Hesiod, *Works and Days*

Introduction

Personality traits linked to the practice of a trade. European examples. In the absence of professional specialization, these links follow other criteria. European beliefs leave out the potter. Possible explanations for this gap, which the present book will attempt to fill. Enumeration of the issues under study.

*

Returning by ship from the United States in 1947, I sometimes conversed on the promenade deck with a French orchestra conductor who had just given a series of concerts in New York. One day he told me that in the course of his career he had observed that the personality of a musician is often in harmony with the one evoked by the timbre and technique of his instrument; to get along well with his orchestra, a conductor has to take that into account. Thus, he added, in whatever country he might be, he could expect the oboist to be prim and touchy, the trombonist to be expansive, jovial, and good-natured.

I am always struck by statements that establish a link between realms otherwise unlikely to be associated. Popular thought has always strived to discover such analogies—a mental activity in which we will recognize one of the prime impulses of myth creation.

In short, my conductor was reviving, in his own field, some old and widespread beliefs that there is a homology between two systems: that of professional occupations and that of temperaments. Even today one can wonder whether these beliefs are totally arbitrary or whether they may not be based to some degree on experience and observation.

Nearly a century ago Sébillot broached this topic. His book, *Légendes et curiosités des métiers,* lists basic personality traits traditionally associated with the practice of various crafts. These traits are of three kinds. First, the physical aspect: perhaps because they worked in a sitting or squatting position, weavers and tailors were depicted as dwarfs or cripples. Tales from Brittany are apt to depict the tailor as a hunchback afflicted with crossed eyes and a red mop of hair. Butchers, for their part, were reported to be strong and healthy fellows.

Trades were also differentiated according to moral criteria. Almost unanimously, old European folklore brands weavers, tailors, and millers as thieves who pilfer the raw materials their patrons give them—yarn, cloth, or grain—before returning them in the form of yards of cloth, clothing, or flour. Whereas these three professions are reputed to cheat on the quantity of products, pastry cooks—who hold a reputation as panderers, if not procurers—are believed to offer for sale goods of dubious quality under an attractive appearance.

Finally, distinctive psychological traits are attributed to each category of craftsman: tailors are braggarts and cowards but are also sly and lucky, like shoemakers, who, in their turn, are pranksters, merrymakers, and ribalds; butchers are boisterous and arrogant; blacksmiths, vain; lumberjacks, rude and unpleasant; barbers, chatty; house-painters, bibulous and always cheerful; and so on.

An old saying, quoted by Sébillot, epitomizes these beliefs and introduces a few variants: "Were there a hundred priests who did not love to eat, a hundred tailors who were not merry, a hundred shoemakers who were not liars, a hundred weavers who were not swindlers, a hundred blacksmiths who were not thirsty, a hundred old women who were not chatterboxes, there would be no fear in crowning the king."

To explain the English phrase "As mad as a hatter," mental disorders provoked by chemicals used in processing fur have been cited. Whether this is a rationalization or not, it is clear that, in all these cases, popular thought, while claiming to be based on experience, is also bringing into play various processes of symbolic equivalence that belong to the metaphorical realm. The actual starting point is not always easy to trace. According to Montaigne, "the Greeks decried women weavers as being hotter than other women: because of the sedentary trade they perform, without much bodily exercise." He himself, however, was of a different opinion; he attributed their temperament to "the joggling that their work gives them," that is, to the movement of their legs at the pedals of the loom. Pre–Columbian Americans did not know the pedal loom, but the same connection between weaving and lewdness was made by the Aztecs and embodied in their moon goddess, Tlazolteotl, and Ixchel, the Mayan goddess of women weavers, presided over pregnancy. In their myths the western Canadian Bella Coola assigned this function to carpenters. The Tzotzil Indians of southern Mexico, akin to the Maya, seem to have shared the Aztec's ideas but applied them to an earlier phase of the textile industry: at the winter solstice, grandmothers gave young women yarn-spinning lessons in order to encourage them to be good sexual partners for their husbands.

In the societies that anthropologists study, professions are much less highly specialized than they have been in Europe, the East, and the Far East for hundreds, if not thousands, of years. However, these societies exhibit the same inclination to establish correspondences, though between different categories. For them, physical appearances, together with temperaments, are associated with clan membership, assumed geographical origins, or places of residence. In the Torres Straits between Australia and New Guinea, islanders were grouped into clans bearing animal names; they believed in the existence of physical and moral resemblances between the members of a clan and its eponymous animal. In North America the Ojibwa believed that the members of the clan of the Fish, often beardless and bald, lived to be very old; that those of the clan of the Bear had long, thick black hair, which never turned white with age, and an irascible, fierce temperament; and that the people of the clan of the Crane were noted for their sonorous voices and made good orators. In the southeastern United States, the Creek also characterized clans according to the habits of their eponymous animals or to the specific geography of their places of residence. Thus, even in societies that, for lack of specialized professions, could not associate occupations with distinct social species, people would perceive themselves, or be perceived, as belonging to specific groups, and these groups were constituted on the basis of models in nature.

In South America—a part of the world that will be of particular interest to us—several peoples, mainly of the Carib linguistic family, give animal names to foreigners and assign them corresponding physical traits, personalities, and behaviors. The Toad people have long legs and fat bellies; the Howler Monkeys are bearded; and so on. Within the Carib family, the Waiwai (to be discussed below, pp. 94–95, 124–25), explain differences between animal species, between animals and humans, and between the various tribes by an elaborate system of combinations and blendings. In the beginning a small number of beings, animals-to-be, got married to each other or to future humans. At first all these beings could hardly be distinguished from one another. Matings between potential animals, between potential animals and potential humans, or between the latter only gave rise to more and more highly differentiated species. This continued until all the human and animal species—spread out on the table, as it were, in the manner of a game of solitaire—offered the image, finally complete, of the great game of creation. They analyze and discuss each stage of this genesis in order to justify the particular traits and distinctive habits of each species and the correspondences in behavior and temperament between each human group and its pedigree. The mating of male quadrupeds with female vultures produced sedentary Indians; between male opossums and female humans, Indian hunters of large fowl. Male coatis and female vultures produced foreign tribes. Among the latter, those born of male macaws and female vultures were stronger than the Waiwai. A few male agoutis begot Indians who were not only foreigners but wild and cruel people as well.

Such theories, which could be called evolutionist, are fairly common in South America, as Tastevin pointed out in his work on the Cashinawa (Indians from the upper Juruá, whom I will often discuss): "In contrast to [Herbert] Spencer, [they] consider that animals are descended from humans, instead of the other way around" (Tastevin 1926: 163). The same notion is prevalent among the Guarayo of the Rio Madre de Dios. According to them, some of the species considered most noxious derive directly from humans. Others evolved from humans through a series of intermediate forms: the tortoise from the monkey, the monkey from man. The tapir and the agouti stem from plant species. Conversely, in the northernmost part of Brazil, the Surára say that the tapir is a former coatá monkey who, after falling from a tree, failed to climb back up again, and for them wild pigs used to be cuxiú monkeys.

The twenty or so tribes of the Uaupés Basin, members of the Tucano linguistic family, interact in very specific ways. First, any member of a given clan can marry only within a clan of equal rank in another tribe. Also, each tribe believes itself to be descended from an animal ancestor, some of whose distinctive features it retains. To one of these tribes, for instance, tapirs are "fathers-in-law"; white-lipped peccaries and pacas are two kinds of "foreign brides"; agoutis are "sons-in-law." All these animals speak dialects that reflect their place within the network of intertribal alliances: the tapir speak Tukano, the paca speaks Pira-Tapuya, etc. Characteristics in the natural realm and the social realm reflect one another; indeed, if human groups show animal traits, these traits correspond less to objective properties than to what might be seen as philosophical and moral values. The Tukano classify animals according to habitat, mode of locomotion, color, and smell. The first two criteria pertain to experience; the others refer to symbolic values. Animals pass on their empirical characteristics to the human groups who consider them to be their ancestors; conversely, the human groups apply their systems of values and their categories to the animal realm.

In this respect, classifications according to smell are particularly interesting. Furthermore, they are not limited to America; one need think only of the smell-calendar of the Andaman islanders. According to the Desana in the Uaupés area, smell can be absent or present, pleasant or unpleasant. The author whose ob-

7

servations I quote adds that "the concept of smell is not limited to plain sensory experience. It includes what might be called an 'air,' a vague sense of attraction, repulsion, or fear. The Desana make that clear when saying that smells are not perceived through the nose but constitute a kind of communication which involves the whole body" (Reichel-Dolmatoff 1978: 285–86).

Again in South America, another system of classification by smell has been extensively described and analyzed (here the word "smell" is intended to mean more than "olfactory sensation"). It is found in a group belonging to the Gé linguistic family, the Suya, who differ from the Tukano in all respects. These Indians not only assign distinctive attributes to the inhabitants of the long houses that make up their village—fine and straight-haired people, resembling whites; people with beautiful raven-black hair; tall people; extremely active people; people who have a special relationship with rain; etc.—but also classify animal and vegetable species and humans (themselves grouped by sex, age, and political function) according to a fourfold system of smells. The researcher translates these four categories as "strong and gamey," "pungent," "bland," and "rotten." These classes of smells do correspond not so much to sensory categories as to moral values. (After all, don't we say, almost always figuratively, that someone "exudes an odor of sanctity"[1] and, referring to a situation, that "It stinks"?) As the same author writes:

> Odor may be less a mode of "objective" olfactory classification than a way of expressing power, force, or dangerousness. . . . Terms that refer to odor in the olfactory sense . . . have a variety of referents relating to qualities, states, and olfactory stimulation at the same time. [Thus,] odor pertains to the social as well as the natural realms. [Seeger 1981: 92–93]

1. I.e., "He is in a state of spiritual perfection." A reference to the pleasant smell allegedly exuded by saints after their death. Hence, also, "He enjoys a good reputation."—Trans.

8

Other South American peoples classify their clans or those of their neighbors according to more or less imaginary linguistic features: as deaf, mute, or stuttering or as talking too loud, too fast, in a pleasant tone, or with disrespect. The Sikuani of the llanos of Venezuela, attribute an abundance of nasal vowels to their neighbors, the Saliva, who, according to their myths, took refuge in an earth-oven during the flood, whereas they themselves, who managed to stay afloat on a raft, possess an abundance of oral vowels. The same opposition between dark and light phonemes is found in Australia, where the Yalbiri, or Lander Walbiri, are regarded as speaking "high" or "clear," that is, with voiceless consonants, whereas other groups speak in a "heavy, weighty" manner.

In his own way Sébillot shows that in our societies, also, there was, and maybe still is, a tendency to consider social categories as natural species. At the same time, however, a problem arises: over thirty trades are listed by him, but among them there is no mention of the potter. Yet pottery and weaving rank among civilization's greatest arts. For thousands of years, pottery in various forms—as glazed or unglazed wares, faïence, stoneware, porcelain—has been in every home, humble or aristocratic. Ancient Egyptians even went so far as to use "my pots" to mean "my belongings"; and the French, when talking about paying for damages of whatever kind, always say they are "paying for the broken pots."

How can we explain this omission? Is the author's documentation in fact incomplete, or must we assume that potters, male or female, had no particular place in the inventory of professional idiosyncrasies? Given the scope of Sébillot's knowledge and his scrupulous exactness, it is highly unlikely that he overlooked available information. To support the first hypothesis, then, two sorts of considerations come to mind.

First, in traditional European societies, pottery was often practiced by a group instead of by isolated individuals. There were families of potters, and everyone put a hand to the wheel, so to speak. Or, again, a potters' workshop, sometimes a group of workshops, would select a spot outside the village, close to the clay deposits necessary to their trade. In such cases, potters formed a small society distinct from the village community; they did not embody a typical, personalized function within that community. One went to the blacksmith's, the shoemaker's, the saddler's to have an article mended or to order a new one; not so to the potter's. The potter took his products to the market or the fair or left them with a retailer. In their day-to-day activities, people did not come into close contact with him.

Second, one might conjecture that, in contrast to ancient China, where potters and blacksmiths were on an almost equal footing, popular European thought viewed the potter's work as a paler version of the smith's art. The latter would then become the sole repository of the magical and mystical values that—as the American data prove—might also have been conferred on pottery. Smithing and pottery are the two great arts of fire; however, one digs deeper for ore than for clay, metal requires higher temperatures, and, on the whole, when compared to the smith's, the potter's work looks far from heroic.

Elsewhere in the world, pottery and smithing are frequently associated. African ethnic groups often specialize in some craft, recalling castes in this respect; some of them are known for practicing both pottery and smithing. There are also endogamous castes, in which men are smiths and women are potters. Among certain populations of northern Asia the smith and the potter, who handle material substances, are together opposed to the shaman, who manipulates a spiritual substance.

Southern Asia provides additional support for this idea. The proto-Indochinese mythology of central Vietnam gives a prominent place to the goatsucker,[2] both as a smith-bird, at the service

2. The goatsucker belongs to the same family as the nighthawk and whippoorwill.—Trans.

of thunder, and as a rice-grower; he knows how to reap good crops and how to fill his belly, which is why he is called "the one who eats his fill." We will also see that South American myths connect the goatsucker with the origin of potter's clay.

In short, proto-Indochinese myths elevate the goatsucker, so to speak, from the realm of pottery to that of metalwork; at the same time, as we will observe in South American myths, its characteristic greediness takes on positive rather than negative connotations. However, it is not without caution that I submit this interpretation. For if one adopts the explanations given by some ethnographers, namely, that the mountain people of Vietnam represent the goatsucker as a blacksmith only because its cry evokes the pounding of the hammer on iron, then one need not have recourse to any other considerations.

The forest and savanna people of tropical America, who are the main focus of this book, knew nothing of working metals. Their use of fire was limited to cooking and pottery. This may be why the notion of a cosmic struggle, still unattached to any specific representation, was associated with pottery, as a kind of prefiguration of the smith who steals fire from the gods to put it in the service of mankind.

In the four volumes of *Mythologiques* I have shown that, in America, what is at stake in this struggle between the people Above and the people Below is cooking fire. We shall now see that, for these Indians, potter's clay, which has to be "cooked" and which therefore also stands in need of fire, is at stake in another struggle, this time between a celestial people and an aquatic or subterranean people. The humans are passive witnesses of this conflict and happen to profit from it. In another version, in meeting the people of the water, humans are granted the knowledge of pottery, but on certain conditions and not without risk to themselves.

The notion that the potter, along with the products of his or her industry, mediates between two powers—the celestial opposed to the terrestrial, the aquatic, or the chthonic—is not restricted to American cosmogony. I shall limit myself to an example from an-

11

cient Japanese mythology, which I choose because it rests on a set of beliefs and representations that might well have left traces on both sides of the Pacific.

In the *Nihongi,* Emperor Jimmu Tenno, first human in a line of divine origin, left Kyushu to conquer Yamato. One night he had a dream: a celestial god promised that he would be victorious if he used clay taken from the top of Mount Kagu—located halfway between the world Above and the world Below—to make eighty bowls and an equal number of jars, in which he should offer a sacrifice to the gods of heaven and earth. But one never procures potter's clay without trouble, as American myths will confirm. Highwaymen (i.e., enemy peoples) were blocking the road to the mountain. Two of the emperor's companions dressed up as a peasant couple: the highwaymen did not bother to stop them. They brought back the clay, and the emperor himself made the prescribed number of jars and bowls. He sacrificed to the gods of heaven and earth near the source of a river. Divinatory tests confirmed the god's promise. These rites are of particular interest to the Americanist, for they bear a peculiar resemblance to so-called "poison fishing," or fishing with drugs, found in both South America and Southeast Asia.

My purpose, however, is not to undertake a worldwide comparative study of the ideology of pottery. This book, devoted to the myths of the Americas, will pose and try to resolve three problems, which I list here not in the order in which they make their appearance in the book but in the order of their increasing scope. One problem pertains to ethnography; I shall try to highlight analogies of structure and content between myths from widely distant areas: southern California and, in the other hemisphere, the eastern piedmont of the Andes, from the Jivaro in the north to the Chaco tribes in the south, passing by way of the Campa, the Machiguenga, and the Tacana. It is as though, in the two Americas, one could spot along the mountains an ancient trail, which here and there left vestiges of the same beliefs and representations. Another problem is the internal logic of myths. This was first discussed in a course I taught at the Collège de France in 1964–65 (see *Paroles Données,* pp. 109–11), and it is the starting point of this book. I will focus on a very localized myth, one that at first sight seems to associate completely random elements at whim. Step by step I will examine the observations, empirical deductions, analytic and synthetic judgments, and the explicit and implicit thinking that account for this association. The third problem is presented in the last chapters, which deal with mythic thought in general and show how distant structural analysis is from psychoanalysis, on this as well as on other issues. Finally, I suggest that, far from being an outmoded form of intellectual activity, mythic thought operates whenever the mind asks itself what signification is.

1

A Jivaro Myth

A Jivaro myth and its variants. Theory of the shapeless. Woman and pottery. First issue under study.

*

The Jivaro Indians, who became famous as head-hunters, no longer practice their art, but several tens of thousands of them still live on the borders of Ecuador and Peru, at the foot of the Andes and on the eastern slopes.

In one of their myths the Jivaro say that the Sun and the Moon, who were human beings, used to live on the earth; they shared the same dwelling and the same wife. She was named Aôho, which means Goatsucker; she liked to be embraced by the warm Sun but shrank from the Moon, whose body was too cold. Sun tactlessly remarked on this difference; Moon took offense, and climbed up to the sky on a vine; at the same time, he blew on Sun and eclipsed him. Aôho's two husbands had disappeared, and she thought she had been abandoned. She started to follow Moon into the sky, taking along a basketful of the clay that women use for pottery. Moon saw her, and, to get rid of her forever, he cut the vine that was linking the two worlds. The woman fell with her basket, and the clay scattered over the earth, where it can now be found. Aôho turned into the bird bearing her name, and at every new moon one can hear her plaintive cry as she implores the husband who left her.

Later Sun also climbed up to the sky on another vine. Even up there, Moon continues to evade him; they never move together and cannot be reconciled. That is why we are able to see the sun only during the day and the moon only at night.

The myth says:

If the sun and the moon, instead of quarreling for possession of the woman, had been able to agree to have her in
common, then among the Jivaros also two men would
now be able to have one woman in common. But since
the sun and the moon were jealous of each other and engaged in controversy about the woman, the Jivaros are
still jealous of one another and fight for possession of the
woman. [Karsten 1935: 520]

The clay used in ceremonial jars comes from Aôho's soul, and
women gather it from the places where she dropped it during her
fall, when she was quickly changing into a Goatsucker.

Karsten, the Finnish ethnologist who collected this version at
the beginning of the century, published another version that differs from the other in three main points: (1) the sun plays no role
in it; (2) the woman, Aôho, married to Moon alone, provoked the
anger of her husband, who left her because she kept the best parts
of the pumpkins he had ordered for his dinner; (3) Moon cut the
vine his wife was climbing, in order to catch up with him in the
sky, but, instead of clay, she was carrying the pumpkins, which fell
to earth, originating the plants the Indians still cultivate today.

The same researcher collected a third version among the Canelo Indians, who speak Quechua, are neighbors of the Jivaro, and
have been influenced by them. In ancient times, the Goatsucker
was a woman whom Moon secretly visited at night, hiding his
identity. In order to find out who this mysterious lover was, she
stained his face with genipa sap (the juice of the fruit turns black
in contact with the air). Unable to wipe off the stains and ashamed
of having been identified, Moon went up to the sky. The woman,
who has now turned into a Goatsucker, mourns the loss of her
faithless lover at every new moon.

Father J.-M. Guallart, a Jesuit missionary, published a very short
version, consolidating Karsten's first two versions into one story
while changing the protagonists and their relationship. Instead of
two men married to the same woman, we have one man, Moon,
with two wives. One of them did not get along well with him. One
day he asked her to go and pick ripe squash from the garden; she

made soup, ate it, and brought back three unripe squash for her husband's dinner. Furious, he climbed up to the sky on a cotton rope. As she was following him, he pulled up the rope, and she crashed to the ground in the shape of soft clay. This is the origin of potter's clay.

A Jivaro tribe, the Shuar, add one detail to the same story: on her way up to the sky, the woman was carrying a basket full of earthenware; the sherds became lower-quality clay, while the victim's body turned into good clay.

A few years ago, Ph. Descola heard a different version from the Achuar. (They, too, are closely related to their Jivaro neighbors, but they are not to be confused with the Shuar.) They say that in the old days it was always light because Sun and his brother, Moon, were living together on the earth. People could not sleep or even stop working. Night first alternated with day when Moon went up to the sky. He was married to Auju (*Nyctibius grandis,* an American goatsucker), who kept eating all the ripe *yuwi* squash (Karsten: *yui = Cucurbita maxima*), leaving him the unripe squash. Moon caught his greedy wife in the act, but she had sewed up her lips with chonta palm thorns and claimed that she could never have swallowed all the squash with such a small mouth. Moon wasn't fooled; he climbed up to the sky on the vine that was then linking the two worlds. Auju followed him, but he had the *wichink* squirrel (*Sciureus* sp.) cut the vine:

> The woman was so taken aback that she started to defecate here and there, and her excrement turned into banks of *nuwe* (potter's clay). Auju became a bird, and Moon now shone at night. (When Auju makes her characteristic lament on moonlit nights, she is mourning the loss of her husband.) Since then, the sky has moved up much higher, and, as the vine has been cut, it is impossible for men to go up there. [Descola 1984: 272]

When he was doing research among the Jivaro in 1930–31, M. Stirling discovered that the various myths previously gathered and published were actually fragments of a long native Genesis, almost forgotten in those days. Still, Stirling managed to elicit a few parts of this Genesis from an old man, who gave him a dramatic account, "with much gesturing, pantomime, and voice modulation, and with the display of considerable emotion" (Stirling 1938: 123). The informer admitted to frequent memory lapses; according to him, the story was much longer, and he could remember only the main outline. Later, additional fragments appeared in the work of Father Guallard and, more extensively, in the publications of Father Pellizzaro and his collaborators in the Salesian missions, who have started an impressive collection of Shuar traditions.

I will later come back to this essential myth and for now will simply sum up the episode corresponding to the versions we have just seen.

In the beginning, there were the Creator, Kumpara, and his wife, Chingasa. They had a son, Etsa, the sun. One day, his father, putting a bit of mud in his mouth, blew it on Etsa while he was sleeping. It turned into a woman—the moon, Nantu—whom Etsa could marry, since she was not a blood sister. There is no doubt that this myth is a reminiscence of the Bible, for the Jivaro were first in contact with the Spanish in the sixteenth century, and Jesuit missionaries settled among them as early as the eighteenth century. The themes seen above reappear in the rest of the story.

Auju, the Goatsucker—here a man "who was active only in the nighttime" (Stirling 1938: 123)—fell in love with Moon and tried to conquer her, but in vain. Etsa was also courting her without much success, and Moon, tired of her suitor, took advantage of a moment when he was busy painting his face red and went up to the sky. There she painted her body black so that it became the night. And she ran on, "climbing over the curving vault of the sky" like a jaguar.

Auju saw her escape and wanted to try his luck. He started climbing a vine that was hanging from the sky. But Moon cut the vine, "which fell and became entangled in all the trees of the jungle, where one may see it now" (Stirling 1938: 124). In the sky, the moon, Nantu, made a child out of clay and took great care of it. This increased Goatsucker's jealousy, and he smashed the child to

17

pieces, which became the earth. Etsa, the sun, was more successful than his rival: he managed to reach the sky and forced Moon to
marry him. The rest of the story deals with the birth of their children and with their adventures and those of their parents. One
day, Moon found herself buried underground (under circumstances we will examine later); Goatsucker freed her and threw
her back into the sky, losing her again—this time for good. Since
then, the disconsolate bird has been calling to his beloved in the
moonlight.

$$*$$

Before delving further into these myths, we must examine one difference between these versions: they claim to explain the origins
of three different things: potter's clay, cultivated squash, and forest
vines.

Cucurbitaceae are creeping or climbing plants. They resemble
vines in this respect. Moreover, although cultivated in gardens,
they remain akin to the wild varieties. The Aguaruna Jivaro call
wild Cucurbitaceae *yuwish,* from the name given to the squash
they cultivate, *yuwi.* According to an expert in Amerindian agriculture, "The habit of the plant further suggests that it may have
come in as a volunteer into primeval fields, there been tolerated,
and then deliberately associated by man with the main field crop"
(Sauer 1950: 505). Pending further evidence, we can consider
cultivated Cucurbita as combinatory variants of wild forest vines,
for they remain close to the wild species and grow in a way similar
to vines.

Let us now consider the vine/potter's clay alternation. A number of clues indicate that the Jivaro attribute one common characteristic to them: both belong to the category of *amorphous* elements. This category has negative connotations and seems to hold
a prominent place in the minds of Indians.[1]

1. Compare the subsequent remarks with this: the French word *moche* (a pe-
jorative adjective meaning "ugly") probably derives from the Frankish *mokka,*

One thing is obvious: potter's clay comes first in a shapeless mass, and the task of the potter consists precisely in giving shape to amorphous matter. Pottery can be correlated and opposed to metalwork by the fact that with fire the potter makes soft matter hard, whereas the smith, also using fire, makes hard metal malleable. In Guallart's version, clay is characterized by its softness. Similarly, vines appear as an unorganized mass, randomly tangled among the forest trees.

Most of the plants used by the Jivaro for so-called poison-fishing are vines, such as the wild varvasco. Karsten points out that "when, among the Jivaros and the Canelos Indians, men plant the varvasco, they afterwards abstain from eating the intestines and blood of animals . . . , also parts like the heart, the lungs, and the liver; they cannot eat these because then the plant would rot away" (Karsten 1935: 141). Further observations by Karsten confirm that there is indeed a feeling of repugnance for blood and viscera because of their soft consistency and formlessness:

> If the women eat the intestines of various animals, the plants [they cultivate in their gardens] will soon fall asunder in small pieces and be spoiled. The same will happen if they eat things that flow or that easily melt away and vanish, like blood, the fat of swine, and the sweet liquid contained in the sugar cane; or that are of a very loose consistency so that they easily dissolve, like tadpoles, fish roe, and the flesh of the crab and the snail. The plants will lack consistency, dissolve, and be spoiled. For the same reason the women must abstain from eating the palm top, which consists of loose fibers and easily falls asunder. [Karsten 1935: 138]

Given this, it is easy to conceive that for the Achuar, according to Ph. Descola, "Garbage connotes dense underbrush, forming an impenetrable maze of shrubs, bushes, and arborescent ferns."

"shapeless mass." *Moche* originally referred to "a bundle of spun silk not yet dyed or starched" or to a "bundle of worms on a fishing line, used as a bait."

The Machiguenga are another sub-Andean people, settled along the upper parts of tributaries of the Amazon. They establish an even more direct link between animal and vegetable shapelessness: a hunter must never eat the entrails of a monkey he has killed, for "they would turn into vines, and the hunter would get tangled up in them" (Garcia 1935–37: vol. 17, p. 223). The disease the Machiguenga fear most is the one that causes the intestines to rot instantly. Female relatives must abstain from spinning yarn in the house of a dying person, for the yarn would undergo a secret transformation in the intestines of the corpse, which would then escape from the body; these would become attached to those present in the house, and all would die. The main demon feared by the Machiguenga is called Kientibakori: "He has a bulky mass of intestines, which resemble *inkiro* tadpoles." Mme. F.-M. Cazevitz-Renard, who specializes in research on the Machiguenga, indicates that this word also designates the gelatinous mass of tadpole eggs that is thrown into the pot and used as seasoning for sweet manioc. (As we have seen, the Jivaro are stricter and forbid women to eat tadpoles.)

It is also notable that in some myths that we will discuss later on there is an opposition between vines or cotton rope, the one-time connector of heaven and earth, and bamboo, which becomes the means of opening a passage between the terrestrial and chthonian realms. These myths tell how Uyush, the Sloth, went underground by descending into a bamboo stalk, whose joints were formed by his defecating at regular intervals. We have seen that, for the Achuar, potter's clay comes from the excrement of the Goatsucker woman. This associates excrement with the shapeless, and we will see later that some myths set the Sloth and the Goatsucker in opposition. This opposition is based on the fact that the Sloth relieves himself at intervals of several days; he is thus linked to the notion of discontinuity.

Similarly, the contrast between sinuous vines and straight, hollow, and jointed bamboo stalks (that is, the contrast between well-formed elements and shapeless ones) parallels the opposition between the continuous and the discontinuous. I have dealt with this opposition at length in *Mythologiques,* first in *The Raw and the Cooked* (pp. 50–55 and passim). My analysis showed that, not only in America but elsewhere in the world, demanding, jealous, and vindictive gods are the direct cause of the passage from the continuous to the discontinuous. We thus have a first clue to understanding why jealously has such a prominent place in myths about the origin of pottery. The potter—or woman potter—imposes restraints on shapeless matter, breaking it up into pieces and molding it into shape.

However, to be precise, one must add that Jivaro myths bring in a third type of communication between the various levels of the universe. They say that an ogre attempted to kill Etsa, the sun, by pinning him down with one of the posts from the house that the two of them were building. These posts were made from the trunks of *paeni* trees (*Minquartia punctata,* an Oleacea). Using his magical powers, Etsa hollowed out the trunk by which he was held prisoner, got inside, and climbed up to the sky, where he became the sun. We thus have a triangular oppositional system: first, vines or flexible ropes are opposed to stiff bamboo and posts; then, jointed bamboo is itself opposed to smooth posts.

At any rate, it is clear that even in the "squash" or "vine" versions of the myth concerning the origin of pottery, earth or clay are present, and they are a constant in all the versions. The Jivaro name for the Genesis collected by Stirling is *Nuhino;* following his informer's explanations, he translated it as "Earth Story." In the myth reported by Karsten, the Jivaro name for clay is *nui.* Stirling's Genesis starts with the creation of the world; the Jivaro represent this creation—in the Chinese fashion, one might say—as the work of a potter: the sky is a great blue ceramic bowl. It was with mud that the Creator made Nantu, the Moon, whom the Sun later married; she in turn used clay to model her son, who was almost instantly destroyed by the Goatsucker. This son was named Nuhi (cf. *nui,* "clay"), and his body became the earth, where we now live.

In the same myth it is said that Sun and Moon had three sons, the Sloth, the Dolphin, and the Peccary, and one daughter, Manioc.

Then Sun and Moon became sterile, and their mother gave them two eggs. One of them was lost; the other produced a daughter, Mika, who later married her brother, Uñushi, the Sloth. Mika is the ritual name of the tall jars used for storing the *chicha* consumed during ceremonies; Mika is also the patron of potters. Karsten emphasized this link between women and pottery: "The Indian woman has to fabricate the clay vessels and manages these utensils because the clay of which they are made, like the earth itself, is female—that is, has a woman's soul" (Karsten 1923: 12). He also points to the phonetic similarity between *nui,* "clay," and *nua,* "woman." According to him, Indian women themselves are aware of this link, for in another report he says: "As I have pointed out elsewhere, there is an interesting connection between a woman, who alone has to make the clay vessels, and the earth and clay of which they are made. The clay vessel, according to the idea of the Indians, 'is a woman'" (Karsten 1935: 492).

The same thing is implied by our myths when they derive potter's clay from the excrement, the dead body, or the soul of a woman or from the basketful of clay she dropped during her fall; or when other myths, told by the Shuar, say that the Mistress of Pottery created female genitals from clay.

Jivaro myths nonetheless present us with a puzzle, for they closely link one of the arts of civilization, a moral feeling, and a bird. What relationship can there be between pottery, marital jealousy, and the goatsucker?

2
Pottery, a "Jealous Art"

Pottery, a "jealous art." Its mythical origins. Masters and Mistresses of clay in the Americas. The Hidatsa's jealous potter. Pottery at stake in a cosmic struggle.

*

We will attempt to solve the problem in stages. First, is there a link between pottery and jealousy? (We already have a few elements of the answer to this question.) Second, what about the link between jealousy and the goatsucker? If we can show cause for a relationship in these two cases, we will be able to establish a link between pottery and the goatsucker through what I have recently called transcendental deduction. We will thus verify what the myths seem to postulate: these three terms are linked by a transitive relation.

All of the research on the art of pottery in South America shows that it is a matter of concern, governed by numerous rules and prohibitions. The Jivaro, whose myths we have been studying, employ only a special kind of clay, which is found in just a few spots along the river. Karsten points out that this raw material has "a magical significance. . . . A whole primitive 'philosophy' is connected with the making of these important utensils" (Karsten 1935: 100). Also among the Jivaro, Stirling noticed the "considerable care . . . taken in the locating of outcrops of suitable potter's clay" (Stirling 1938: 94).

The Yurucaré, who also lived at the foot of the Andes but much further south, took strict precautions regarding the craft of pottery. It was practiced exclusively by women, who went in great solemnity to look for the clay, but never during the harvest season. For fear of thunder and in order to keep out of sight, they hid away in a remote spot, built a hut, and performed rituals. Once

23

they got down to work, they remained completely silent, communicating only by signs, in the conviction that their pots would crack during the firing if they uttered a single word. They also had to stay away from their husbands; otherwise all the sick would die.

We will see later on that some observations made in North America explain the antagonism between thunder and pottery, and certain Peruvian beliefs can shed light on the prohibition against collecting clay during the harvest season. These beliefs oppose the farmers in the well-watered areas to the people living at higher elevations, who, lacking water, cannot grow plants and so use the earth for making pots. In terms of water, pottery and agriculture could thus be seen as antagonistic techniques. Hence their incompatibility for the Yurucaré.

G. M. Foster, the great pottery specialist, writes that in Mexico, even today, "Wherever pottery is made, potters appear to deprecate themselves, and they are looked down upon by nonpotters. . . . Almost everyone agrees that farming or storekeeping is preferable to this traditional craft" (Foster 1965: 46). Along the same lines, the Machiguenga oppose the "good, black" earth, created by the good demiurge, to the earth created by the bad demiurge, the "red earth used for making pots, which is worthless, where good manioc cannot grow" (Garcia 1935–37, vol. 17, p. 223).

The Peruvian myth I mentioned earlier tells the story of a princess who reigned over potters and was adamant in the defense of her art. One of her neighbors, the prince of farmers, asked for her hand. One day he sent her an ill-looking jar containing water that could give birth to the springs lacking in her country. Offended by the poor quality of the container, she threw it away without deigning to look at its precious contents. Here, again, a representative of the potters demonstrates their narrow-mindedness and inability to consider anything beyond what is related to their trade.

The forest-dwelling Indians are potters and do not lack water. Pottery and agriculture are thus compatible for them. Therefore, among them a different system of opposition prevails: between wet clay from the river banks, good for pottery, and the hard, dry earth of the termite hills. Amazonian beliefs illustrate this connection between pottery and water. The Tukuna, a tribe of the Rio Solimões (a branch of the Amazon River), know two different rainbows, both subaquatic demons: the Rainbow of the East, master of the fish, and the Rainbow of the West, master of the potter's clay. Their Yagua neighbors also have two rainbows, one large and one small; the small rainbow meets the earth and is the Mother of Earthenware.

A widespread Amazonian myth says that Boyusu, a female snake identified with the rainbow, came out of the river one day, disguised as an old woman, to teach an incompetent Indian potter. She taught her how to coat her pots with white slip and paint over it in yellow, brown, and red. Once upon a time, Boyusu snakes and humans indulged in doubtful relationships. Women raised male snakes in jars, making the jars larger as the snakes grew; finally, they set them free in a lake, calling them back occasionally in order to use their "sons'" shapes and colors as models for the decorations they painted on their pots. They also took them as lovers. Men also had lovers who were snakes "turned into women of unmatched beauty" (Chaumeil 1893: 188, n. 34). Two details correspond to the Jivaro myths: red ocher, which occurs in small, compact nodules, is called "Boyusu's excrement," and there are mentions—unhappily, quite vague—of a fight between two Boyusu "over a matter of jealousy" (Tastevin 1925: 172–206).

In addition, the Jivaro also have myths about two orphans or a woman despised by her people for not knowing how to make pots. Nunkui, mistress of gardening and of women's crafts in general, taught them the art. The same myths stress the quasi-ethical value Indians place on pottery. In order to be worthy of marrying a good hunter, a woman must know how to make good earthenware, in which she can cook and serve the game he brings back. Women unable to make pots would be seen as literally damned creatures.

Like the Yurucaré, Guiana Indians imposed very tight restrictions on pottery:

They are convinced that clay can be extracted only during the first night of the full moon. . . . Large gatherings take place that night. At dawn, the natives take enormous quantities of clay back to their villages. They firmly believe that vessels made from clay extracted at any other time would tend not only to crack but to provoke various diseases in those who ate from them. [Schomburgk 1922: vol. 1, p. 203]

The Waura are Indians of the Arawak language family, living along the upper reaches of the Xingu River. A recently reported myth of theirs traces the origins of pottery to a supernatural snake carrying various kinds of receptacles, who, after a lot of wandering around, ended his journey in an area rich in clay. When extracting this clay, you have to be very careful and slow. If any noise is made, the snake will come up and eat you: "There, one must not make the slightest noise. It is dangerous, yes, very dangerous. For a long time the Waura have avoided mining clay in that place" (Penteado Coelho 1984: 12–13).

The Urubu, Tupi Indians of the Maranhão, are among the few South Americans who assign the craft of pottery to men.

When these men want to make pots, they isolate themselves in the forest so as not to be observed. During the entire time that they are at work, they do not eat, drink, urinate, or have sexual relations with women. They make pots of good quality, but many of them crack when being fired. The men think that this failure has its source in the spirit of the artisan, not in the techniques he has used or in the raw material. [Huxley 1956: 247]

Rules and prohibitions surrounding the art of pottery are found throughout the world. Briffault compiled a list of them in order to prove that this art (which is much more elaborate than one might think, given the properties of different kinds of clay and the choices to be made of temper, fuel, temperature, and firing techniques) is a female invention. However, the Urubu example show that men are subjected to exactly the same restrictions as women are in Guiana and among the Yurucaré. Leaving aside the question of its origins, pottery is indeed mostly women's work in the Americas, and there, more than elsewhere, there is a wealth of myths that account for the great care taken in the making of pottery and that shroud the various operations in a mystical imagery.

Other myths confirm the examples already given. Like the Jivaro, the Tacana live at the foot of the Andes, but further south, in Bolivia. They say that the Grandmother of Clay taught women how to build clay pots and make them strong by firing them. But she was also a demanding goddess. She insisted that the women keep her company and invited them to her home; in order to keep them there, she went so far as to bury them, causing the ground above the clay beds to cave in. One woman, collecting clay by the river during the night, was buried, along with her child, for another reason: the Mistress of Clay could not stand being disturbed in her sleep. Since then, a medicine man always supervises the extraction of clay, and coca leaves are thrown into the pit to placate the goddess. She also exercises her surveillance beyond the limits of her own territory: a woman, they say, left her house without filling her jars with water, and the Mistress of Clay and Earthenware punished her for her negligence by confiscating all her pots.

Moving north into Jivaro country, we see that Shuar women must pay due court to the Mistress of Pottery so that she will give them access to good clay; otherwise, she will deceive them by hiding it under clay of poor quality. Further north, in southeastern Columbia, the Tanimuka or Ofaina believe that the Earth, Namatu, the primordial woman, introduced the art of pottery. She is the Mistress of Pots; they cannot be made without her permission. Women fetching clay for the first time leave a small vase and some coca—an offering to Namatu given as payment, in exchange for her consent.

The large clay bowls used for baking manioc loaves are made with the utmost caution and in accordance with many restrictions. The work is done in a prescribed spot in the village; pregnant or menstruating women, being "too hot," must stay away (Hilde-

27

brand 1976: 181–87). If the firing takes place during the day, the children are shooed off, and complete silence is observed. The potter does not eat or drink, does not bathe, abstains from sexual intercourse, and gathers her hair in such a way that not a single hair will fall on the clay. No one may enter the village wet, for the bowl is susceptible to the cold. For the firing, it is placed in the center of the collective house, supported by three clay-poles, which symbolize the cosmic pillars; if they were shaken by the snake coiled around them, the stability of the human world would be threatened and that of the other worlds as well. The center of the dwelling is indeed the center of the world. It is a sacred space, closed off to traffic and work in the daytime; at night, the men gather there to chew coca and tell myths.

Whatever her name—Mother Earth, Grandmother of Clay, Mistress of Clay and Earthenware, etc.—the patron goddess of pottery is a benefactress. Depending on the versions, humans are indebted to her for the precious raw material or for the shaping, firing, or decorating techniques. But, as we have seen, she is jealous and fussy. She can be the source of occasional jealousy among spouses, as in the Jivaro myth; sometimes, for the Jivaro and others, she puts a high price on her favors; she herself can be jealously fond of her pupils: in order to keep them near her, she buries them. She sets countless constraints on the proper times (of the year, the month, or the day) for extracting clay; or she imposes precautions and prohibitions (such as chastity for women in Guiana and Colombia, for men among the Urubu) under various penalties, which range from the cracking of pots to the death of the sick and to plagues.

The link between pottery and jealousy is even more obvious in North American myths, which expand the theme to cosmic dimensions.

I showed in part one of *The Origin of Table Manners* that a South American myth coming from the Tukuna Indians closely corresponds in form and content to North American myths about a woman clinging to a man's back and refusing to let go. According to these myths, the woman resembles the burrs of certain plants. Some say that she is at their origin. For the Oglala Dakota, burrs are the symbol, if not the magical cause, of jealousy and envy.

Among the Penobscot Indians of North America there is a reversal of this same myth. The heroine is a supernatural creature, well known among other eastern Algonquians, and here she is the one who is trying in vain to get rid of a stick that she has foolishly fastened to her waist in order to use it as a husband; and here it is the man, represented by the stick, who is clinging to her. In both cases the myths reduce the man to a thing (in the one case he is paralyzed; in the other he is a stick). As for the woman, she is sometimes the jealous person, sometimes the object of jealous behavior. Algonquian myths call this supernatural creature Jug woman or Pot woman. Her name has also been translated as Scab woman; but, in support of the other expressions, it is interesting to note that, for the Ponca, the clinging woman is a potter.

The belief system I am trying to outline here appears in its full scope among the Hidatsa of the upper Missouri River Basin, who are members of the Siouan linguistic family. For them, pottery was a mysterious and sacred art. It could be practiced only by a woman who had obtained the right from another woman, generally her mother or the sister of her father; this right had been passed down from woman to woman, starting with a remote ancestor who was supposed to have received it from the Snakes. There had indeed been a time when only the Snakes made pottery. We have already encountered this theory in South America, where some Amazonian tribes say pottery was introduced by a chthonian snake; we find its celestial counterpart among the Tukuna and the Yagua, for whom the rainbow, conceived of as a subaquatic demon, was the Master of Clay and Pots.

The Hidatsa say that a long time ago the Snakes took an old couple to the clay beds. They taught them how to mix clay with sand or grit made from stones taken from the hearths and ground up. Making pots was such a sacred occupation that no one could

29

come near the potter while she was performing rites in honor of the Snakes and singing sacred songs. She forbade access to her hut, and before settling down to work she made a public announcement so that no one might venture in and breach her secrecy.

She worked in darkness; her door was closed, and the smoke hole was partially covered: she was impersonating the Snakes, who were believed to live in dark places, far from the Great Birds, who preyed on them. Before the firing, the pots remained covered with damp hides until the clay had set.[1] If someone walked into the hut unannounced or, unknown to the potter, uncovered the pots, then the Great Birds, who were ceaselessly flying about looking for the Snakes, were bound to destroy the pots, before or during the firing. Or the pots would be brittle and break when they were used. The potter's work thus triggered a contest between the Great Birds and the Snakes.

In the village of Awaxawi there was a summer ceremony, called "Tying the Pots," during which two decorated pots, one male, one female, were ritually prepared. This ritual can be compared to a presumed Amazonian practice associated with the myth of the Boyusu snake: "The jars in which the snakes were raised had sexes. . . . In the male jar, snakes were raised that would change into men for the women" (Tastevin)—that is, to be their lovers; the reverse was true for the female pot. The Hidatsa stretched skins over the openings of their sacred jars, which they used as drums; the name of the ceremony comes from the tying of these drumheads on the jars. During the rest of the year the jars were kept in a well-sealed pit, and they had to be protected from sunlight when they were removed to an earth-covered hut. This ceremony was a ritual asking for rain. The performers ran a vibrating instrument along a tree trunk carved to represent a snake with notches on its back; the noise they produced sounded like the Snakes when they bring rain. Drummers also played on the two

---

1. To allow for progressive drying and to avoid cracking; the pots must be completely dry, all moisture eliminated, before they are fired.—Trans.

jars. The leaders of the ceremony are reported to have had the right to make pots decorated with certain patterns.

A myth accounts for the origin of these rites. There once was a handsome young man who scorned women. One day, when he woke up, he saw a woman leaving his bed. She visited him four times, and the hero decided to follow her. She walked toward the north. At nightfall she saw a killdeer bird flying away at her approach. The woman identified it as a scout for the Great Birds, and she asked her companion to cut a chokecherry branch (*Prunus virginiana*), snake-like in shape, which they placed at the opening of a cave, where they probably took shelter. At night, the thunder roared. Then they knew that the Great Birds were attacking the branch.

After the storm they continued their journey, walking toward the northeast, and finally came to a lake. The hero followed the woman deep into the water. He came in sight of a country inhabited by Snakes, for the woman was actually the daughter of the Snake Chief. From this subaquatic world, thunder could sometimes be heard, and lightning was seen in the distance. The Snakes said that the bolts were Thunder Birds trying to kill them; but they did so in vain, for lightning could not penetrate the water.

The hero married the woman and, after some time, expressed the wish to go back to his people. His wife agreed to follow him. In the Indian village she hardly ever left her hut; there was no water there to protect her, and she was afraid of thunder. She spent her time doing embroidery with porcupine quills and never went out to fetch wood or water or to work in the gardens.

She forbade any woman to touch her husband, even very lightly. But one day his sister-in-law touched his robe in jest. Though he carefully cut out the section of his robe that had been touched, his wife knew what had happened. She disappeared soon after the incident.

The hero went back to the lake and attempted to dive down to his wife's country, but at every dive he was pushed back to the surface. He cried and moaned so much that in the end his wife appeared out of the water, holding two pots. She explained that

31

the larger one was a man, the other, a woman, and that they were to be used as drums for bringing rain. She taught him the details of the ceremony and the songs; also, when not in use, the jars were not to be moved around but stored away in a deep, well-covered pit, sheltered from thunder.

∗

Centered on a jealous deity, the Hidatsa myths about pottery are particularly well structured and rich in details, but similar beliefs are found among other Amerindians. The Pueblo Indians believe that all their pots have souls, and they see them as personalized beings. This spiritual essence is part of the pot as soon as it is shaped, before the firing. Hence the offerings placed in the kiln, next to the pot. When a pot cracks during the firing, one is hearing the sound the living being makes in escaping.

Like the Hidatsa, the Honduran Jicaque associate pottery work with a form of jealousy: "The Earth does not like to be used for making clay pots. . . . She takes her revenge: when someone is making pots, his body is seized by cold" (Chapman 1967: 209–11).

As for the notion of a cosmic battle between the Thunder Birds and the chthonian Snakes, in which pottery is the stake (or one of the stakes), it is of well-known importance in the myths and beliefs of the Algonquian-speaking peoples: the Menominee, who live between Lake Michigan and Lake Superior, say that clay pots belong to "the powers from below" (Skinner 1921: 285–86). We have just seen that these beliefs spread even further. They may offer an explanation for some prohibitions imposed on culinary practices. The Mandan, who speak a Siouan language like their Hidatsa neighbors, used to hang meat on a rope to roast it, for their pots were used exclusively for cooking vegetables. A clay vessel ought not to hold fat, and it would not fail to crack if it were used to cook meat.

So far we have demonstrated that myths and beliefs establish a link between pottery and jealousy. In their myth on the origin of potter's clay, the Jivaro also explain how marital jealousy came about: clay comes from a woman whose two husbands fight in order to possess her; the fight can also be between her husband and a suitor. Elsewhere, woman herself—Earth woman, initiator of pottery or giver of the sacred pots—shows a lover's or an owner's jealousy toward those under her protection (in this respect she resembles other benefactresses coming from distant places); she can also be demanding, petty, and finicky. The connection between pottery and jealousy is directly or indirectly linked to the cosmic struggle between the Great Birds, the powers Above, and the Snakes, the powers Below. This connection is a fundamental feature of Amerindian thought. We now need to turn to the next thing on our agenda: the connection between jealousy and the goatsucker.

3
Goatsucker Myths in South America

The Goatsucker, the bird of death, in South American myths. Connection with the cycle of the struggle between the stars. Three main themes: greediness, marital jealousy or strife, and splitting.

*

The suborder of Caprimulgi, order of Caprimulgiforms, comprises four families and one subfamily. In the New World, the Nyctibiideae and Caprimulgideae families and the Chordeilineae subfamily are represented by several genera and about sixty species, present mainly in the Southern Hemisphere. Following standard practice among naturalists, I will freely refer to all members of this family as goatsuckers. Throughout this book, then, this word will connote a category in which American mythical thought includes various genera or species, to which identical or very close semantic values are attributed.

Even in Europe, where the family of Caprimulgideae is limited to one species, *Caprimulgus europaeus,* the goatsucker is present in numerous popular beliefs, attested to by the names that designate it and by the significations they reflect. In French, it is called *engoulevent* ("wind-swallower"); *tête-chèvre* ("goatsucker," a translation of the Latin scientific name); *coche-branche* ("branch-treader," for its sleeping position; i.e., its perching lengthwise on a branch is reminiscent of a rooster treading a hen); *crapaud-volant* ("flying toad," because of its wide mouth); *hirondelle de nuit* ("night swallow"); etc. In Italian it is called *succiacabre;* in Spanish, *chotacabras;* in Portuguese, *engolovento, mãe-de-lua,* etc.

Its English names are goatsucker, bullbat, nighthawk, nightjar, and poor will or whippoorwill (an onomatopoetic evocation of its cry: five notes, only three of which are heard). The Germans call it *Ziegenmelker, Kuhsauger, Kindermelker,* i.e., the milker, the goat-, cow-, or childsucker; *Nachtkröle* ("night toad"); *Totenvogel* ("death bird"); *Hexe* ("witch"); *Hexenführer* ("witch leader"); *Tagschläfer* ("day-sleeper"); *Wehklage* ("moan"); etc.

A semantic frontier seems to separate Romance and Germanic languages from Slavic languages. Slavic words corresponding to the Latin *Caprimulgus* are derived from scientific language. In Russian, Polish, Czech, Slovak, Serbo-Croatian, Bulgarian, and so on, popular speech uses related terms, all derived from Old Slavic *leleti* or *lelejati,* literally, "to stumble" or "to swing," hence the figurative sense of the noun *leletik, lelejek, lelek,* "dummy," "good-for-nothing," "nitwit."[1]

Names of the *engoulevent* ("wind-swallower") type refer to the bird's huge mouth, which stretches from the eyes to under the ears. The bird can swallow enormous insects, such as moths; these get trapped behind the spiky hairs along the edges of its beak, which form a kind of portcullis, and they are also held fast by the glue that coats the inside of the beak. Names of the goatsucker type perpetuate the common European belief—dating back to antiquity—that the goatsucker hovers around goats in order to suck their milk and make them dry. A whole mythology is revealed through these appellations, as well as by others (Death Bird, Witch Leader, and Nitwit, Good-for-Nothing, which find equivalents in America). This mythology draws on the bird's nocturnal character; its gloomy, secretive character; the fact that it does not build a nest; and especially on its grasping and gluttonous nature, displayed in three kinds of appetites or feelings: avarice, jealousy, and envy, which are often designated by the same name in the languages of so-called primitive peoples.

Goatsuckers are prominent in myths of the New World, perhaps because these species are so well represented there. Lehmann-Nitsche was the first to set up an inventory, but he did not try to interpret his data. In Brazil these birds are called *mãe-de-lua, manda-lua,* or *chora-lua,* i.e., "moon mother," "moon-

---

1. I am indebted to Mrs. Anita Albus and Mr. Dietrich Leube for their help with German, and to Mr. Ludwik Stomma for Slavic languages.

searcher," or "moon-cryer" (they are reputed to sing in the moonlight). In tropical and subtropical America they have native, most often Tupi or Guarani, names, which vary according to the area, genus, or species; *urutau* or *jurutau,* translated as "ghost bird" or as "wide mouth"; *ibijau,* "earth-eater"; *bacurau; curiango;* etc. In the sixteenth century Jean de Léry had already noticed that the coastal Tupi Indians gave special attention to a bird that was heard mainly at night, "no larger than a pigeon and with ash-gray feathers . . . and a penetrating voice, even sadder than a wood owl's." They said that the birds bore good news and encouragement from dead friends and relatives.

Less optimistically, the Tukuna believe that the souls of the dead come back in the shape of goatsuckers in order to suck out the blood, flesh, and bones of the living, leaving them only their skin. The Kalina of Guiana believe that people have several souls and that the one that remains connected to the earth sometimes appears in the shape of a goatsucker. For the Taulipang, the goatsucker is the servant, or the familiar spirit, of the water genie. Still in Guiana, the Arawak believe that goatsuckers are the pet birds of the spirits of the dead. They are often seen near graves and are never hunted. A goatsucker perching near you is an omen of death. The goatsucker is also an evil spirit pursuing humans with his cries, biting and killing them too. The *tu'io,* a Caprimulgus, augurs death, according to the Desana of the Uaupés River Basin. Similar beliefs, along with the same prohibitions, are found as far as Argentina, among the Tehuelche.

In the early nineteenth century, Humboldt and Bonpland reported beliefs concerning a cave inhabited by these birds, the cave of Caripe, la Cueva del Guacharo, in Venezuela: "The natives associate mystic beliefs with this cave, which is inhabited by nocturnal birds. They believe that the souls of their ancestors live deep in the cave" (Humboldt, in Brehm n.d.: vol. 2, p. 571). These birds are an aberrant genus of Caprimulgiforms, *Steatornis;* they are gregarious, eat a diet of fruit, and are hunted for their abundant fat; but Ph. Descola, in his study of the Jivaro, noted that Indians fear these hunting expeditions into deep caves inhabited by thousands of birds—that is, into a chthonian world.

Such ancient connections with death and the underworld do not preclude other functions, attested as early as the eighteenth century. In the Amazon a goatsucker feather was a talisman that brought success in love. This is close to a Carib belief from Guiana: the goatsucker, who flies only at night, symbolizes solitude and debauchery (this, by the way, calls to mind the Japanese word *yotaka*, "night falcon," which refers both to the goatsucker and to low-class prostitutes).[2] Again in the Amazon, the virtue of pubescent girls was protected by sweeping the area under their hammocks with goatsucker feathers, stuffing a dead bird in their hammocks, or obliging them to sit on a dead bird for three days. These practices could be interpreted as a homeopathic treatment—*similia similibus curantur,* like things are cured by like: a tempting interpretation, for Brazilian Indians often compare the bird's wide mouth to a vulva, and some say that the goatsucker's crest was made of women's pubic coverings in what the researchers themselves described as an obscure myth (however, see pp. 44–45, 61).

Finally, other characteristics of the goatsucker have caught the attention of the Indians. According to Guiana Indians, it has four eyes, probably because of an ocellate pattern on its wings. The female lays two eggs on the bare ground or on a stone, and (again in Guiana) it is forbidden to steal these.

American myths concerning goatsuckers are so dissimilar that it is hard to classify them. I will try, nevertheless, to distinguish a few of the main themes.

In the *Popol Vuh,* the sacred book of the Quiche Maya of Guatemala, the lords of the infernal kingdom of Xibalba have their gar-

2. Professor Moriaki Watanabe gave me the following details: these prostitutes worked on the ground, and, according to old popular belief, they were quick to pocket their clients' money.

dens watched by nocturnal birds that can be identified as goat-suckers: their mouths were slit wide open in punishment for having let the divine twins pick flowers in the gardens—hence their appearance. The Amazonian Tupi raise the goatsucker to a higher rank: the *urutau* Goatsucker is one of the four deities sur-rounding the Moon, the goddess of plants. The Makiritaré make fun of the ugly *Nyctibius grandis* but still place him among the three supernatural birds living in the sixth sky. His brother, a cul-tural hero, stays with his friend the Sloth, soon to be added to our bestiary. In Columbia, the Catio also have three sacred animals: a bird of prey (a kind of eagle), the praying mantis, and the "owl" (in Spanish, *lechuza,* which could be a goatsucker). Such a con-jecture is supported by the fact that one of the Campa's sacred birds is a goatsucker (*Steatornis* sp.) whose feathers were used in men's headdresses, and it is highly probable that the "sacred bird" whose feathers decorated the Inca's diadem was a goatsucker. Moreover, for the Catio themselves, this "owl" used to be the wife of a god who, disguised as a leper, caught her deceiving him and turned her into a bird. This god was plagued with ulcers, and a Kalina myth from Guiana attributes to the Goatsucker the power of healing ulcers.

Other myths, which do not include the Goatsucker in a pan-theon, still provide explanations as to his origins. Amorim re-ported the following very obscure and intricate one from the Ama-zon Basin (it is in *lingua geral* but is attributed to no tribe in particular). Once upon a time two supernatural girls came from the sky, and a great chief and his son fought each other to possess them. These girls were also egrets, and, though they had no va-ginas, they became pregnant, one by the chief's son, who had be-come her lover, the other by the chief himself, who had been transformed into a tree, under which the girls had fallen asleep. This girl exploded and gave birth to fish: the other was trans-formed into the insects that announce the coming of summer—cicadas, dragonflies, and butterflies. Then both girls turned into rocks, one facing the sun, the other facing the river. The chief's son, in his grief, gathered the white feathers his lover had plucked

Fig. 1   The South American goatsucker *Nyctibius grandis*
(After Brehm 1891: vol. 2, p. 230)

off, soiled them with dirt, put them on, and disappeared. The legend says that he turned into an *urutauhi,* a small species of goatsucker.

In his article about the goatsucker (*urutau*) Teschauer reports a Guarani myth, from the Uruguay River region, that appears to invert Amorim's myth. A chief's daughter and an Indian were in love, but her parents opposed the unequal match. One day she disappeared. She was found in the hills among animals and birds. Embassy after embassy was sent to persuade her to return to her people, but in vain, for she had gone deaf and senseless with grief. A sorcerer declared that the only way to bring her out of her lethargy was to give her a shock, which he accomplished by announcing the pretended death of her lover. She leaped up and disappeared, changed into a Goatsucker.

Both myths deal with an impossible union, one between a chief's son and a supernatural creature, the other between a chief's daughter and a common man, sometimes described as a prisoner or a foreigner. In the one case the hero, in the other, the heroine, turns into a Goatsucker on learning of the death or disappearance of the person he/she loves.

Lehmann-Nitsche mentions or summarizes several variants of the second myth, in which the heroine, changed into a bird, is associated with the Moon, her lover with the Sun. This seems to be related to a belief, found in southern Brazil, Paraguay, and northwestern Argentina, that the goatsucker keeps its eyes open in its sleep in order to follow the path of the sun in the sky. Although unfounded, this belief is doubly interesting. It supports the hypothesis that these two myths are inverted variants of each other: the first myth calls one of the supernatural women Mother of the Sun (and calls the other Mother of the Fish), while the second myth associates the sun with the male partner. Moreover, this brings us back to our starting point, the Jivaro myths that stage a conflict between the Sun and the Moon over a Goatsucker woman; here, however, a third party enters the conflict between a solar and a lunar character, and the latter becomes a Goatsucker.

I would stray too far from my topic were I to demonstrate how Jivaro myths are related to the North American cycle discussed in parts 4 and 5 of *The Origin of Table Manners,* the cycle of the quarrel between heavenly bodies. I shall simply point to a few key features. The main version of the Jivaro myth starts with two husbands, Sun and Moon, quarreling over the wife they share. The most typical versions of the North American cycle, for their part, revolve around a disagreement between two male gods, also Sun and Moon, over the respective merits of two kinds of females: humans and frogs. In both cases, the myths account for the origin of the spots on the moon. In the Jivaro myth, where Moon is the Sun's sister, she paints her face black, hence the spots. In the North American myths, on the other hand, the Sun's frog wife (who turned out to be a good-for-nothing) was being sneered at by her brother-in-law, the Moon, and in revenge clung to his chest: she can still be seen there, making dark spots on the shining surface.

In South America, among the Jivaro themselves, one can find intermediate stages that bring further evidence for this connection with North American myths. In Bolivia, the Cavina—also a sub-Andean people—tell the story of a man whose wife, a Boa, was as beautiful as she was hard-working. But a Toad woman was also in love with the Indian, and the two jealous women engaged in a fight. Boa lost and returned to the lake she originally came from. Toad took on her appearance and passed herself off as her rival. However, she turned out to be so lazy and empty-headed that the man was not fooled; he killed her and went to look for his first wife. Along the same lines, a variant of the Jivaro myth, collected by Wavrin, attributes several frog wives to the Sun. One of them proved such an inept cook that the Sun went up to the sky to get away from her. Thus, it is not only in European languages that (as in *crapaud-volant,* frog-mouth, *Nachtkröte*) a batrachian can become a combinative variant of the goatsucker.

We also witness here a tendency I first discussed in *Mythologiques,* namely, that North America's great cosmological themes sometimes reappear in South America in the form of domestic squabbles, which might be seen as miniature images of major conflicts that took place before the universe was brought into order.

*

Though less clearly etiological than Amorin's and Teschauer's versions, summed up above, there is a second body of myths that focus on marital jealousy and strife. This was precisely the first feature to catch our attention, and it was present in the myths we have just examined.

First, jealousy. A Karaja myth, studied in *The Raw and the Cooked* (M_{110}, p. 184), says that one night the older of two sisters expressed her admiration and yearning for the evening star. The following morning the star came into her hut, disguised as a decrepit old man with white hair and a wrinkled face, and offered to marry her. Horrified, she turned him down. Out of compassion for the old man, her sister accepted his offer. The next day they found out that his body was just a shell hiding a handsome young man, in magnificent attire, who knew how to grow edible plants as yet unknown among the Indians. The older sister was jealous of the younger one's luck and so ashamed of her own stupidity that she turned into a wailing Goatsucker.

Other myths deal with marital discord. For the Arawak of Guiana, the goatsucker is the reincarnation of an adulteress whose child died while she was running away from her husband. Tupi-speaking Mundurucu live along the lower Tapajoz; they tell the story of a man who insisted that his mother feed him the way birds feed their young. He was married, but he kept turning down the food his wife cooked for him. She was puzzled and started to spy on him. Revolted by what she saw, she refused to have any-thing further to do with her husband. He turned into a great goat-sucker. In another Mundurucu myth an Indian was in the forest with his wife, picking wild berries; he gradually strayed away and finally disappeared, changed into a small goatsucker. (In another version his wife also becomes a bird.) These myths thus combine two forms of marital discord with a trait that can be attributed to goatsuckers through empirical observation, namely, *orality*. In-deed, in the first myth, it is the hero's oral fixation that estranges him from his wife and keeps him closer to his mother: the former serves regular meals, the latter is willing to feed him like a nest-ling. In this context, a Tenetehara myth from northwestern Brazil ends in a particularly significant way: the hero, a hunter, having lived through a great number of adventures, rushes back to his mother's lap and then cannot detach himself from her (there are variants of this among the Kayapo, the Shipaia, the Cavina, and the Tembé, who describe the hero as a hunter of goatsuckers). Let me skip briefly to an altogether different geographical area: in Hok-kaido, the northernmost island of Japan, the Ainu call the goat-sucker *habu-totto* or *huchi-totto,* imitating his cry, which means, according to the myths, "Mother! Nurse me!" or "Grandmother! Feed me!"

We thus come to a third group of myths, focusing on greediness and gluttony. Lehmann-Nitsche studied forty-three versions—lit-erary and highly modernized for the most part—of a Quechua myth from northwest Argentina. This myth plays on the homophony between the Quechua name for goatsucker, *cacuy*, and the Quechua phrase for "Make some flour!" An unusually voracious young woman fed her brother very sparingly and kept ordering him to make *algarrobo* flour (from a leguminous plant of the *Prosopis* genus). One day, tired of being ill-treated, the boy made his sister climb to the top of a tree, claiming that she would find honeycombs up there. Then he cut off the lower branches so that she couldn't get down. She turned into a goatsucker, and one can still hear the bird cry out: "Make some flour! Make some flour!" Hence its name.

This Quechua heroine who deprived her brother of food finds a counterpart in a Kayapo myth in which the hero is a man who treated his wife like a slave and would not give her meat or water. At night she suffered cruelly from thirst. She wanted to sneak out of the hut while her husband was asleep and then, guided by the croaking of the frogs, find a waterhole; but she was afraid he might discover her absence, so she managed to split herself into two parts: her body remained in their bed, while her head, using her long hair as wings, flew out to quench her thirst. But her husband woke up, understood her trick, and stamped out the embers on the hearth. The head was unable to find its way back to the house, which was now plunged in darkness. It flew all night long, looking for its body, which the husband made into smoked meat; the head kept on flying and turned into a goatsucker. We have thus moved from the theme of selfish greediness to that of decapitation.

The beheaded goatsucker becomes a beheader itself in a Timbira myth in which the bird cuts off the head of one of two cultural heroes and sets it up in the fork of a tree, near a bees' nest. In another myth, widespread among the Carib and Arawak of Guiana, a hunter of land crabs, caught in the rain, protected himself by cramming a calabash on his head, down to his eyes. An evil spirit came along and admired the hunter's smooth, polished head. The hunter offered to make the spirit's head just as beautiful: he scalped him. Later the two enemies met again. The spirit wanted to take his revenge, but the Indian managed to convince him that he was dealing with the wrong person. He ended up crushing the spirit's head against a flat rock. The brain was smashed to pieces, each of which became a goatsucker. This is why the Indians fear these birds, born from spirits of the bush, bearers of evil.

A much less dramatic kind of split occurs in a Tukuna myth, set in the days when the Indians did not know of sweet manioc or fire, which were the exclusive possession of an old woman. She had received the former from the ants, the latter from her friend, the Goatsucker, who kept it hidden in his beak. The Indians liked the old woman's cooking and wanted to discover her secret; when they questioned her, she claimed that she used the heat from the sun to bake her manioc cakes. The Goatsucker found her lie very funny, and, when he burst . . . into laughter, they saw flames coming out of his mouth, which they then forced open in order to take the fire. That is why goatsuckers have such wide mouths. As we have seen, the Indians often compare the bird's wide beak to a vulva (see above, p. 37). In Guiana myths about the origins of cooking fire, an old woman is the sole possessor of fire, which she keeps hidden in her vagina.

Beheading (or splitting) and fire are thus two motifs that hold a prominent place in the mythology of goatsuckers. This appears even more clearly among the Ayoré of the Bolivian Chaco. Unfortunately, we have only fragments of their myths and know almost nothing of a very important ritual cycle in which the Goatsucker plays the main part. In May, at sunset, when Arcturus rises in the East, the Ayoré announce the "closing of the world." This is a dangerous period: "It shall not rain; the forest shall be dry and burnt. Most small birds and other animals shall disappear. The nights shall often be cold." This "taboo of the forest" lasts for four months, until the full moon in August, which is when the Goatsucker begins to sing again. Her cry[3] is anxiously awaited, for it announces the "reopening of the world." As soon as they hear it, men and women separate. They flood the hearths with water and light new fires. The men take offerings to the Goatsucker—peanuts, corn,

3. It soon becomes clear that in this myth the Goatsucker is a female.—Trans.

calabashes, and beans—so that she will keep them from starving in the year to come. They go out to collect wild honey and bury it, also as an offering to the bird, so that she will provide them with honey in abundance. The men do not eat or drink for one day and one night. The women, for their part, weave belts of fibers, dyed red, for their husbands or lovers. When they come back from collecting honey, the men are whipped by the elders so that evil spirits will stay away from them. The following morning marks the opening of the New Year, and the men go back to their wives. Soon the rains begin, the forest turns green again, the animals come back, and it is time to begin planting.

For the Ayoré, the Goatsucker is thus the Mistress of Honey, and this brings to mind the Quechua myth of the woman whose greed for honey turned her into a goatsucker. Add to this the fact that in Argentina, in the province of Catamarca, the cry of the goatsucker is a sign that a nest of honeybees is not far off. As for the strict fast imposed on the men, it recalls the Quechua and Kayapo myths in which the hero or heroine is deprived of food and drink. The Goatsucker is the mistress not only of honey but of fevers, convulsions, and other diseases and of torrential rains and devastating fires. The Ayoré see the bird as a female deity, a jealous and fussy one, who cannot tolerate facial hair or, among other things, the faintest trace of fresh blood in meat. To please her, one must cook game before gutting it. The coming of the goddess is hoped for because she brings the dry season to an end and announces the great renewal; yet she is also feared, for she belongs to the world of the dead and is their messenger.

The Goatsucker named Assoojna (Asohsná, Asoná) appears in myths sometimes as a man, sometimes as a woman; in the latter case she is the wife of Potatai, a goatsucker of a different species. As a woman, Assoojna once smashed a stone and threw the flakes at a group of lazy servants. These flakes changed into fire and killed the offenders; then the fire went into the trees of the forest, where it can still be found today, when two pieces of wood are rubbed together to kindle fire. The lazy servants' relatives wanted

45

to avenge their death, and Assoojna and Potatai had to hide from them. Their children, who were iguanas, found themselves without providers and had to steal food in order to survive: "That's why the Ayoré are thieves." In the end the children found their father squatting in the tall grass and their mother crouching in a hole, and that is why goatsuckers always hide during the day.

As a male character, Assoojna also threw burning stone flakes, but at enemies. Those who were not killed by fire were plagued by fevers that still bring death to Indians today. Other diseases came about—in short, everything that shortens human life—following a flood that turned the land where the survivors had taken refuge into an unhealthy place. They finally settled on dry ground, but their descendants are still subject to the same diseases.

According to a third version of the same myth, Assoojna and Potatai, then Ayoré, were being threatened by enemies and hid underground. Their son, the Iguana, warned them of the approach of their enemies, and the three of them went up to the sky. In order to erase their tracks, Assoojna called for rain. She and her husband changed into two different species of goatsuckers.

All of these versions, which associate a myth with a great ritual cycle in which the Goatsucker takes on a cosmic function as a major deity, seem to be a thousand leagues away from the petty squabbles between husbands and wives to which the myths of other South American tribes trace the origins of the bird. However, the Ayoré have their own share of such stories, and they occur in a parallel series. Here are two examples. According to one myth, Assoojna used to be an Ayoré woman; she was beaten to death by her husband, and that is why she keeps coming back to bring diseases to the Indians. In another version, Assoojna, the most beautiful girl in the tribe, fell in love with the son of a foreign chief and married him. Contrary to the local rule of matrilocal residence, the husband's father insisted that the young couple live with him. The mother-in-law was jealous of Assoojna, treated her unkindly, and even contrived to drive her son away from his wife. Despair drove Assoojna to suicide, and her spirit became the Goatsucker, who returns every year to punish her persecutors. We are again very close to Amorim's and Teschauer's versions (see above, pp. 38–39). South American Goatsucker myths seemed so diverse at first sight that we could see no way to classify them. But one can actually make a transition from one to the other: there is a continuity.

4

Potters' Kilns and Cooking Fire

Potters' kilns and cooking fire. Goatsuckers and pottery: the theory of the
Ovenbird. Myths from the Chaco and elsewhere. Application of
the canonic formula.

*

The theme of splitting is better represented in North American
myths (split brain, splitting one's sides laughing, split stone) and
will be left aside for now. Let us move to other considerations.
Starting from the Jivaro myths that set up a triangular pattern with
jealousy, pottery, and the Goatsucker, I have shown that there are
connections in South American Indian thought between pottery
and jealousy on the one hand, jealousy and the Goatsucker on the
other. The first connection results from the fact that in the most
elaborate of indigenous theories about pottery this craft is seen as
the stake in a conflict between celestial powers (Thunder Birds)
and chthonian or, rather, subaquatic powers (the Great Snakes).
Sketches or traces of these theories appear elsewhere as well.

One of the conclusions of the four volumes of *Mythologiques*
was that myths of the Americas find a common paradigm in a
struggle between humans and nonhumans over the possession of
cooking fire. That is what I referred to as "one myth only" in *The
Naked Man*. Like cooking, pottery requires the use of fire: clay
vessels must be fired. But Indian thought makes a double distinction between the two kinds of fire. First, cooking fire was con-
quered by humans, who had to fight either animals (i.e., nature
opposing culture) or the people Above (in that case, earthlings
still in their natural state oppose supernatural, celestial beings).
On the other hand, when pottery is at stake, humans do not identify with either side of the conflict. Placed *between* the Snakes and
the Birds, they act more as witnesses to a battle that does not in-

volve them. Instead of taking responsibility or initiative in the action, they become passive beneficiaries or victims. At best, they are protected by one of the two parties, or they act as associates or accomplices.

Second, except in one instance, which I will discuss later, all the myths about the origin of cooking fire agree on one point (actually, they agree with experience, too): conquering fire was a difficult achievement for humans, but, once they had succeeded, fire was theirs forever. But in their possession and practice of pottery, they are, on the contrary, constantly challenged, for the rivalry between the powers Above and the powers Below never comes to an end. Small as their part may be in the cosmic struggle, men are contaminated by the spirit of jealousy that animates these contending powers. Consequently, the practice of pottery is subject to countless rituals and fussy, cautionary measures, and this does not fail to affect the craftsmen's moral disposition.

The myths of the Chaco indirectly support these considerations. Their geographic origin is all the more significant because the theory of pottery outlined above is based mainly on North American myths (see pp. 28–33), and, according to Métraux, who knew the Chaco very well, there are striking analogies between the myths of this region of the Southern Hemisphere and those of the Northern Hemisphere: "It is probable that . . . the Chaco Indians represent an ancient population which, until recently, has preserved several features of a very archaic culture that in remote ages might have been common to primitive tribes of both North and South America" (Métraux 1946b: 213–14). Moreover, these cultural similarities go hand in hand with physical similarities.

Now, one finds among several peoples of the Chaco—the Chané, Choroti, Lengua, and Ashluslay (and also the Guarani of Paraguay and the Tupi-speaking Apapocuva of southern Brazil)— the North American belief that supernatural birds cause thunder. The Ashluslay even go so far as to say that cooking fire used to be the exclusive property of the Thunder Birds, and when man discovered their secret, the birds were so jealous that they became man's worst enemies. Consequently, where cooking fire is concerned, the Thunder Birds display the same hostility they generally display in myths concerning the origin of pottery. Conversely, such an attraction can operate in the opposite direction. Mr. Thor Anderson, whom I met in Berkeley, kindly told me a myth he had collected in Mexico among the Chamula Indians. In the past, they say, the jaguar used to terrorize humans because he was invulnerable to their weapons. As soon as he detected the smell of roasted meat, he rushed to the house from which it emanated and ate all the people in it. But today, thanks to the Lord who created earthenware for the good of mankind, the jaguar can no longer smell roasted meat.

Thus, contrary to the many South American myths in which humans obtain fire *from* the jaguar, they already have it; and it is pottery they obtain *against* the jaguar. But the consequences are the same, for in both cases the jaguar is left on the side of nature and henceforth will eat his meat raw. The existence of these two intermediate forms confirms the parallels between the myths on the origin of cooking fire and those on the origin of pottery.

The second connection—that between jealousy and the Goatsucker—is easier to establish. As I said, it results from an empirical deduction that attributes a gloomy disposition and a ravenous appetite to the bird because of its solitary life, its nocturnal habits, its lugubrious cry, and its wide beak, which allows it to swallow large victims.

However, the demonstration remains incomplete at this stage. If these three terms are to form a system, they need to be linked in pairs. We have established that the Goatsucker and pottery are both related to jealousy. Now, what is the relationship between pottery and the Goatsucker?

Here we are faced with a problem requiring careful consideration, for its solution brings into play some fundamental principles of the structural analysis of myths. In order to prove the connection between the Goatsucker and pottery, we must have recourse to a bird that has no place in the myths we have examined up to this point. But this procedure is justified in two ways. First, this bird is present in other myths that entertain a relation of transformation with the former myths. These new myths are connected to those about the Goatsucker not only logically but geographically: they come from the Chaco, where the Ayoré live, in whose rites and myths the Goatsucker plays a major role. Second, according to travelers and zoologists, this new bird's habits contrast with the Goatsucker's in several respects. In short, I will submit two birds and their corresponding myths to a treatment similar to the one I applied to two masks and their myths in *The Way of the Masks*.

This new bird is the ovenbird (*Furnarius* sp.), of the family Furnariidae, a subfamily of the Furnariinae that includes five genera. Some species of the *Furnarius* genus, found mainly in Argentina and Brazil, are of special interest to us because their habits are diametrically opposed to the goatsucker's.

According to the myths, the Goatsucker cries only a few months during the year and at night, especially when the moon is out. The ovenbird, on the contrary, is extremely vocal. Quoting Burmeister, a nineteenth-century traveler, Brehm writes that it even seems to

> take pleasure in interrupting conversations; they [ovenbirds] start crying out as soon as two people walking together stop to talk. This has often happened to me in the garden of my friend, Dr. Lund. When the birds started to cry, my host often said: "Let them finish; we will not be able to speak a word in their presence." [Brehm 1891: 541]

I have already mentioned that the goatsucker does not build a nest; it lays two eggs directly on the ground or on a stone. The only way to protect them is for the female to hover over them, and, if a man or an animal approaches, she will pretend she has a broken wing and will flop to the ground, at some distance, in order to draw the intruder away from the eggs or the young. Just

51

the opposite of this, the ovenbird builds a clay nest on a branch (Brazilian peasants call it *João de Barro, Maria de Barro,* "Clay Jack" or "Clay Mary," or *pedreiro,* "the mason"). This nest is remarkably large and well designed; it has a hall and a separate chamber, padded with dry weeds, feathers, and hairs, in which the female lays her eggs.

Finally, the Goatsucker is associated in myths with marital jealousy. More precisely, this bird has a prominent place in all myths dealing with the separation or gap between the sexes caused by jealousy among men over the same woman, the jealousy of a rejected lover (man or woman), the inability of two lovers to be together, or marital discord. Even in myths where the Goatsucker is the agent or the result of a beheading, these themes are not completely absent, for decapitation also involves separation. Like the two halves of a separated couple, the body and head, split apart, suffer from the loss of each other.

These themes are radically opposed to what we know about the ovenbird, for male and female ovenbirds share the work of building their nest, which is, according to Brehm, a masterpiece, "considerably different from the nests of all other birds." Unlike the goatsucker, the ovenbird likes to be close to humans and, what is more important, he constantly chats with his female. Ihering, a remarkable observer, writes that

> the male cries out and the female immediately answers half a tone lower; two sounds of equal length thus alternate with such speed, such rhythmical accuracy, that the listener is filled with admiration, especially on thinking how difficult it would be for humans to practice this kind of musical exercise at prestissimo speed. A professional musician listening to a pair of *João de Barro* with me particularly admired the perfect timing of the second voice, achieved with no prompt from the first singer. Human musicians need the cues the conductor gives them with his baton, whereas these birds, even at some distance from each other, seem to answer automatically and instantly. [Ihering 1940]

Indeed, observing such fervor, Indians could not fail to take it for what it actually is, the mark of perfect harmony in a couple; this couple is diametrically opposed to those others, described in the myths, in which one member, or a third party, who brings about conflicts between a man and wife is or becomes a Goatsucker.

Though a sacred bird in Brazil, the ovenbird appears in very few myths. These come mainly from the Chaco, and a rapid inspection will be enough to show us that they are connected through a transformational relationship with the neighboring Ayoré myths, examined in the preceding chapter, in which the hero or heroine is a Goatsucker. In those myths we saw a male or female Goatsucker unleash destructive fire against disobedient servants or enemies. This fire threatened to exterminate the entire population; once the danger was over, the survivors founded a new settlement.

We find more or less recognizable inverted forms of this myth among the Toba, the Mocovi, the Tumereha, the Mataco, and others. When compared to the Ayoré's, the Mataco versions show some particularly interesting features. Instead of the fire-makers holding leading roles, with their victims as secondary characters, the parts are now reversed. Long ago, they say, when humans and animals did not form distinct zoological families, there was an inextinguishable fire burning at the end of the world, with huge pots full of food cooking day and night. In another version, this whole setup is replaced by a people of giants made of fire. In both cases, approaching the fire or the men of fire required special precautions: either "one must never speak of prairies with high grass, for the fire would hear and would spread itself through the world," or the fire giants were "very sensitive" and "the men who walked in that country were not allowed to make any noise, to speak, or to laugh" (Métraux 1939: 10–11).

In this latter version the animal people, ancestors of the Indians, once went to visit the fire giants. The Ovenbird liked to laugh (we have seen that he is a cheerful bird), and he could not contain himself at the sight of the giants' children: they were squatting in front of the houses, with flames coming out of their behinds. The children went and complained to their parents. So the giants set the whole world on fire. The earth was devastated; there were no more trees. A little bird who had hidden in a hole managed to make them grow back with his songs.

A Toba version explains that the Indians protected themselves from the fire by digging a large pit, lined with clay, where they stayed for three days and three nights without food. This shelter brings to mind the nest of the ovenbird and perhaps also some beliefs concerning the beginnings of pottery. In fact, in North America some Algonquian peoples (Blackfoot and others) say that, a long time ago, they used the same procedure in making a coarse, brittle type of earthenware, now no longer to be found.[1]

At any rate, with this inversion of the protagonists (and of other details—fire in the trees, trees in the fire; authors or victims of the fire seeking refuge in a hole, etc.), it is clear that the Mataco and Toba myths in which the Ovenbird is the main character are the mirror image of the Ayoré's Goatsucker myths.

There is more. In the Mataco myth the Ovenbird sets off the great conflagration by laughing; he is thus an inversion of the Goatsucker in the Tukuna myth (see above, p. 44), who was hiding fire in his mouth and betrayed himself by laughing, which allowed men to take possession of his fire. In this case, hidden fire is exposed; in the other, a fire that is all too visible triggers the laugh of the Ovenbird, who should have acted as though it were hidden. Finally, cooking fire, a constructive fire, comes out of the Goatsucker's mouth, an anterior and superior orifice. Destructive fire comes out of the anus of the young giants—a posterior and inferior orifice. In spite of the distance separating the Mataco from the Tukuna, these two myths are counterparts.

Closer to the Mataco, and even more so to the Ayoré, the ancient Mojo of eastern Bolivia have a myth whose hero is an Ovenbird. The Father of Men, Moconomoco, a gluttonous god, had

1. A reference to the process of pit firing, in which a pit is dug in the ground; the pots are piled up, along with fuel (wood or dried dung), and the pit is covered until all the fuel has burned down, exposing the pieces. This is a low-temperature firing that yields a quite fragile ware.—Trans.

eaten up the grain supply and then drowned, leaving the Indians to starve. The Eagle led them to the spot where the god's body was lying in the river. They pulled him out of the water, the Ovenbird ripped open his stomach, and they retrieved the grain. As a rescuer and food-provider, the Ovenbird is here again opposed to the Goatsucker, a greedy and gluttonous bird (Moconomoco is thus congruent with him), who, as we have seen, deprives his family of food and drink.

The Cashinawa live much further north, but they belong to the Pano linguistic family, which also includes the Mataco, according to some studies. Like the Ayoré, they associate the great fire with the shortening of human life. Moreover, they describe this fire in the same terms as the Mataco do: the trees were all reduced to ashes, and that was the main effect and practically the only one mentioned in either story. Such similarities might help reconstruct the cultural history of the sub-Andean regions through which the Pano-speaking peoples advanced. Now, the Cashinawa also give a prominent part to the Ovenbird: in the times when their ancestors were leading primitive lives, sleeping in the open and eating only roasted meat, the Ovenbird taught them how to build houses and make pots. They worship the bird, and it is forbidden to kill it.

*

After showing that jealousy, pottery, and the Goatsucker are parts of a system in a large group of Jivaro myths, I attempted to discover the reason for such a system. I proceeded through a series of stages, first establishing a link between pottery and jealousy, then between jealousy and the Goatsucker. In order to close the system, I still had to link pottery and the Goatsucker.

The preceding notions concerning the Ovenbird lead one to think that there is indeed a link between the two terms, and this is corroborated by the Cashinawa myth about the origin of pottery. However, it is an indirect link, going through another bird, one whose habits, and the myths concerning it, place it in correlation with and opposition to the Goatsucker. For this bird, in whom all the semantic valences of the other are reversed, takes us straight back to pottery.

Is this a legitimate procedure? This remains to be proved, for I am suggesting that we complete a transformational cycle with a stage that is absent in the myths that illustrate the other stages.

However, can we say that the Ovenbird is completely absent from these myths? Though its main habitat is a huge southern area, including the Chaco, where most of the myths concerning it belong, it is often found in other parts of South America and beyond, and the Cashinawa myth is only one example of the Ovenbird's sacred status in Brazil as a whole. The bird likes to nest quite close to human settlements, and the building materials and the size and perfection of its nest are striking:

> When crossing the high, mountainous ranges separating the great coastal forests in Brazil from the prairies of the Campos, . . . everywhere along the road, on tall, isolated trees near the houses, one can see big lumps of dirt on the thick horizontal branches, looking like melons with bulges all over them. There is something extraordinary in their aspect. They look like termitaries. [Brehm 1891: 540]

There is no doubt that the Ovenbird was on the Indians' mind even when it did not show up in their stories. And, as I have demonstrated, its habits were bound to be seen as being completely opposed to the Goatsucker's.

Still, another kind of difficulty remains. So far, I have been postulating the existence of a transformation in five stages:

woman → jealousy → pottery → goatsucker → ovenbird

From a formal point of view, there is something disturbing in this sequence: a bird follows a bird at the end. Whereas the first three stages are heterogeneous, the last two are homogeneous. They thus appear redundant in this respect (for a similar problem, see

From Honey to Ashes, pp. 265–66). Such a redundancy would disappear if the logical positions of the birds in the system were themselves heterogeneous. Now, that is the direct result of a formula I established in 1955, which I called a "canonical formula," for it can represent any mythic transformation.

At first, the Jivaro myths presented us with the following problem: What is the relation between the Goatsucker, who "functions" as a jealous bird or as a cause for jealousy, and a woman whose function is to explain the origin of pottery? Hence the following formula:

$$\frac{F}{jealousy} : \frac{F}{potter} \; :: \; ?$$
$$\text{(Goatsucker)} \quad \text{(Woman)}$$

We need to note that this is a negative function: mankind obtains clay only because the woman loses it and dies; that is, her human self dies, and she turns into the bird whose name she used to bear.

Here, now, is the solution to which we are led:

$$\frac{F}{jealousy} : \frac{F}{potter} \; :: \; \frac{F}{jealousy} : \frac{F}{Goatsucker} -1$$
$$\text{(Goatsucker)} \quad \text{(Woman)} \quad \text{(Woman)} \quad \text{(potter)}$$

In other words, the "jealous" function of the Goatsucker is to the "potter" function of the woman as the "jealous" function of the woman is to the "reversed Goatsucker" function of the potter. What does this mean?

In order to follow the Jivaro myth and be able to establish a relationship between a woman and a bird, on the one hand, and between jealousy and pottery, on the other, here is what is needed: (1) a congruence must appear between the woman and the bird with respect to jealousy; (2) the register of the birds must have one term congruent with pottery. The Ovenbird meets this need;

it is thus legitimate to introduce it into the system, provided it is seen as an "inverted Goatsucker," as it is in fact seen in the myths. Indeed, the Ovenbird myths are inverse transformations of the Goatsucker myths.

As I have shown, the "jealousy" function of the Goatsucker depends on what I have elsewhere called an empirical deduction: it is an anthropomorphic interpretation of the bird's antomy and observable habits. As for the Ovenbird, it cannot be considered as a term in a relation, because it does not appear as such in the Goatsucker myths. It is present as a term only in those myths that invert the former ones. However, by using it as a function, one verifies the system of equivalences obtained through a transformation into an empirical deduction of what started out as only a transcendental deduction (namely, that the Goatsucker may be at the origins of pottery, as is claimed in the myth): in the light of experience, the Ovenbird is a master potter as, in the light of experience, the Goatsucker is a jealous bird.

This shift is accompanied, in the rhetorical realm, by a transformation that is comparable to the transformation of a function into a term: a supernatural creature that used to be a Goatsucker only in name—that is, figuratively—actually turns into this bird when, in disappearing physically, she leaves mankind with the raw material used in making pots, namely, clay, which, *sub specie naturae,* only her opposite, the Ovenbird, knows how to work.

5
Goatsucker Myths
in North America

Goatsucker myths in North America. We find there the three themes spotted in South America. The theme of splitting illustrated by the story of the moving rock, which brings us back to marital strife and jealousy.

*

Goatsuckers are represented by sixty to seventy species in South America but by only six in North America, and these six do not correspond exactly to those we have already encountered. The *Nyctibius* genus is the most important one in the Tropics, but it does not go any further north than southern Texas. In North America the *Caprimulgus* genus (with a rounded tail) and the *Chordeiles* genus (with a forked tail) are predominant. Indigenous languages generally make a distinction between the two genera. English versions of the myths most often translate the first one as Whippoorwill and the second as Nighthawk or Bullbat.

Despite this extremely uneven distribution of goatsuckers in the two hemispheres, and although the *Chordeiles minor* species is the only one represented in the whole of the Northern Hemisphere, with the exception of the arctic and subarctic zones (the distribution of *Caprimulgus vociferus* is limited to the eastern half of the United States; in the western half it is replaced by *Phaloenoptilus nuttallii,* called poorwill), Goatsucker myths from the two Americas display a remarkable homogeneity. This is yet another proof supporting the thesis defended in *Mythologiques,* namely, that American mythology is one. In North America we will indeed find, variously illustrated, all the themes that appeared in our analysis of the South American myths.

Like the Indians of Guiana, some North American peoples, differing in languages and cultures, agree in considering goatsuckers lazy: they do not build nests but lay their eggs directly on the

Fig. 2   The North American goatsucker *Chordeiles minor*
(After Brehm 1891: vol. 2, p. 227)

ground or on stones.[1] As we have seen, it is partly because of this peculiarity that South American myths oppose the Ovenbird to the Goatsucker.

The Penobscot Indians of Maine designate *Caprimulgus* by the word *wi'pule'su* (attested under related forms in other northern languages of the Algonquian family: Malecite, Saint Francis, Micmac, etc.). According to popular etymology, it is derived from the word *li'puli,* "Ejaculate!" We have here a counterpart of the relationship, frequent in South American myths, between the Goatsucker's mouth and the vulva. The Penobscot, on their part, hear their word for "vulva" in the cry of the thrush, a bird that, like the goatsucker, is the herald of evils and death.

In the Great Lakes area the Menominee, also members of the Algonquian linguistic family, believe that the death of a goatsucker accidentally hit by a hunter augurs imminent danger. But if, on hearing its cry, one manages to point one's finger toward the exact

1. I must add that the poorwill (*Phaloenoptilus*), called "the Sleeper" by the Hopi, is a hibernating bird, at least in the southwestern part of the United States.

spot where the bird is sitting, it will stop crying and leave. The Omaha and the Dakota—Plains Indians of the Siouan linguistic family—say that a goatsucker, when consulted by a human, foretells an imminent death if it stops crying, a long life if it goes on crying. The eastern Cherokee, who are distantly related to the Iroquois linguistically, neither kill nor eat goatsuckers. They fear these birds—hate them, even—for their cry is an ill omen, and sorcerers often take on their appearance when practicing evil.

We have seen that South American Indians also establish a link between the Goatsucker and death, but not without some ambiguity, for the coastal Tupi gave the Goatsucker a positive connotation (see p. 36). Up to a certain point, the Iroquois may also have given the Goatsucker a positive connotation by making it the leader of their initiatory quest; the Algonquian-speaking Fox, neighbors of the Menominee, may also have done so and likewise the Hopi and the Zuñi in the southwestern part of the United States, as is perhaps suggested by the prominent role played in their rites by the bird itself or by its feathers.

Finally, I have pointed to a transformation in Jivaro myths: *moon wife → goatsucker wife → frog wife.* Now, the Ute Indians of the Great Basin see in the Whippoorwill a nocturnal deity who was ordered by the council of the gods to turn the Frog into the Moon.

∗

A myth whose distribution seems restricted to central and northern California (Maidu, Achomawi, Modoc) deals with the origin of the goatsucker. In the Maidu version that I will follow here, it is called Nighthawk (in the others, it is simply Hawk). One day an Indian sent his two daughters off to marry a great hunter. They would be able to tell his house by the skins of the black bear that hung by the door. However, he added, they were not to go to the wrong house, for just across the way lived Nighthawk, a lazy, good-for-nothing man. The two girls set off. Nighthawk saw them from a distance and stole the bearskins, which he tied up by his

61

own door. The girls went into his house and spent the night there. They discovered their mistake only the following morning, for in the meantime the good hunter had returned and retrieved his bearskins. The girls immediately went to the other house.

Nighthawk was furious at the loss of his wives, and he called down a storm. It rained and rained. The whole country was flooded. Water came into the houses. This lasted until the new husband cut off the evil man's head: "The evil Night-Hawk-Man long ago, getting angry because of women, caused the water to rise in flood." And, speaking to him: "That is what you are. You shall be one who shall not disturb mortal men. You are Night-Hawk, you shall be a bird, unable to do anything. It shall be a world where, lying to women, (people) can marry them" (Dixon 1912: 195–97). The Achomawi version gives a different moral: by beheading the one who caused the flood, they created the right to kill evil shamans.

The Modoc version presents some disconcerting aspects. It obviously derives from the other versions but seems to replace the Nighthawk with a small Hawk (provided the Modoc words are the exact equivalents of those used by their Klamath neighbors, for whose language we have more comprehensive grammars and lexicons). However, this version very strongly emphasizes the traits attributed to the Goatsucker by the South American myths, as we will now see.

We must first note that, for the Modoc, the Hawk embodies a supernatural spirit with a greedy character of remarkable tenacity. The main character in this myth is named Hawk. He was a bad hunter who, when invited, ate his fill of meat without taking anything back to his family. The other hunters liked to make him open his mouth and then gorge him with pieces of meat, especially the liver and intestines they themselves disdained. This grotesque, despised character once managed to fool two sisters who had been sent to the village by their mother in order to marry Eagle, a great hunter. Hawk passed himself off as Eagle by soaring high into the sky, a performance that nearly cost him his life.

Then, since he had no food to give to his wives, he cut flesh from his legs and brought that to them—a scanty and execrable fare. They watched him, saw him being fed by the hunters, realized their mistake, and went to the good hunter.

Eagle and Hawk each had four brothers. The two camps got into a fight. The Eagles won, decapitated the imposter, and threw his head up into the sky. The women had been forbidden to look, but they disobeyed, and the head dropped back down, killing the Eagles. The head became the husband of the two women. The elder took on the task of carrying it around in her basket. She pulled it out every time it asked to fly out to kill game. One day, in tears, weighed down by all the meat she had to pile up in her basket, she no longer alerted the head when she spotted game and went for help to Kumush, the great cultural hero. He took the head out of the basket and put it in a sweat lodge full of red-hot stones. The head begged to be let out. When Kumush ignored its plea, it broke through the stones piled on the roof of the sweat lodge and died of exhaustion. The sweat lodge was carefully opened, and the body of a handsome young man was found inside. They burned it on a funeral pyre, and this is the origin of the cremation of the dead.

In this myth the villain is gluttonous and selfish. Like the South American Goatsucker, he eats all the good food and starves his family (see p. 43). Let us note the following resemblance as well: seeing their man being stuffed with food (here by his fellow hunters, there by his mother) provokes the greatest indignation in his wife or wives. It is this sight that prompts the Mundurucu woman (or women), on the banks of the Amazon (see p. 42), and her Modoc counterpart, on the borders of California and Oregon, to leave so dreadful a husband.

This person, according to the North American versions, is then beheaded. The head severed from the body can fly, like the head of the Goatsucker woman in a Kayapo myth (see p. 43). The rest of the Modoc version illustrates the theme of the clinging woman (here it is a clinging husband), which I have already discussed (see p. 29). As for the incident of the head breaking through the stones on the roof of the sweat lodge, other North American myths will soon show that it plays a central part in Goatsucker myths. Consequently, the fact that the Goatsucker in the Ayoré myths kills his opponents with shattered stones is not an insignificant detail or even a secondary theme. In both North and South America the theme of split stones is a constant in Goatsucker myths.

In several versions of the North American myth, the bird-man causes a flood, and according to the Ayoré of the Bolivian Chaco the anger of the Goatsucker also provokes such a catastrophe. Finally, the story of a jealous rivalry between two men over one or two women clearly takes us back to the Jivaro myth and to our starting point. Jealousy stems from the husbands' fear of being left by their wives. In the Maidu version, this theme is doubled by a symmetrical one: the men will henceforth lie to women in order to coax them into becoming their wives. Here, a lie brings about the union of the sexes; there, jealousy manifests their disunion.

Let us attempt to go further in this search for parallels between the myths of the two hemispheres, risky as this may be. In the Modoc myth, Eagle warns the two sisters that he is going to cut off his rival's head and "take it above the sky." Let us suppose, even though it is not mentioned in the text, that the head, once high in the sky, will turn into a heavenly body. Thus the two sisters whose sin was to look up into the air will remind us of a Karaja myth already mentioned (see p. 41), particularly because, in both cases, one of the women rejects an ugly husband, while the other accepts him (the elder sister in the Modoc myth; the younger, according to the Karaja); moreover, in both cases (though *post mortem* in the Modoc myth), the repulsive husband turns into a handsome young man.

Are we not dealing here with the fragments of one and the same mosaic, arranged differently? It is difficult not to admit it, and one can scarcely avoid concluding that two versions of a myth on the origin of the Goatsucker, separated by thousands of miles, were independently drawn into the orbit, so to speak, of the Pan-American cycle of the star-husband (see *The Origin of Table Man-*

ners, pp. 203 ff.). This cycle is itself part of a greater one, the cycle of the quarrel between the stars, which we have already encountered in our discussion of the Jivaro myths.

∗

The cycle of the star-husband is especially well represented among the Algonquian and is also found among small groups, of various languages and cultures, found in a limited area in what is now the western parts of Oregon and Washington; the latter are thus close to the Modocs, whom we have just discussed. These two population groups, then, together with some of their neighbors, share a myth in which Goatsuckers play a strategic part. To examine over twenty versions one after the other would be tedious. Let us simply say that they all start with a quarrel between the Trickster (a deceiving half-god) and a rock endowed with speech and movement. The causes of the quarrel do not vary much from one version to the next: the Trickster has given his blanket, his shirt, or his knife to the rock and now wants them back because it is about to rain or because he needs the knife to cut his meat; the Trickster had given the rock a blanket soiled with excrement, but, now that it has been cleaned by its new owner, he would like to have it back; the Trickster steals the blanket from the rock or else he relieves himself on the rock and soils it. The rock has no use for robbers or litterers. He also thinks that one cannot give something and then take it back. The Blackfoot version contains the following maxim: "What was given to the great rocks can never be taken back." So the rock starts rolling, chasing after the Trickster, catches up with him, and traps him under his huge weight. Summoned by the cries of the victim, several animals come to his rescue, but they all get killed by the rock; or else the victim calls directly to the Goatsuckers (to *Caprimulgus* alone, or to *Caprimulgus* first and then to *Chordeiles*). The last bird he implores manages to shatter the rock, almost always by farting violently. The rock is reduced to little pieces. This, says one version, is the origin of all the stones that one sees today in the world.

Algonquian words for the bird *Chordeiles* generally stem from the root *pist-*, which seems to inspire numerous puns among the Blackfoot, since their word for "fart" is *pistit*. However, the episode of the Nighthawk's farts is not limited to the populations belonging to this linguistic family, so the link between these two notions is probably more than strictly phonetic.

In its twenty-odd versions, the myth covers a considerable area. It includes the Micmac, the Kickapoo, the Cree, the Blackfoot, the Gros Ventre, and the Arapaho, all belonging to the Algonquian language family; then, south of the Arapaho, the Siouan tribes, like the Dakota (for whom the hero, the victim of a Rock woman clinging to his back, is freed by his son, who, having been turned into "Hawk," shatters the rock with an arrow) and the so-called village tribes of the Upper Missouri River: the Arikara, Pawnee, Mandan, and Hidatsa; then, further west, in the Great Basin, the Ute and, to the northwest, the Salish of the interior: the Flathead and the Coeur d'Alene.

The myth claims to explain the birds' current appearance rather than their origin. They have a wide mouth and a flat head because the Trickster wanted to beautify them, to reward them for their help, or, more commonly, he transformed them out of ingratitude and in jest, after being freed by them. The latter version (in which the Nighthawk gets his mouth slit wide open in a fight) is echoed as far away as the Klamath.

In the South American myths, we saw that the Goatsucker reveals that he is hiding the fire in his mouth when he bursts out laughing and that he shatters stones and pelts his opponents with the flakes. This splitting theme becomes even more prominent in the North American myth, in which one or several Nighthawks shatter a big rock (thus producing, according to one version, all the stones in the world), and they do so by themselves exploding—but through a different opening: instead of laughing, they fart.

What the Indians interpret as a loud flatulence is apparently the sound of the bird's wings vibrating in the air when it swoops on its prey. We find this explanation in a peripheral version from the Ute

Indians. Audubon, who describes the same phenomenon with a different image, says that, when the bird reaches the middle of its plunge, the wings take a new direction and open suddenly in the wind, violently hitting the air like the sails of a boat (Audubon 1848). The Algonquian versions, which hold a central position in the whole set, associate the sound of the bird with thunder and see the Goatsucker as a mediator between the celestial powers and the chthonian powers (let us not forget that they are engaged in a fight in which pottery is at stake). In an Assiniboine version, the thunder itself breaks the rock. In a version from the same origin, the Trickster promises the hand of his daughter to whoever will set him free, only to admit flatly, once he has been freed, that he has no daughter. He is reputed to enjoy deceiving women. This is reminiscent of the moral of the Maidu myth (see p. 62). We find another, independent, analogy when comparing a Blackfoot version of the myth about the vindictive rock with the Hidatsa myth about the origins of pottery and marital jealousy. In the latter myth (see p. 31) the hero has been "soiled" by the touch of a seductress and tries to hide the incident from his wife by cutting off the part of his shirt that his sister-in-law had touched. The hero of the Blackfoot myth, the Trickster, does the same thing when the Nighthawks defecate on his shirt in retribution for the misshapen faces inflicted on their young; he strips off piece after piece, ends up stark naked, his body covered with ordure, and is finally obliged to go and wash himself off.

This Blackfoot version calls for two remarks. Despite the distance, it is strikingly similar to a myth found among the Parintintin, the Tupi-speaking Indians who live along the Rio Madeira in the Amazon Basin. One day an old man made fun of the Goatsucker (*bucurau*) because of his wide mouth. The bird took him up into the sky, then dropped him. During his fall, the old man opened his mouth, and the bird defecated into it: "That's why old men's mouths stink." Second, in the Blackfoot myth, the story takes place at a time when men and women lived apart and marriage did not yet exist. In fact, it is at the end of the Trickster's adventures—and one of them is the incident with the Nighthawks—that women finally decided to take husbands. We are thus taken back to the link between the Goatsucker and the issue of the relation between the sexes, which, at the beginning of our investigation, we found illustrated in the theme of marital jealousy in Goatsucker myths.

In Canada, the Dakota Indians, neighbors of the Algonquians but speaking a Siouan language, give the name *p'isko* to a certain bird (the nighthawk, according to Rigg's dictionary; for Wallis, conjecturally, whippoorwill), and *p'isko* is derived from a root that is phonetically close to the one we have seen in Algonquian. In one of their myths, this bird yielded to Spider a magical power he had received from the Thunders. For this reason, the Thunders held a grudge against him, and the Indians do not bring him offerings of tobacco. The Nighthawk (a goatsucker) stands halfway between the Thunders, masters of the celestial world, and Spider, master of the terrestrial world: he bears the responsibility for the conflict between these powers.

The Apache, southern Athapaskans, live on the periphery of the area in which we find the myths about the vindictive rock defeated by the Nighthawks. Here, again, these birds hold a prominent place. According to the Apache, one species—probably *Chordeiles minor*—with a name close to the Algonquian, *piše,* flies so fast that lightning cannot catch up with him. Thus, "during a thunderstorm we go, 'piš, piš.' . . . It is just like making believe that we are that bird during the lightning, and then it is hard for that bird to hit us too" (Opler 1941: 195). The Nighthawk is deified; rites are performed in his honor. The Apache also celebrate a cult of the *gahe* or *jajadeh,* from the name of another goatsucker (the poorwill: *Phaloenoptilus?*). Gahe or Jajadeh, spirits living inside the mountains, are impersonated by masked dancers. During the day these spirits take on the appearance of poorwills; at night they turn into women who are child-abductors and flesh-eaters. It is interesting to point out, by the way, that Flathead versions of the myth of the vindictive rock replace the Nighthawks, found elsewhere, with two old women. These women also break the rock to pieces, and they are cannibals. They are killed by the

Trickster (here Coyote). Remember that one version of the California myth links the origin of the Nighthawk to the murder of bad shamans (see p. 62). Goeje's obscure indication, based on Penard (Goeje 1943: 54) according to which the Kalina of Guiana "say the Whippoorwill originated in slander," may be traced back to the same set of beliefs assimilating Goatsuckers to evil sorcerers.

The prominent part given to Goatsuckers by the Apache, not only in myths but also in major rites, recalls the importance of Goatsuckers for the Ayoré in South America. This is all the more significant because the Goatsucker, at the top of the Ayoré pantheon, is a jealous deity, and observers of the present-day Apache stress that the notions of jealousy and envy are crucial to an understanding of their psychology and daily behavior. Moreover, according to these observers, in the Apache language there is only one word for the notions of jealousy, envy, and greed, and in their current life this people seems to blend the three into one feeling.

6
Oral Greediness and Anal Retention

Oral greediness and anal retention: the Goatsucker and the Sloth. Back to the Jivaro creation myth: cosmic conflict and war among humans. The Sloth, an old enemy. A brief look at his role in various South American myths.

*

Selfish, envious, jealous, miserly, guzzling: literally or figuratively, the Goatsucker in the myths of the Americas connotes oral greediness. We may wonder, however, how this trait leads to farting or defecating. It would not be enough to say that, in order to explode, whether through laughter or flatulence, one needs to be morally or physically stuffed to the point of being unable to hold back; for besides the fact that the myths do not place these two dispositions in a cause-and-effect relationship but alternately stress the one or the other, there are other reasons for thinking that the connection between them is established at a deeper level.

To present oral greediness as a category of mythic thought invites the question whether this category exists as such, by itself—whether it is a whole in itself—or whether, in disengaging it from the material under analysis, we may have isolated a fragment of a semantic field, one stage among others in a transformation.

Following the hypothetico-deductive method applied in *Totemism* (1936b:16–18), I will try to draw a table of commutations in which oral greediness is but one element and then check this system against the facts.

Oral is opposed to anal. Psychoanalytic theory has accustomed us to this opposition, but we will see that mythic thought had anticipated this much, much earlier. The *oral/anal* opposition has to do with body openings. These can be open or closed, and according to their state they can fulfill three different functions: if closed, they retain; if open, they absorb or evacuate. Hence a system with six commutations: oral retention, oral greediness, oral incontinence, and anal retention, anal greediness, anal incontinence. We will not postulate that there necessarily are myths representing each case. Some cases may remain unrepresented, and this will require an explanation. We must first examine which elements are actually represented.

Various animals immediately appear as potential candidates after the Goatsucker. However, even before bringing them before us, this way of tackling the issue sheds light on the ambiguous character of the Goatsucker. Indeed, if this bird connotes *oral greediness,* it doubly reverses *anal retention* and must demonstrate some form of *anal incontinence,* which is generally exemplified by farting and/or defecating. A whole group of myths studied above (pp. 65–67) confirms this transformation. Oral greediness results from an empirical deduction; not so with the anal incontinence attributed to the Goatsucker, which results from a transcendental deduction, a process of logical deduction, not inference from observation. We will see later—this time through empirical deduction—that another animal, the Howler Monkey, connotes anal incontinence in myths. For the time being we will focus on anal retention, which stands in diametric opposition to oral greediness in the table representing our system of commutations. In South American myths, the animal assigned the job of connoting anal retention is the Sloth.

This opposition between the Sloth and the Goatsucker immediately appears as paradoxical. Goatsuckers, though their species vary greatly, in types and numbers, from one hemisphere to the other, are present in both of the American continents, except for the arctic regions. We have also been able to confirm that the myths in which these birds appear are remarkably homogeneous throughout the New World.

In contrast, the sloth—an edentate mammal, a member of the suborder of the Xenarthres, along with the anteaters and armadillos, and represented by the genera *Bradypus* and *Choloepus*—suffers from a poor thermal regulation system, which restricts its habitat to the warmer zones of the continent, where the tempera-

ture remains almost constant. Moreover, sloths, especially those of
the *Bradypus* genus, feed on a very limited number of vegetable
species, among which the leaves of *Cecropia* hold a prominent
place: "Some thinke that this beast lyveth onely with leaves of a
certaine tree," Thevet wrote, in the sixteenth century. These two
factors confine the sloth to a forested zone extending, roughly
speaking, from eastern Bolivia to Guiana, including the Amazon
Basin.

We are thus lucky to find that, in the very heart of this zone,
Jivaro myths, the starting point of this book, give the Sloth a privi-
leged place beside the Goatsucker. The fact that the two animals
are put on the same footing supports the hypothesis that they form
a pair of terms in the correlation and opposition. In chapters 1
and 2 I examined a few fragments of the Jivaro Genesis myth. I
will now take it up again at its beginning.

*

The Creator and his wife had two children: Etsa, the sun, and
Nantu, the moon. According to Stirling's version, Auhu, the Goatsucker, was assiduously courting Moon (remember that, in other
versions, Sun and Moon, both men, were jealous over their wife,
the Goatsucker).

In Stirling's version, Sun and Moon, married at last (see pp. 17–
18, 21), had four children: first, Uñushi, the Sloth; then Apopa, the
Amazonian Dolphin, appointed to come to the rescue of his older
brother every time this forest-dweller was in danger on the water;
then Huangañi, the Peccary; and, finally, a daughter, Nijamanche,
the Manioc (or manioc bear), a companion and friend to the
Indians.

As Sun and Moon seemed unable to procreate any more, their
mother, the Creator's wife, gave them two eggs. The Egret stole
them; in the fight that ensued, one of the eggs was broken. The
other hatched into Mika, the earthenware pot, who became the
Sloth's wife. Their parents taught them their marital duties, and

they became the primordial couple. But the husband, faithful to his name, was lazy, and that is why women today have to take care of the hardest tasks.

On a canoe trip, they had a son, Ahimbi, the Water Snake, who first went roaming the world, then came back to his parents. He met his mother, who was lost in the forest, and committed incest with her. Sun caught them and banished them. They had many children; but the animals, who had been helpful to them until then, abandoned them.

Uñushi, who had also lost his way, finally heard the unfortunate news. For no apparent reason he accused his mother, the Moon, of having helped the offenders, and he beat her and then buried her in a hole. Goatsucker, the Moon's unlucky lover, appeared. On the advice of the Dove, he made a horn out of a shell, crept into the hollow trunk of a dead palm tree, and blew his instrument. Responding to the call, Moon burst out of the hole, sped through the hollow tree like a dart through a blowpipe, pushing Goatsucker out of the way, and flew straight up to the sky. Not a word of thanks for Goatsucker. Since then, he can be heard moaning in the moonlight.

When the children of Mika and Ahimbi heard about all this, they went after the Sloth, cut off his head, and shrank it. To avenge him, Mika killed her children. In the midst of raging storms, Ahimbi the Snake fought his mother, the killer of their offspring. These family feuds are the origin of war and of the division of the Jivaro into hostile groups, some on Mika's side, others supporting Ahimbi or Uñushi.

Sun and Moon came back to earth in order to put an end to this strife. They stuffed Ahimbi into the hollow trunk of a palm tree, which they spun slowly while blowing into it as into a blowpipe. This maneuver turned Ahimbi into a boa. Sun and Moon tied him up and left him at the bottom of the river rapids. Returning to a better disposition, the Snake tried to demonstrate his peaceful mood by creating the rainbow, a symbol of unity. All in vain, though, for the war-spirit cast a cloud over it and applied himself to stirring up discord among the tribes. The Creator's wife, the Snake's great-grandmother, tried at last to free him. But the Snake, blinded by rage, did not recognize her, sank her canoe, ate her up, and so lost his last chance to recover his freedom.

*

One must admit that this story is quite confusing. As was noted in the partial summary (see pp. 14–18), characters change sexes from one version to another. Moreover some episodes, probably key ones, are missing, and others, recently published by the Salesian missions, do not tell the known events in the same way, or else they tell of different events, whose links to each other and to already known episodes are not very clear.

Let us proceed in stages, first clarifying two points.

One of the episodes of the myth relates the origins of head-shrinking, the art practiced with great skill by the Jivaro. The first shrunken head, or *tsantsa,* was that of the Sloth. Actually, for lack of human heads, or simply when the occasion presented itself, the Jivaro did shrink the heads of sloths and valued them almost as much. Indeed, as is clearly indicated in the myth, they saw the Sloth as an ancestor, but a member of an enemy group. What is more, his slowness and his grayish coat pointed to a very old age, which proved his strong attachment to life, and, the hardier the opponent, the greater the victory: by shrinking so valorous a head, one gains a soul of superior quality. An informant from a Jivaro group, the Shuar, gives the following explanation: "You wonder why we shrink the head of the Sloth? Well, we see him as a former Shuar, an old enemy who has been transformed; that is why we kill him and honor his *tsantsa*" (Pellizzaro 1982: 59). In Guiana, the Kalina also attribute great tenacity to the Sloth, but they see this under a different light. To them, the three-toed Sloth (*Bradypus*) is the strongest of all underwater spirits:

When people in their boat hear the shrill "ai, ai" of the [*takini*-spirit, akin to the three-toed Sloth-Grandfather]

Fig. 3   The sloth *Bradypus tridactylus*
(After Brehm 1890: vol. 2, p. 647)

they get terribly frightened. Those spirits twine their invisible arms around the boat and pull it down to the bottom of the river, where they crush the people in their deadly embrace. [Goeje 1943: 47]

Now to the second point: eggs. Supernatural creatures hatched from eggs are not limited to Jivaro mythology. The theme can be traced northeast, up to Guiana (Makiritaré), southwest into ancient Peru (Huamachuco), and to a point near the Chaco, among the Mbaya. It also reaches across the Pacific: it can be spotted in Oceania, Indonesia, Korea, China, and even India. We will not delve further into this geographical distribution; let us simply point to a sort of rationalization of this theme, provided by a Shuar version that hints of a love affair between the Sun's mother and a

Duck. Her husband killed her, it seems, and opened up her womb, in which he found eggs. In an Aguaruna version, a duck took over and hatched the eggs.

Let us now return to the Jivaro myths, analyzed earlier, that are part of this set. In ancient times the sky and the earth were connected; the Indians' ancestors could freely pass from one to the other. This ceased when Sun and Moon climbed up to the sky and cut off the vine. As we saw, they wanted to prevent the Goatsucker woman from catching up with them. Here the Shuar version is quite explicit: "If the vine had not been cut, it would still be hanging down from the sky, and we could also have reached the sky" (Pellizzaro 1980a). These happy days are gone, but they have left their mark on the earth: the potter's clay the Goatsucker woman dropped or into which she herself was transformed while falling.

There is thus a striking parallel between these myths and those on the origin of cooking fire, which I summarized and analyzed in *The Naked Man*. For just as cooking fire, now found on earth, is proof that the world Above and the world Below used to be connected, so also does potter's clay—which presupposes fire to harden it—act as a mediator between the two worlds.

In the Jivaro myths this term is present under three distinct modalities. One of them is the Goatsucker woman, the unwitting creator of potter's clay. Stirling's version successively presents two others: first, Nuhi, the son that Moon fashioned of clay before she married the Sun. He was smashed by the jealous Goatsucker (here a man), and his dead body became the earth on which we now live. Second, there is Mika, the earthenware jar.

From this point on, the architecture of the myth becomes a little clearer. As in other myths, seen earlier (see pp. 28–32, 48–50), pottery is here at stake in a struggle between celestial and chthonian powers. Mika is doubly connected to the sky: she issued from an egg that was given to two celestial bodies, Sun and Moon; this egg was then rescued by a bird. Though still connected to the sky, this creature was pulled down below into an incestuous relationship with her son, the Water Snake. As a consequence, Moon, Mika's mother, was buried (in the earth) but finally reached the sky, there to remain. Mika's son, the Snake, in return for eating his celestial grandmother, who had wanted to set him free, was sent for good to the bottom of the water, in the world Below.

In the middle of all this strife, however, something new comes to light: the separation into tribes, and war—two themes that will gradually take over the second part of the story. For, in the end, the sole winner is war: "Having successfully prevented this threat of peace [whose symbol was the rainbow], Masata [the war-spirit] once more started visiting each of the tribes, hurling out his slogan: 'Make war! Make war!'" (Stirling 1938: 129).

(Though it is contingent on a reversal of the polarity of water, *up → down*, there is a striking symmetry between this myth and a myth of the ancient Mayas, illustrated on the page of the Dresden Codex that serves as the frontispiece of this book.)

In short, the Jivaro (in the Roman fashion, one might say, referring to Georges Dumézil's research) change the cosmic conflict between the celestial and chthonian powers into a political conflict, in which the tribes become the opponents. But hadn't the Jivaro myths on the origin of pottery already accomplished this transposition, and even more directly? Indeed, in these myths the ancient connection between heaven and earth was cut off following a polyandrous conflict between two husbands fighting over the same woman. This primeval conflict is perpetuated in and by the extremely jealous temper of Jivaro husbands, noticed by modern observers, which gives rise to conflicts both within the tribes and with strangers. The myths and local informants alike stress this aspect of native life. A short Aguaruna tale asks why the Indians are so jealous of their wives—which means that they actually *are* jealous. A Shuar informant, commenting on the Goatsucker woman's bad conduct—which he deems responsible for today's disputes between men and women—explicitly links these private disputes with war: "When a married woman meets another man, her husband and this man don't limit themselves to quarreling; they declare war on each other and fight until one of them kills the other. That is why husbands today must keep a jealous watch over their wives, in order to avoid confrontations" (Pellizzaro 1982: 59). I was not overinterpreting the myths when I suggested that disputes arising from marital jealousy might be seen as models, representations of wars to come, for we can see that the Indians themselves offer this interpretation.

*

Nothing in all this seems to account for the place of the Sloth in the Jivaro Genesis tale, and this problem will detain us for some time. As a preliminary, I will introduce a few myths from other populations; their interest lies in the Sloth's presence in them and in the fact that they can be linked to the myths we have already discussed. After this circling maneuver, we will make a frontal attack on the problem.

The Jivaros are not alone in South America in seeing the Sloth as one of their ancestors. The Motilon, a people of Colombia, say that at the beginning of the world the Sloth was a man. The Ipurina, Arawak-speaking Indians who live in Brazil, in the basin of the Rio Purus (some six hundred miles southeast of the Jivaro), believe they are descended from the Sloth. According to one of their myths (myth M_{331} in *From Honey to Ashes*), there used to be a large pot in the sun, and in it was boiled the garbage collected throughout the world by a multitude of Storks. Once this rotten stuff was cooked and had floated to the surface, the Storks ate it.

One day the chief of the Storks, the Creator of all birds, threw a round stone into the almost empty pot. The pot immediately filled with boiling water, boiled over, and flooded the earth, burning all the trees "and even the rivers." The sole survivors were human beings and one tree, of the Senna family (*Cassia* sp., used by the Indians as a purgative). The Sloth, who was then human, climbed this tree in search of fruit with which to feed his starving companions. The sun and the moon had disappeared, and it was pitch dark.

The Sloth picked the fruit and dropped the seeds it contained. The further they fell (first on the ground, then into deeper and deeper waters), the more clearly the sun reappeared; at first very small, it slowly grew to its present size. The chief of the Storks gave the seeds of nutritious plants to the Sloth, and the Indians were able to start cultivating gardens. The chief of the Storks ate the men who refused to work, at the rate of one a day. The pot is still in the sky, but it is now empty.

At first sight, there is no connection between this myth and the ones we saw earlier, but let us take a closer look. For the Jivaro, clay fell from the sky to the earth, to provide the raw material for pottery. But, for the Ipurina, pottery in its manufactured state already existed in the sky at the beginning of time. A temporal transfer corresponds to the spatial transfer: the pot is not used to cook fresh produce but rather garbage and various rotten stuff—stuff that belongs to the end of the culinary cycle instead of the beginning, in a sort of reversal of the cooking process. Here the Storks do not ingest food; rather, as consumers of waste, of the refuse of ordinary cooking, they reabsorb nonfood.

We see a round, intact, stone being dropped into an almost empty pot and filling it with water so hot that it consumes the world when it boils over. Is this not a striking reversal of the Ayoré myths from the Bolivian Chaco (see pp. 45–46), in which stone flakes either turn to fire or cause a blaze? And here is yet another proof of the reversal of the same terms from one group of myths to another: in the myths from the Chaco about the great fire, the only surviving tree is an *algarrobo,* an important food plant of the Mimosa family. In the Ipurina myth it is a *Cassia,* also a leguminous plant, used not as food but as a purgative. Finally, the stone-thrower, responsible for the catastrophe, is a Goatsucker for the Ayoré, a Stork for the Ipurina.

These myths are thus linked through a transformational relationship. No one, I think, will contest the notion that a universal conflagration, caused by boiling water (consuming even rivers!), cannot represent the first stage of the transformation. Rather, it comes as the final result of a series of unconscious operations effected on an initial stage that was necessarily inspired by a blaze set off by fire. It is now clearer why the Ipurina myth is set in a world where everything is reversed: where earthenware, preexisting the art of pottery, is used in "anti-cooking" and where boiling water instead of fire sets the world ablaze.

The Ufaina or Tanimuka, a small tribe in southeastern Colombia, belong to the Tukano linguistic family. One of their myths is symmetrical with the Ipurina myth. Instead of overcoming the long night, the Sloth initiates it, and he starves the Indians instead of feeding them. This Ufaina myth runs as follows. The Sloth, who still had a human shape, climbed to the top of a tree, then up to the sky on a vine. He clung to the sun, obscuring it. Darkness fell upon the earth, and it started to rain: the old man was urinating. Everything was flooded; there was nothing to eat. A fruit from the *Micrandra* (a tree of the spurge family) fell into the water and set it boiling. They bombarded the old Sloth with darts and finally cut him in two. One half fell into the water and turned into an aquatic bird; the other got caught in a branch and became the two-toed sloth (*Choloepus*). The sun shone again.

The fact that a mythical being is split into an aquatic bird and a Sloth calls for special attention because, in the Ipurina myth, the chief of the Storks was paired against the Sloth. Along the Upper Paraguay River, the Umutina, who are linguistically and culturally close to the Bororo, tell a myth in which boiling water—an element in the Tanimuka myth—ignites a fire, as in the Ipurina myth. This water belonged to otters, also water creatures. In the days when Sun and Moon lived on the earth as friends, the river otters (*Pteronura brasiliensis*) used large pots to boil their fish in water. Sun coveted the most beautiful pot; he changed into a rat and stole it. But it was too heavy and hot, and he had to call on Moon for help. Moon clumsily dropped the boiling vessel, which set the forest on fire. To escape the flames, Sun turned into a *gavião-tesoureiro* (a bird of the falcon family whose tail ends in two long feathers; this myth was reported in Portuguese), and Moon turned into a *corujinha* ("small owl"). But instead of flying out of the blaze, Moon hid in the brush and was burned to death. Sun gathered his bones and brought him back to life.

Fig. 4   The Sloth *Choloepus didactylus*
(After Vogt 1884: fig. 240, p. 496)

These two birds could be doublets or combinative variants of
the large and small goatsuckers. Like this falcon, some large goatsuckers of tropical America have two long tail feathers (in Portuguese, *Curiango tesoura; Macropsalis* and *Hydropsalis* genera);
and we have already met with a bird identified as an owl that
seems to be a goatsucker (see p. 38). Both families are nocturnal
and have soft feathers that make their flight noiseless. In the Bororo version of the myth (M_{120} in *The Origin of Table Manners*),
aquatic birds—instead of mammals—stored their drinking water
in large heavy jars. Sun came by to ask for a drink and, lifting a jar

carelessly, dropped it, letting the water spill out. The birds were angry, and, bothered by the heat of the Sun, they started fanning themselves. Sun and Moon were blown up into the sky by this wind and remained there. As in the Jivaro myths, the final separation between the world Above and the world Below results from a quarrel between celestial bodies and one or several birds—here, aquatic birds, there a Goatsucker. This quarrel either arises over earthenware or brings about the creation of potter's clay.

Let me digress here and suggest the following. In the Bororo myth, the drinking water contained in the jars clearly represents cultural water, the equivalent—in "water clef," so to speak—of cooking fire in the myths about the origin of this fire. In South America many of these myths say that cooking fire used to belong to the jaguar. Here, cooking water—i.e., drinking water—formerly belonged to aquatic birds. Losing fire condemns the jaguar to eating raw meat. Similarly, losing cultural water condemns the aquatic birds to feeding from natural water, i.e., rivers and swamps. Here is what the Bororo myth says: "You shall not need pots any longer. From now on you shall be water birds, and you shall feed from the lakes. You shall eat crabs, small fish, silt, and water plants" (Albisetti-Venturelli 1962–76: vol. 2, pp. 1139–67).

That we are indeed dealing here with a distinction between nature and culture *through pottery* is also apparent in a detail that appears at the very end of the Ipurina myth: henceforth, the chief of the Storks will punish lazy gardeners. Now, in volume two of the *Encyclopédie Bororo,* the myth that we have just analyzed is followed by another (one that may well have been collected immediately afterward) concerning the punishment of careless peasants. The myths thus establish a link between agriculture and the use—the *proper* use—of pottery.

Let us now get back to the animals who are the protagonists in all these myths. Aquatic birds here take the place of the Goatsucker. These myths also refer to a time when the Sun—who was still living on the earth (Bororo) or had fallen to earth (Ipurina)—was sent (back) up to the sky for good by aquatic birds (Bororo) or by the Sloth (Ipurina). The Tanimuka version, a reversal of the

Ipurina myth, follows the same pattern while arranging the elements in a different fashion: a personage separated the Sun too much from the earth; to bring things back to normal, this evil being was cut in two, and one of the halves brought forth an aquatic bird (*perico d'agua,* in the narrator's unpolished Spanish), the other, the Sloth. This regression thus ends with a reinstatement of the pair that appears in the Ipurina myth (see p. 78).

Across the border between Colombia and Brazil, the Tukuna, who live along the Rio Solimões and are linguistically different but not too remote from the Tanimuka, tell a strangely similar myth. At the beginning of time, they say, darkness ruled over the earth, for a great tree obscured the sky (a tree of the kapok family, apparently the same as the one the villain climbed to attack the sun in the Tanimuka myth). Every day the Nocturnal Monkey paid a visit to an *arara tucupy* tree (*Parkia oppositifolia,* a leguminous plant) and ate its fruit. Each time that he relieved himself at the base of the tree, one could see a glow. This cultural hero, by bombarding the foliage of the tree with the hulls of the fruit, made a thousand openings that let the light shine through. That is how stars came about.

Convinced that there was light above the tree, the cultural hero and his brother cut its trunk with the help of the ants and the termites. The tree remained hanging from the celestial vault. They wondered what was keeping it up there. The little Squirrel found out that it was a two-toed Sloth. He blinded him with a handful of ants, and the animal let go of the tree, which crashed to earth.

One remark about the *arara tucupy.* This leguminous plant bears tiny pods eaten only by animals. From the human point of view, it is thus a *non*food, opposed both to the *algarrobo,* a very important food plant in the Chaco, and to the tree of the *Cassia* genus, which, used as a purgative, is an *anti*food. As for the *Micrandra,* it is not a leguminous plant, and I lack information about its use. However, considering the fact that Euphorbiaceae are often used as purgatives or emetics in South America, the *Micrandra* could be seen as a combinative variant of the *Cassia.*

In the Ipurina myth we saw the Sloth throwing seeds from the tree in order to feed his starving companions. However, he feeds them purgative *Cassia* seeds—antifood, as we said—and, as a feeder, he reverses his action of defecating; this will be confirmed in the next chapter. Similarly, the luminous feces of the Nocturnal Monkey prefigure the Sloth's feces, which change into comets or igneous meteors when he cannot go down to earth to defecate, as we will also see.

The scene has been set. Now let the Sloth come on stage.

7

The Sloth as a
Cosmological Symbol

The Sloth as a cosmological symbol. The excrement of the Sloth. The
Indians' knowledge and the naturalists' knowledge. Other correlations
and oppositions between the Sloth and the Goatsucker.
Pottery vs. weaving.

＊

Tanimuka, Tukuna, Ipurina: these Indians give the Sloth a cosmic
function. This function is even more prominent further south,
among the Tacana of eastern Bolivia, who may be linguistically related to the Pano family. As we will see later, the Tanimuka, Tukuna, and Ipurina myths are on the fringe of a mythological system in equatorial and tropical America that is principally situated
along the Andes and then curves northeast toward Guiana.

Here is the Tacana tale. In the days when humans did not know
fire and fed on wind, one Indian brought back a Sloth for his two
little boys. This animal ate the leaves of the *davi* tree (of the kapok
family, like the tree in the Tanimuka and Tukuna myths) and was
almost always up in this tree. The children played at preventing
him from coming down to relieve himself. The Sloth, irritated by
this game, threatened to kill them, along with many other people.
As the children did not stop harassing him, he let himself fall to
the ground and relieved himself. The ground started to smoke;
soon flames appeared, the fire spread, and the ground broke
open and swallowed up all of the human beings.

Not all died, however, and one of the survivors was an old
woman, who said the disaster had been caused by the children's
having prevented the Sloth from leaving his tree to defecate. At
such times, she said, the animal must be allowed to climb down in
peace.

When the blaze subsided, a new mankind emerged from the
underworld by climbing a series of sticks placed end to end.

These beings were shorter than present-day men, but they are our ancestors. It is in that fire that the male sloth got the yellow spot he bears on his back. If this fire had not happened, men would still be feeding on wind.

Some variants support the old woman's theory. If, in order to relieve himself on the ground, the Sloth had to descend too fast or drop from his tree, he would make a hole in the ground. If he dropped his excrement from high in the tree, it would hit the earth like a comet. The earth would pivot, and all living creatures would die; or else it would break open, and water would spring forth and flood everything, causing total destruction.

In another version, red Howler Monkeys settled in the top of a tall tree, fed on its fruit, and did not hesitate to urinate and defecate without leaving the top. They marveled at the habit of the Sloth, on a nearby tree, who always climbed down to relieve himself, and they asked why he did that. The Sloth explained that, if he followed their example, the earth would pivot; then the Idsettideha (literally, "Sun men," inhabitants of the chthonian world) would mount to the surface, while the present inhabitants of the earth would go to live in the underworld. That is why sloths always relieve themselves on the ground.

It will be recalled that in an Achuar myth (see p. 20) a miraculous baby—later to become Uyush the Sloth—when molested by children, descended into the underworld through a hollow bamboo stem. He created the joints in the stem by defecating at regular intervals. In their version of the same myth, the Aguaruna, another Jivaro group, say he created flatulence.

Tacana beliefs about the Sloth find an equivalent in Guiana also, where the small sloth (*Bradypus tridactylus*) is called *kupírisi,* "sun sloth," because of the yellow spot between his shoulder blades. Brazilian peasants call him *ai de bentinho,* "scapular sloth," for the same reason. The Kalina phrase *kupirisi yumañ,* "Father(?) of the Sloth," refers to a star that appears low on the horizon early in the long dry season: "The Carib then says: 'The Sloth [the star bearing this name] comes down to earth to relieve himself; he has

Fig. 5   The red howler monkey *Alouatta* (formerly *Mycetes*) *seniculus*
(After Vogt 1884: fig. 14, p. 50)

not relieved himself for one year.' The Sloth cries out when the
star nears the horizon; that is why the star is called *kupírisi yumañ*"
(Ahlbrinck 1956: art. "Kupirisi").

The Yagua (neighbors of the Tukuna) believe that two Sloths
with human heads, born from menstrual blood, hold up the
world at both ends. Any wrong move on their part would threaten
the balance; the world could tilt, and a cataclysm would follow.
Halfway between the Jivaro and the Tacana on the piedmont of the
Andes, the Campa and the Machiguenga call the great Magellanic
Cloud "the Sloth." [1] According to the Machiguenga, it was the only

1. According to Webster, the Magellanic Cloud is "either of two conspicuous
nebulous appearances . . . near the South Pole, resembling thin white clouds. They
are composed, like the Milky Way, partly of star clusters and partly of true nebu-
lae."—Trans.

luminary in the sky before the moon came to shine on the earth (see below, p. 146).

Astronomical connotations also seem to be attributed to the Sloth in the great myth of Poronominaré, the cultural hero of the Baré (Arawak-speaking Indians living on the border between Brazil and Venezuela). I have stressed elsewhere the affinities between this personage and the moon (see *Mythologiques,* vol. 1, p. 164; vol. 3, p. 127; vol. 4, pp. 421, 515). Poronominaré was an inveterate womanizer and adventurer, envied by the Indians, who attempted to kill him. He defeated them one after another and turned them into animals, allotting to each the physical appearance and life-style it would henceforth have. Sloth, his last opponent, was sly and swore to his good intentions. He talked the hero into climbing to the top of a tree and then threw him down. Poronominaré, propelled by his weight, crashed through the ground like a meteor and reached the underworld. The Sloth rejoiced: he saw himself as the sole master "over the sun, the moon, the stars, the earth, waters, birds, and other animals, everything . . ." (Amorim 1928: 138–45). He intended to eat his victim, make a flute from one of the bones, and attract girls with his music.

In the underworld, Poronominaré was welcomed by the Cicadas. They said they would take him back to earth with them at the end of the summer, at the new moon (the season for cicadas starts toward the end of August or the beginning of September). On the appointed day the Cicadas helped Poronominaré climb up to the earth through the interior of his blowpipe. He saw the Sloth singing under the moon, boasting of having killed him. The hero riddled him with darts from his blowpipe, and the Sloth fell into the underworld. Poronominaré climbed the tree, unhooked his enemy's hammock, and threw it to the ground, where it turned into the sloth as we see it today: "From now on you shall never sing under the moon; you shall whistle in the silent night. You shall be the chief of the sloths" (Amorim, ibid.).

Known in numerous versions, in which the hero sometimes bears another name or the details of the plot differ, the myth of

Poronominaré has spread over a vast territory, incuding northern Brazil, southern Venezuela, and Guiana. This territory is thus quite remote from Tacana territory, and yet the same pattern appears in both places. Hurled from the tree by the Sloth, breaking through the ground like a meteor, Poronominaré plays the part that the Tacana myth assigns to the animal's excrement, dropped from the top of the tree. In both cases, the ground breaks open, giving access to the underworld, from which will emerge, in the one myth, the Idsetti-deha, founders of a new era, in the other, the Cicadas, harbingers of the new season.

*

From the Tacana in eastern Bolivia all the way to the Kalina in Guiana, passing, on the way, through a whole series of other peoples, the Sloth thus stands as a cosmological symbol. It is particularly clear in the Tacana myths, but in others, too, that this role is linked to the animal's habits, especially to those concerned with the functions of elimination.

We now need to ask the question we asked in the case of the Goatsucker myths: By which process do these myths attribute certain peculiar habits to the Sloth? Is it through empirical deduction or transcendental deduction? There can be no doubt on this point, for in all the myths that we have examined the Indians have shown themselves to be excellent naturalists.

Like the European travelers of the sixteenth to eighteenth centuries—and sometimes later—we remain half way between observation and fantasy. Let us, all the same, compare the Sloth's fate at the hands of Poronominaré with observations made by Oviedo y Valdes during the first half of the eighteenth century:

> [The sloth's] voice is very different from that of all the rest of the animals of the world: because it sounds only at night, and as a whole, in continued chant, from time to time, singing six notes, one higher than the other, always descending: so the highest note is the first, and from that

one he descends, lowering his voice; as one might say la
sol fa mi re do, this animal says ha ha ha ha ha. [Quoted in
Britton 1941: 14][2]

The indications given by the myth are confirmed more directly by
a contemporary naturalist, at least for the *Bradypus* genus: "The
cry holds the note re sharp for several seconds. One can imitate
the cry by whistling, but the animals will answer in response only
to the note re sharp; that is, they will not react to mi, fa, or do, or
even to re natural" (Beebe 1926: 35–37).

Ulloa, a sixteenth-century traveler (quoted ibid., p. 15) claims,
along with a Tenetehara myth, that the sloth drops the fruit he
picks from the trees, then rolls up into a ball, falls to the ground,
and eats the fruit there. Schomburgk, who wrote in the nineteenth
century, said that the sloth, unable to walk on the ground, moved
about from branch to branch. These two observations are contradictory. However, all naturalists confirm the Tacana account of the
peculiar way in which the sloth defecates.

A sloth observed in captivity

emptied [her bladder] at approximately six-day intervals,
and the colon a few minutes after the bladder. Dipping
the hind-quarters in cold water and allowing the water to
run off while holding her up by her forelegs induced
evacuation. After we learned of this reaction, this was
done every five days. [Enders 1940: 7]

Superfluous solicitude! For according to other observers, the
sloth's digestive cycle requires at least a week and sometimes
even two:

[Food] . . . may remain in the stomach from 70 to 90
hours, and even longer, after ingestion. During this time

2. I am indebted to Professor François Boulière for his help: twenty years ago,
for a course I was teaching, he gave me a list of sources concerning the biology of
the sloth.

small amounts of the digested foodstuffs may be slowly passed on to the intestine, and towards the end of the period food residues begin to appear as small rounded pellets in the rectum. In some cases a week or so may be taken to make the transit of the alimentary canal! The rectum of the animal has often been found greatly distended with hard fecal pellets, a centimeter or so in diameter. The living animal may accumulate for several days and later excrete large masses of this material, up to a pound or two in weight at one time. [Britton 1941: 195–96]

This same observer reports that the sloth's stomach, with its enormous capacity, "may be found to comprise more than a quarter of the body weight" (ibid., p. 32).

Yet another observation:

After a storm, in a grove of tall Ficus trees [*Würgfeige*], I observed the way four sloths climbed down from various sides, with the help of vines. Once they reached the ground, they relieved themselves on a heap of excrement left by other sloths. The process took a long time, and each animal released a considerable amount of feces. During the operation, the four of them were squatting, their upper bodies erect, holding on to roots; most kept their eyes closed. They were in no way disturbed by the presence of onlookers and appeared not to see them. Whether this case of defecating on the ground at a fixed spot can be generalized, I do not know. The fact that these animals all came down at the same time was probably due to a sudden drop in temperature, which must have induced a speeding-up of peristaltic motion. [Krieg 1939: 291]

Krieg hesitates to generalize from his observations, but other naturalists corroborate the fact that the sloth always defecates at the same spot, in nature as well as in captivity. This is also what is implied in the Tacana myths, as well as by the Shuar, who, when they want to kill a sloth and shrink its head, encourage the animal to climb down its tree: "Come! Come! Come down, my friend, so you can defecate at ease" (Pellizzaro 1980b: 32).

As for the temperature drop during the storm, it is confirmed in a saying of the Arawak of Guiana: "When the wind blows, Sloth walks" (Roth 1915: 369). The Trumai, of the Xingu area, give the same name to the sloth and the wind, *suut;* they believe that the sloth is the master of the wind and that he can bring about storms.

If sloths excrete only at long intervals, the reason is that they eat very little, sometimes only every other day; they can even fast for several days in a row. We have seen that *Bradypus* feeds almost exclusively on *Cecropia* leaves; *Choloepus* takes a more varied diet.

Such frugality did not go unnoticed by travelers in the old days, who sometimes drew extreme conclusions. Thevet wrote about the sloth: "Another thing there is worthy of memory, that this strange beast was never seen eating, for the wild men of the country have watched her to see if she would feed; but all was in vain, as they themselves have showed me" (Thevet 1878: chap. 52). Also in the sixteenth century, Oviedo y Valdes declared: "I have had him at home, and what I was able to understand of this animal is that he must sustain himself on air. . . . He has never been seen to eat a thing but continuously to turn his head, or mouth, toward the wind" (cited in Britton 1941: 14). Here is what Léry said, in the same time period: "I have heard, not only from savages but also from interpreters who had stayed in that country for a long time, that this animal was never seen eating, in the fields or in houses; so that some think he feeds on wind" (Léry 1975: chap. 10). We have already met with living creatures presented as wind-eaters (see p. 85) and will soon see them again.

The sloth can store his waste in a large rectal pouch, which holds a considerable amount of feces, and he eats so little that it was thought he fed solely on air. Here again we were able to verify that seemingly foolish mythical speculations were founded on an actual knowledge of zoology and botany. Without an intense curiosity about living creatures and all things around them, men could never have acquired this knowledge. However, mythic thought goes beyond these observations. It jumps to conclusions that are not verified by experience but satisfy men's imagination and reflection.

According to the Carib of Guiana, the Sloth, like other animals or supernatural beings to be mentioned later, has no anus; or, rather, he no longer has an anus. When order was finally being imposed on the world, the animals had to prove that they could swim. The Sloth failed the test, for he kept farting; so his anus had to be plugged up with mud (sloths are poor walkers but good swimmers). Like the Nighthawk in North American myths (see pp. 66–67), the Sloth was originally given to farting, but these two animals differ in that the Sloth has lost this capacity. Myths, then, establish a correlation and an opposition between the Sloth and the Goatsucker in terms, respectively, of *anal retention* and *oral greediness* (the Sloth eats little or, according to some, nothing).

This is not the only way in which myths proceed to establish this double relationship. The Modoc personage (see pp. 63–64) who can be assimilated to the Nighthawk found in other California myths (the bad hunter who feeds his wives with meat from his legs) finds his counterpart in South America in a Mundurucu myth in which an Indian behaves similarly. While hunting, he strays away from his companions, cuts some flesh from his thigh, and claims that he has killed a deer. One day he was found out, and it was discovered that "he brought back only bad meat, taken from his own body." Once the truth was discovered, the man wrapped himself in his hammock, gripped it with hands and feet, and became the first Sloth. It is true that the Tenetehara tell the same story about the Tortoise, but in this tribe the Sloth takes the place of the Tortoise in a set of Amazonian myths in which the Tortoise fools the Jaguar. The Sloth and the Tortoise are thus commutable, and the same thing is seen also in Tacana myths, where either is assigned the role of opponent to the Howler Monkey.

The Goatsucker and the Sloth are both connected with jealousy. I have already proved the case for the Goatsucker, and the Carib of Guiana say that the Sloth originated in jealousy—that in fact it is jealousy incarnate. Various myths attribute a male or female human lover to a female or male Sloth who displays vindictive jealousy. For instance, in an Arawak myth from Guiana we see a Sloth (*Choloepus didactylus*) treating his human lover badly, clawing her and pulling her hair because they had been seen by an Indian, who kept spying on them. The Indian killed the animal and became the lady's lover in his place. A Mundurucu myth tells the story of a young Sloth lady, called Araben, who resisted the advances of an Indian. She claimed that her suitor's first wife or the other women in the village made fun of her ugly teeth—or might do so. But she was wrong in her accusations, and this is why the members of the clan of the Sloth are liars and jealous persons, given to railing at each other. In a myth mentioned above (see p. 6), the Vultures were jealous of the Sloth and coveted his wife. They attempted to get rid of him several times, but the Sloth always managed to survive: he dried up a lake, pumping the water out with his blowpipe, and he escaped from a fire by fleeing through a lizard-hole, the entrance to a long tunnel that brought him back close to his house.

The Sloth and the Goatsucker are correlated and opposed in yet another way: both are associated with a technical activity. We saw that the Jivaro myths put the Goatsucker at the origin of pottery. The Sloth is associated with weaving. A Tacana myth tells the story of the younger of two brothers who fell in love with a female sloth at the time when sloths and humans were alike. No woman could match her skill at weaving hammocks, bags, and belts. The older brother hated his sister-in-law but failed to break up the marriage. The myth concludes by saying that female sloths make better weavers and better wives. The Waiwai myth quoted above

94

claims that, originally, only Indians and the *Choloepus* Sloth knew how to make clothes out of fibers.

The fact that the two animals are doubly opposed—in terms of greediness and retention and in terms of orality and anality—is doubtless enough to let us infer that if one animal is associated with one of civilization's two great arts, then the other is bound to be associated with the other art. But the Sloth's association with the art of weaving is justified more directly.

In his common position, hanging head down from a branch, the sloth resembles a hammock. According to the Mundurucu myth, summarized above, the sloth resulted from the gradual transformation of a man wrapped up in his hammock. The myth of Poronominaré says that the first sloth was a hammock turned into an animal.

This interpretation can be taken even further. A Warrau myth (M_{327} in *From Honey to Ashes*) opposes the two wives of an Indian: one was a good weaver but was sterile; the other bore children but was inept in the practice of any craft. As a good worker and a sterile woman, the former is completely on the side of culture; for the opposite reasons, the latter is entirely on the side of nature. Now, the South American Indians give a social and moral value to the functions of elimination. It has been observed that in some groups the men induce vomiting when they wake up, in order to evacuate any food left in the stomach overnight; almost everywhere in South America, Indians prefer to wait until nightfall to relieve themselves: "[The Indian] knows how to control his natural needs better than the white man, and seems to abide by the following maxim, given to me in rough Spanish by an Indian from San Carlos: 'Quien caga de mañana es guloso,' i.e., 'Whoever defecates in the morning is a glutton'" (Spruce 1908: vol. 2, p. 454). To abandon oneself to natural urges is to prove oneself a bad member of society.

In the Warrau myth, the sterility of the skillful worker transposes, in terms of the reproductive functions, the virtuous retention practiced by the men in their eliminating functions. In this respect, the Sloth—a small eater who excretes at long intervals and always in the same spot—is seen by the Indians as a "naturally well-bred" animal who can serve as a cultural model. It is therefore not surprising that they attribute to him a remarkable skill in weaving, the most complex, the most refined, of the great arts of civilization, and one that even societies at an early stage of technical development brought to a high degree of perfection.

8

In Quest of Zoemes

In quest of zoemes. The Anteater, a combinative variant of the Sloth.
Squirrels, Kinkajous, Coendous, Opossums. A theory about tree-dwelling
animals.

*

The sloth suffers from poor thermal regulation. The *Bradypus*
genus, about which accurate measurements are available, has an
average body temperature of 32°C., which can drop to 20° when
the surrounding temperature reads 10°–15°; the animal then falls
into a state of torpor. Its temperature reaches 40° when it is 30°–
40° outside, in which case it suffers from hyperthermia. This peculiar physiology limits the habitat of the sloth to the equatorial and
tropical zones of the New World, where variations in temperature
are minimal.

One therefore cannot expect to encounter the sloth in North
America. Now, if we suppose that the South American myths devoted to the Sloth, or those in which it has a prominent place,
have equivalents in the Northern Hemisphere, we will need to
find out what transformations they undergo there.

We can be confident in our search, though, for we know that
mythic thought is never at a loss when facing situations of this
kind. Operating across enormous distances, meeting with variations in geology, climate, fauna, and flora, mythic thought can preserve or retrieve what, in *The Naked Man,* I called "zoemes": animals given semantic functions. It is these that allow mythic thought
to keep its operations within the same framework. The peoples
who settled the two Americas in a series of migratory waves consciously or unconsciously looked for species, genera, or families
presenting some analogies to the ones they were familiar with in
other regions; if they failed to find any, they looked for creatures

they could substitute for those missing in their new environment and integrated them in their myths without altering the initial network of relations.

In the warm regions of South America, mythic thought was particularly interested in the sloth. It was struck by its unique physiology and habits and probably also by its way of mating; for the act lasts several hours (it is thus easy to observe), and it is performed in a ventral position, a very rare mating posture among wild mammals, which resulted in the attribution of a certain human quality to the sloth. However, even in South America, other animals can be called on to fulfill the same semantic function as the sloth and thus serve as combinative variants of it.

Such is the case with the anteater or, rather, with Anteaters. The same name is used for several genera belonging, like the sloth, to the order of Edentata and the suborder of Xenarthra, whose members are also classified according to size and the number of fingers they possess. The ant bear or tamanoir, *Myrmecophaga jubata*, lives in the savanna. Small anteaters, *Tamandua tetradactyla* and *Cyclopes dorsalis,* are tree-dwellers, found in the forest. It is often difficult to determine which genus is referred to in a myth. Amerindian languages sometimes have a specific name for each genus or sometimes distinguish them by using different suffixes. Goeje observed that, in Carib, "the word for the anteater, *wariše* or *walime,* seems related to the word for the two-toed sloth, *walekole"* (Goeje 1946: 47). It is also related to the word for the tapir, as we will see in our discussion of this animal (see p. 166). The Suya, members of the Ge linguistic family, call the sloth "the evil one" or "the evil anteater"; like the Arawak of Guiana, they say it is an animal of ill omen. Also, they do not eat sloths, because, they say, these animals can pretend to be dead. The Barasana of the Uaupés area, a Tukano-speaking tribe, account for the existence of the great anteater in the same way as the Shuar account for the sloth: originally a man, he was changed into an animal because he intoxicated himself with tobacco. In Guiana the Arawak say that the two Indians who first ventured to taste manioc beer—despite the deity's warnings against the potency of this drink—turned into a three-toed sloth and a two-toed sloth. According to some Amazonian myths, ornaments fashioned of sloth or anteater nails (depending on the versions) give shamans the power to remove themselves to distant places and to call forth rain or storms.

Naturalists point to similarities between the small anteater, *Cyclopes didactylus,* and the sloth: low body temperature and extreme slowness of movement. And, what has been attested by observation in the case of the sloth, some myths claim for the anteater: that it defecates with difficulty, or at least pretends to. This belief may also have an empirical basis: "The dung [of the anteater] has a characteristic odor as well as appearance. It is always surrounded by a strong, impervious sheath that has the appearance of mucus and that holds the matter in shape even when it is deposited in water, as it frequently is." The same observer adds: "If in the anteater, as in other Xenarthra, such as the sloths, there is considerable storage of fecal material before defecation, this coat may prevent the absorption of decomposition products set free by the undigested remains of a high protein diet" (Enders 1935: 494).

Whether this scientific hypothesis holds true or not, there is no doubt that the myths see infrequent or difficult defecation as a trait common to the two animals. Like the Sloth, the mythic Anteater is said not to have an anus, which is why he can eat only small insects. Other myths say that the Anteater does not need an anus because he has such a small mouth; others, still, that his head cannot be told from his rear, so that you never know whether you are in front of him or behind him. Along the same lines, the Caingang-Coroado believe that the Anteater was created by the demiurge in a hurry and so was left unfinished. The Tacana believe that the Anteater's rear gives off a stench that brings strength to sorcerers, and this belief is also empirically confirmed; for according to Enders, "there is a very characteristic odor, which is similar to that of the urine. This is so strong that, after becoming familiar with it, one recognizes it in the forest" (Enders 1935: 494). The Makiritaré mention this smell in their tales.

The Tacana regard the Sloth and the small Anteater as powerful sorcerers. As far as the Anteater is concerned, the same opinion prevails in an area going from Amazonia to the southern parts of Brazil. The small Anteater used to be able to speak all languages; he taught the Caingang-Coroado all their songs and dances, but he has grown so old that now he can no longer speak. We saw that the Tacana, the Jivaro, and the Ipurina say that the Sloth is the ancestor of mankind. The Caingang-Coroado say the same thing about the small Anteater; consequently, in this tribe it is forbidden to kill this animal. On the other hand, among the Guarani of Paraguay, anteater meat was the only kind allowed to menstruating women and to the mothers of newborn children whose umbilical cord had not yet fallen off: a prohibition in the one case, a prescription in the other, but both founded on very similar beliefs. The justification for the prescription is the Guarani theory that the flesh of the Anteater is the epitome of all other kinds of meat. From the Chaco to Amazonia, as a compendium of all creatures, the Anteater is always seen as female, or, to be more accurate, it seems to be a one-sexed species, capable of reproducing itself by parthenogenesis: "'You shall live without a woman,' said the Tacana demiurge to the Anteater, 'and you shall beget children to whom you yourself shall give birth'" (Hissink-Kahn 1961).

The example of the Anteater amply demonstrates that, even within the same region, animals chosen to fulfill one semantic function can be accompanied or replaced by others, acting in their place or simply echoing their functions. But in North America there are neither anteaters nor sloths. When dealing with such widely different environments, how can we proceed to answer the following question: Are there, in the Northern Hemisphere of the New World, any myths that are homologous to the Southern Hemisphere myths in which the Sloth is the main character?

Let us return to these South American myths, particularly the Tacana's, where the cosmological role of the Sloth stands out most clearly. These myths stress the demanding nature of the Sloth. He must be able to climb down from his tree to defecate in peace, and if unruly children force him to let his excrement fall from the top of the tree or to let himself drop down, he or his excrement will hit the ground like a comet, the earth will split open, and, from the chasm, either flames or floods of water will shoot forth and annihilate mankind. Or else the earth will tip over and the Sun men, the Idsetti-deha, will come up from the underworld and live on the surface, and humans will take their place down below. One version deals at length with this last result: when the blaze went out, a new mankind emerged from the depths of the earth; though smaller than today's men, these creatures were their ancestors (see pp. 85–86).

Other myths provide more information on the nature of these Idsetti-deha. They tell the story of an Indian who (after certain events, which vary with each version) crept into the burrow of an armadillo and came out into the other world. This world was inhabited by the Idsetti-deha, who were dwarfs, had no anuses, and fed on the smell of food, according to some versions, or mainly on water, according to others. For these diminutive creatures, wasps were hostile Indians and hares were jaguars. The visitor rid them of these enemies, but the Idsetti-deha were utterly disgusted every time they saw him defecate. They finally dismissed the man, who was guided back to the surface of the earth by an Armadillo.[1]

Thus, in three ways the myths associate the Sloth with a people of dwarfs having no anus. First, he is, in a sense, one of them, for he appeared early on earth, along with other primitive humans who, like him, fed on wind. Second, like the Idsetti-deha, the Sloth has no anus. Third, the Sloth brought about the end of this

1. In southwestern Argentina the Tehuelche also believe in a "People of the Sun" who have no anus. More logically, however, they place them in the sky instead of underground. It is interesting to compare them with the Tacana Sun Men, for the Tehuelche belong to the Chon linguistic family, which is often classified in the literature as part of a so-called macro-Panoan stock, which also includes the Tacana and Mataco languages.

primitive mankind and its replacement by the Idsetti-deha, who were not very different, except in size.

In their myths the Jivaro also associate the Sloth with supernatural beings who are, again, chthonian dwarfs. These are the *nunkui,* tiny spirits of the gardens, who live underground. One of these spirits (or their general representative: in Jivaro, *nunkui* is sometimes a singular, sometimes a collective, noun) took the shape of Uyush, the female Sloth, who brought to mankind the plants grown by a small girl (a dwarf in her own way), also called Uyush. Like the Tacana Sloth, she was harassed by children and finally left the village, to return to the underworld. This symmetry between the Tacana and Jivaro myths goes further. According to the Tacana, a primitive mankind that did not know how to cultivate plants fed on wind; for the Jivaro, it is in losing cultivated plants that the ancestors of today's men acquired, so to speak, flatulence, the opposite of food but also made of wind (see p. 86).

The theme of the dwarfs with no anus, living underground, is found all the way from the Xingu Basin to Central America, passing through northern Amazonia. Thus it is found in the northeastern part of Peru, among the Yagua; among the Catio of Colombia and the Cayapa of Ecuador, for whom supernatural beings have no apertures at all in their anatomies; in Brazil, among the Tucuna; and in Venezuela, among the Yupa and the Sanema.

The Tucuna speak of a people of subterranean dwarfs who feed on the smell of food. An Indian married one of them. She wanted to eat the way her husband did, but she suffered unbearable pain from eating solid food. The Indian used his knife to make her an anus. She was then able to defecate but died soon after.

In a myth very close to the Tacana's (see pp. 100–101), the Yupa say that the sole survivor among a group of Indians prisoners in a cave managed to escape through "a crack between two rocks." On the other side was the land of the Pipintu, dwarfs without anuses who fed on smoke. They had long beards but no hair, because all the humans living above them "let their waste fall down on their heads." In order to consume solid food, they put it on the napes of their necks and let it slide along their backs. They begged their visitor to make them an anus like his. The man tried to operate on them, but all his patients died, for they also had no intestines, and solid food tore up their insides (see Wilbert 1974: 86–90).

Like the Yupa, the Sanema live in Venezuela, and they use almost the same terms to describe a people they call the Oneitib. Nevertheless, these dwarfs, who have the same anatomy as the Pipintu, swallow raw meat without chewing; they also have no intestines and are hollow inside instead of full, which makes them perpetually hungry. Interestingly, in the Yupa myth, the hero explained to his tiny hosts that he was coming from "the cave of the dead," where all his companions had died (they had come to deposit a dead body in this cave, which was used as a ossuary). Now, for the Jivaro the dead are insatiably hungry, like the Sanema dwarfs. These human souls feed exclusively on the souls of the birds, fish, and quadrupeds that the Indians killed and ate when they were alive, and that now are nothing but wind.

The animals of the warmer regions of South America may be lacking in North America, but mythical dwarfs are even more popular there. The Lipan Apache give them anatomical traits very like those described in the South American myths; they have no anus or one no larger than a pinhead, so tiny that the dwarfs cannot defecate, and they feed on the fumes from cooked food. For the Apache, they are unfinished creatures, like the South American Anteaters; they emerged from the world Below before the demiurge had had time to complete them.

On the northern Pacific coast the same dwarfs undergo a *bottom → top* transformation that leaves their semantic function intact: they have no mouth, or a tiny one, sometimes also no eyes or voice, and they have to feed on maggots, minute shells, or the smell of food. In the middle of the continent, the Omaha and the Ponca effect an even more radical transformation: the dwarfs are attributed the power of wounding their enemies under the skin without damaging it: they change from nonperforated to nonperforating creatures. For the Arapaho, the dwarfs are cannibals with children's voices; they are also in the habit of leaving their hearts in their lodgings when they go out and of reversing the meaning of words: for them, "heavy" means "light" and vice versa. These transformations accord well with the general notion of a "world in reverse" that is illustrated in many ways by the dwarfs. The last stage in these transformations appears among the Wyandot, linguistically related to the Iroquois and former inhabitants of the Saint Lawrence Valley. Their dwarfs have no elbow joints, so they can bend their arms only at the shoulders and the wrists; this transformation is found in other myths as far as Middle America.

We now need to ask whether in North America, as in South America, the people of the dwarfs entertain special relationships with certain animals and, if they do, we need to identify these animals. If the answer is positive, the animals of the two hemispheres will be equivalent, despite differences between them, by the fact that in both places they are assimilated to the dwarfs. It will then become possible to enlarge to its true dimensions a semantic field we have only partially explored through the use of the South American materials.

One answer immediately presents itself concerning the animal we started out with—the only one, among those we have considered, that is found in both hemispheres. The Mohegan-Pequot, who are eastern Algonquians, call the chthonian dwarfs *makia'wis,* a word that can be understood literally as "little boy" but that is also used to refer to the whippoorwill. Other phrases found among eastern Algonquians also assimilate whippoorwills to tiny supernatural beings; for instance, an orchid of the *Cypripedium* genus, the lady's slipper, is called the "whippoorwill's shoe" or "whippoorwill's moccasin" in the Mohegan language and on the North American east coast, from the Wanabaki to the Delaware. All eastern Algonquians, as well as the Creek, the Cherokee, and the Iroquois, believe in dwarfs who haunt lakes, mountains, or forests. I have already indicated that the Apache identify poorwills with the spirits of the mountains (see p. 68).

Here, now, are the traits that associate the dwarfs with other animals. The Coeur d'Alene, Salish-speaking Indians of Idaho,

> believe in a race of dwarfs who inhabit the forests and live in trees, which they go up and down with great celerity. People have watched them ascending and descending trees. They always go head first. They are formed just like people, but are very small. They appear to be all red, and most people think they dress in red. They carry their babies upside down on board carriers. People whom they approach lose their senses. Sometimes when they come out of their stupor they find themselves leaning against a tree upside down. Sometimes they missed part of their clothing and, on looking around, would see them hanging from the ends of branches high up in the trees. These dwarfs were fond of playing tricks, . . . [but they] never kept any article they had taken, and never killed or hurt people.
>
> Another kind of dwarfs, often called by the same name as the first but differing from them in appearance and disposition, are of the size of small boys. They live in cliffs and rocky places up in the mountains and were formerly numerous in parts of the Coeur d'Alene and Nez Percé country. They dress in squirrel skins and use small bows and arrows. They often shout when they see people and in this way have often led hunters astray. [Teit 1930: 180]

Two points in this text call for special attention, First, there is the emphasis on the color of the dwarfs: they are red or dressed in red. We find mentions of a color specific to dwarfs in various places within a vast territory, extending from eastern Bolivia and central Brazil all the way to Canada. For the Tacana, the Idsetti-deha, dwarfs of the underworld, have red hair. Some of them are given the task of holding up the world, which would collapse if their hair turned white. We saw that the Yagua give this same cosmic role to two Sloths born from menstrual blood, which associates them too with the color red. In the cosmology of the Tapirape of the Araguaya Basin there are Thunder creatures, the Topü; they

105

are hairy dwarfs, whose headdresses are made from the feathers of the red parrots who fly in the sky in stormy weather. The Topü pelt Indians in the stomach with red flowers that burn like flaming arrows. In the Orinoco delta, a Warrau myth, close to the Poro-nominaré myth (see p. 88), presents demons who have a red spot instead of an anus and climb down trees head first. According to an Arawak of Guiana, if one digs deep into the earth, one reaches a world inhabited by red-haired dwarfs. Their wives cannot give birth normally; their wombs have to be cut open to deliver their children, then sewn back together.

Back to North America. The Lipan Apache talk about a people of dwarfs whose anus is red; they are formed like humans except for their size. For the Coeur d'Alene, as we have already seen, the dwarfs are red from head to toe or dressed in red.

Now to the second point. The Coeur d'Alene dwarfs' most striking characteristic is that they come down trees head first, carry their babies upside down, and place their unconscious victims in the same position. Another myth, from western Canada, puts the Squirrel in the role of a savior because of his ability to descend trees head first. Now, the Coeur d'Alene say that the dwarfs wear clothes made out of squirrel skins. There may then be significance in the fact that in a Wyandot myth an Indian is given miraculous hunting powers by a supernatural female dwarf, whereas before he had been able to kill only squirrels and other small game. In an Iroquois myth, a young boy also meets the dwarfs during a squirrel hunt. Squirrels are negligible game for humans, suitable for children, but they are the largest prey that dwarfs can handle. The Squirrel acts here as a mediator between the two races, which are thus allied by a relationship *sub specie sciurorum*. Squirrels are in fact quite important in the beliefs of North American Indians. They are harbingers of death or former cannibal monsters who still enjoy terrorizing passers-by; more seldom, they act as mascots or comic heroes. Within this context let us make special mention of the Iroquois. They see the Squirrel as a powerful demon, a companion of the Thunders, who feed on the smell of food. Here again—though with a transposition into the world Above—the Squirrel is associated with the people who have no anuses.

∗

All of these traits lead us back to the South American animals. First to the squirrels themselves, which are also found in the Southern Hemisphere. One species of the *Sciurus* genus, called *coatipuru* or *acutipuru* in Amazonia and *sérélépé* or *caxinguélé* in central and southern Brazil, is associated with numerous superstitions. In Tupi the suffix *-puru* is used to form names of lucky plants or animals. In connection with the squirrel, it designates an animal that brings sleep to children and takes the souls of the dead into the hereafter. The Indians admire the squirrel because it is one of the very few animals that can come down trees head first. Several Sciuridae have a reddish fur. Could this account for the fact that the dwarfs are commonly described as red? We will not venture a positive answer. Without subscribing to a simplistic theory, currently in favor, that religious beliefs originated in the use of hallucinogens, we cannot exclude the possibility that men may sometimes have used hallucinatory experiences in order to people their representations of supernatural worlds with sensory images. Several hallucinogenic plants, including those used in the Americas, induce brightly colored sensations. For example, *Sophora secundiflora* seeds—consumed in only one region of North America—are supposed to make everything look red.

In South America, squirrels are not the only animals whose acrobatic moves strike the observers' imaginations: "A most interesting characteristic is that when it [the two-toed sloth, *Choloepus*] decides to descend a tree-trunk or branch it turns around and comes down head first, with the body quite free of the trunk, not half clinging, half sliding, tail first, as the three-toed do" (Beebe 1926: 66). A tropical Procyonidus, the kinkajou, called *jupara* in Brazil (*Potos flavus*) also comes down trees head first. The Urubu Indians fear him: "They say that if you're sleeping in the jungle, and a kinkajou defecates on you, you'll die" (Huxley 1956: 227). Hixkaryana Indians also see him as a portent of imminent death, like the squirrel in western Canada. For the Campa in eastern Bolivia, a dangerous spirit called Yanáite has the appearance of a kinkajou. He is a murderer and a cannibal. Some informants claim that he takes his food through his tail (in symmetry, thus, with Anteater, who is thought to excrete through his mouth and copulate with his snout). However, the Campa call the Kinkajou "Son of God" and say that he is the "mother's brother" of a sacred bird, unfortunately not identified. The Kinkajou thus seems to be marked by the same ambiguity that characterizes the Squirrel of North America. The Marikitaré of Guiana give him a positive role: he was the one who stole the original manioc from the sky in order to give it to mankind.

Brazilian peasants also fear the Kinkajou, but for a different reason: "Kinkajous, they say, are sodomites, and a man sleeping in the jungle should protect himself with a well-placed cork" (Huxley 1956: 227). Thus the Kinkajou behaves sometimes as a perforated being (defecating, eating through his tail), sometimes as a perforator.

Another perforator also makes an appearance: a small animal, the coendou, a rodent. Its body is armed with quills, which it is said to be able to shoot like arrows. (It is, however, different from the North American porcupine, which is a rodent but is a member of the family of Erethizontidae, which is not represented in South America.) It is perhaps this animal that the Campas present in one of their myths. In the days when earth and sky were close together, Pava, the Sun, who was then living on earth, decided to go up to the sky by climbing the vine that was connecting the two worlds. Some of his companions refused to follow him and turned into animals. Those who did follow him were pursued by three fierce warriors: Soróni, the Sloth, Kosámi, the Wasp, and Tontóri, who seems to be the Coendou, for the reason mentioned above. The Sun cut the vine just in time, and the three warriors fell back to earth. Soróni was in the sloth's typical posture; Kosámi had been changed into a wasp; and Tontóri was bristling with arrows, just as he is today. It is because of these ancient warriors that the Campas are so warlike. One version of the myth attributes the failure of the pursuers to the fact that the Sloth started out too slowly and that the "Porcupine" wasted time gathering up his arrows. In Venezuela, the Yaruro have a very similar myth, but featuring Howler Monkeys, *Toninos* (small dolphins), and Caymans as the warriors.

I have made a point of referring to these myths, which have no direct bearing on our current preoccupations, because of the prominent part played by the Campa in this book and because these myths have striking counterparts in western Canada (see *The Naked Man,* p. 477). From now on, I will be led more and more to establishing certain comparisons between a mythology centered at the foot of Andes and one that flourished along the west coast of North America, from southern California to Canada.

At this point, let me simply stress that, with the Kinkajou and the Coendou, we are not leaving the semantic field of the Sloth, who was both "plugged" and a perforator, and the dwarfs who, lacking an anus or a mouth, are therefore nonperforated. To this one can add as a supplementary argument the fact that in two versions of the same myth—one Tukuna (see p. 83), the other Sikuani—which tell of a conflict over the tree bearing all kinds of foods (or the reverse, the tree that brought darkness on the earth), the parties are one or two Squirrels versus the Kinkajou or the Sloth.

It is also through a very clear transformation that we can go from the Sloth, on the one hand, and the Goatsucker, on the other, to a third animal, also prominent in myths and the subject of several chapters in *The Raw and the Cooked.* This animal is a marsupial, known in South America as a sarigue, in North America as an opossum. Now, other South American peoples say that the Sloth was formerly a human (see pp. 74–78), and the Mundurucu say the same thing of sarigues. This belief is also found in North America, in the southeast, where the Koasati Indians attributed to opossums of ancient times the use of articulate speech. I showed earlier that the small Anteater sometimes takes the place of the Sloth in myths and beliefs, and we saw then that various South American peoples believe that anteaters are of only one sex, able to reproduce itself, and in southeastern North America the Creek and the Cherokee have the same belief concerning the opossum.

From his Aztec informants, Sahagun heard some very strange ideas about the opossum, though they will not sound so odd within the context of this book. Opossum meat is said to be edible but not the bones, particularly those in the tail. Whoever eats the tail will lose his intestines; they will slip out of his body. However, since bones have this property of extracting, evacuating, anything stuck inside a cavity, an opossum tail, ground up in water, helps women through hard labor pains, and it is the ultimate cure for constipation, for it can "open the passages, the tubes, to clean them, to purify them, to sweep out obstructions" (Sahagun, book 11, chap. 1, p. 12). And, in a chapter devoted to childbirth, the same idea recurs:

> Once a dog secretly ate a whole opossum. Such is the quality of the opossum that this dog started rejecting everything, casting everything out, defecating all its intestines. Likewise, if someone drank the whole tail of an opossum, he would cast out all his intestines; he would defecate everything. Because of this, if the woman drank the *ciua-patli* [*Montanoa tomentosa*] and the opossum-[tail infusion, and] if her labor pains did not respond, the midwife and the old women considered it very dangerous. [Sahagun, book 6, part 7, chap. 28]

What else can this mean but that the Opossum brings about in others a condition that is symmetrical and opposite to that attributed to the Sloth by South American Indians? The anus must be wide open for the intestines to slip out of the body; this opening is the cure for constipation (a permanent condition for the Sloth), and, when transposed from the anus to the vagina, it makes childbirth easier. The early inhabitants of the Oaxaca region represented the Opossum god as an old man. We have seen that the

Sloth is represented by South American Indians as very old. According to the Carib in Guiana, the Opossum embodies what Goeje calls kleptomania. This belief may be seen as a reflection or an echo of the Mexican idea of the Opossum as an extractor or remover. Consequently, far from leaving it, we are continuing to furnish with new elements the semantic field we are trying to determine and inventory.

Let us now consider the relations between the Opossum and the Goatsucker. In *The Raw and the Cooked*, the comparison between Ge and Karaja myths on the origin of cultivated plants had already pointed to the existence of such relations. In the Ge myth, the Star women who gave these plants to the Indians changes into an Opossum or is indirectly associated with the Opossum in the course of the story. However, for the Karaja, the Indians received cultivated plants from a Star man, and this transformation, $O \rightarrow \triangle$, leads to the transformation of the female character into a Goatsucker (see pp. 41–42). Myths about the human husband of a Star woman and those about the human husband of a Sloth woman have a similar armature:

$$
\begin{array}{ccc}
O & \neq & \overbrace{\triangle \quad \triangle} \\
\text{star,} & & \text{humans} \\
\text{Sloth} & &
\end{array}
$$

And the Karaja myth, seen above, shows a symmetrical armature:

$$
\begin{array}{ccc}
\triangle & = & \overbrace{O \quad O}^{/} \\
\text{star,} & & \text{Goatsucker} \\
\text{humans} & &
\end{array}
$$

We already know that the Sloth can be assimilated to a comet or a star (see pp. 86, 87), and we find confirmation of this in the transformation outlined here. In addition, the Star husband in the Karaja myth turned from a repulsive old man into a handsome young man, like the Squirrel (*acutipuru*) in the Poronominaré myth, who helped the hero come down from the sky. In all these myths, therefore, we are dealing with several stellar personages related through transformations, and each of these takes us back to animals who are themselves linked by transformational relationships we had independently established.

Finally, just as the small Anteater can function as a combinative variant of the Sloth, the Opossum is sometimes replaced by a Mustelidus, the Irára (*Tayra barbara*), who assumes its function. Like the small Anteater, the Irára is a honey-eater; Brazilians often call them by that name (*melero*). Now, in the famous Tupi myth in which the heroine goes to the wrong husband or takes one or several bad husbands before choosing the right one, the Opossum plays the part of the main impostor, and, in the Bororo version of this myth, this part is played by the Irára.

But is it not precisely this myth, common to the two Americas, that we met with in California, among the Modoc and the Maidu (see pp. 61–64)? And there the impostor was a Nighthawk (goatsucker). Wherever we go, we keep meeting the same animals, hands linked in the same dance.

What trait, shared by all these animals, could account for their recurrence and association? Taken together, the goatsucker, the sloth, the small anteater, the squirrel, the kinkajou, the coendou, and the opossum make up a tree-dwelling fauna, to which we can add the irára, which, though it does not live in trees, easily climbs them to steal wild honey. Add also the monkeys and raccoons, who are given the honor in Central American traditions, where they result from the transformation of a people of dwarfs, men's predecessors on earth. The dwarfs who escaped this metamorphosis—which took place following a flood—now live underground, their heads or their whole bodies covered with mud to protect them from the fierce sun of the chthonian world. They are trying to return to earth. When they finally manage to do so, the world will turn over; they will be on top, the humans below. These traditions recall the Tacana myths about the Sloth. The Cayapa of Ecuador, who share these views, say that these inhabitants of the chthonian world have neither buttocks nor anus and feed on the smell of food. In Central America this primitive race is believed to have no joints, an anatomical peculiarity that the Wyandot in North America attribute to their dwarfs (see p. 104).

In sum, all the myths considered so far gather into a kind of micropantheon a group of tree-dwelling animals, living above men and smaller than men. These myths also project this micro-pantheon into the chthonian world, a world in reverse: it is night there when the sun shines on earth, and winter there corresponds to our summer. A people of dwarfs—often assimilated to arma-dillos, animals living in burrows—lives there below the humans, just as these, in turn, live below the tree-dwelling fauna.

However, this is but one stage in a combinatorics (system of combinations). In very general terms it can be formulated as fol-lows: *tree-dwelling fauna and the people of the dwarfs are to hu-mans as they are to each other.*

This formula immediately calls for two others, which I will put forth as questions. For if there is a relationship among three terms—tree-dwelling fauna, human society, and a people of dwarfs—mythic thought will immediately wonder: *Which term is to humans as humans are to dwarfs?* And: *Which term is to hu-mans as humans are to the tree-dwelling fauna?*

The first of these three formulas clearly corresponds to the idea that the world beyond is the reduced image of the terrestrial world. This is true for the Indians of northwestern Amazonia: "This land of the After-Life is a diminutive replica of the ordinary world. . . . Everything is on a smaller scale—stunted trees and pygmy game" (Whiffen 1915: 225–26). The Colorado Indians of Ecuador answer the other two questions:

> The sun goes up in the sky, where men live who are taller
> than we are. . . . Our sun goes down into the sea, travels
> below the earth, and comes back; down below, there are

dwarfs. Everything is smaller in that world, above which we walk. Above us there is another world, where everything is taller: human beings, trees, every single thing. [Wavrin 1937: 515–16]

Inversely, the underworld can be peopled with tree-dwelling animals taller than humans, so that the latter appear as dwarfs in their turn. The relation between the chthonian people and humans, then, becomes symmetrical, in terms of size, to the relation described in myths in which small animals, such as wasps or hares, appear to the dwarfs as hostile Indians or jaguars (see p. 101): "For the Wayãpi [or Oyampi—Indians of French Guiana], the world is flat, and the other side is perfectly symmetrical, peopled with *wɔ'ɔ*, giant sloths—typically humanoid animals. One man who had accidentally fallen from the world above was considered by the people below to be a kinkajou" (Grenand 1980: 322–24).

This last text is fundamental for two reasons. First, it extends northward the range of the attribution of a human nature to the sloth. We have seen that this is the reason why the Jivaro, head-hunters and shrinkers, readily substituted the head of a sloth for that of a human enemy. The Oyampi, who are no head-hunters, reverse this situation, to the benefit of the chthonian Sloths: these are said to have a magic hook with which they decapitate their adversaries. An Indian fell victim to these Sloths; his companion stole their weapon and used it against them.

Among these same Indians the human affinities of the sloth lead to a strange consequence. The vegetable kingdom is "culturalized," so to speak, in order to meet the needs of the sloth; various plants are called the "soap," "cotton," "tobacco," "cassava," and "banana" of the *Choloepus didactylus* sloth, for "The Wayãpi think these animals have humanized functions. They thus need objects to enable them to fulfill these functions" (Grenand 1980: 42). The Jivaro also draw linguistic consequences from the human character of the sloth, but they situate these on the rhetorical level. Formerly, they say, Uyush the Sloth lady was the sole possessor of manioc. Women, who had no gardens then, went to her to beg for it. Uyush tested them; she asked them: "What do you call my claws, my coat, my nails, etc.?" The women were supposed to answer in figurative terms. One woman stupidly answered each time with the literal term and was given inedible tubers.

The obligation to speak politely to the gods is a recurrent theme in American mythology. It is present, here and there, from the Maya in Central America to eastern Brazil and the Chaco (see *From Honey to Ashes*, pp. 312 f., 322 f.). But the idea that courteous speech should use metaphors is certainly not restricted to America. For instance, here is an observation made by Hocart in the Fiji Islands: "There is a polite speech . . . used in addressing people of quality; it consists in using metaphors instead of the proper words for the parts of the body and the kinship relation and habitual actions of noblemen" (Hocart 1929: 47). In North America, the Chinook of the lower Columbia River make the same distinction between the two kinds of speech, but, instead of one for noblemen as opposed to one for common people, they have one for the living, the other for the dead. Figurative speech, in which words have a relative meaning, suits the world of the dead; regular speech, in which words have an absolute meaning, is for the living.

The Oyampi's belief in giant Sloths as masters of the chthonian world is interesting in yet another respect, for it supports the hypothesis that the three realms—that of the tree-dwelling fauna, that of human society, and that of the dwarf people—are mutually convertible. A reciprocity of perspectives is necessary to enable mythic thought to constitute the three realms as a closed system; consequently, each realm gives forth its own image and reflects that of the other two. This mutual mirroring accounts for the fact that, in the world Above, giant humans are to humans as humans are to dwarfs, and, in the world Below, a giant tree-dwelling group of animals—also a necessary part in this ideal set—is to humans as humans are to the real tree-dwelling animals.

Borne by its own momentum, mythic thought generates cosmic levels placed on either side of the empirical level, and such

that the relation of each new level to the preceding one is homologous to the relationship that this preceding level has with the
one immediately above or below *it*. Hence, we see some see-
sawing effects that might sometimes be interpreted as contradic-
tions. According to the Colorado Indians, a people of giants lives
in the sky. Conversely, and still in South America, for the Machiguengua the stars are a people of dwarfs, unable to leave their celestial abode; whereas, in North America, the Iroquois believe that
the Thunders, another celestial people, feed on the smell of food
like those chthonian dwarfs who, in other myths, lack mouths or
anuses. And, in one Tacana myth, the inhabitants of the world Below are described sometimes as smaller, sometimes as taller, than
humans, depending on the version.

9
The Levels of the World

Levels of the world and neighbors' quarrels. The Howler Monkey, a symbol of anal incontinence. Second application of the canonic formula.

*

In a residential building, each apartment's floor is the ceiling of the apartment below, and reciprocally. The same thing is true in a universe made up of superimposed levels. For the Campa, "What to us is the solid earth is airy sky to the beings inhabiting the stratum below us, and what to us is airy sky is solid ground to those who inhabit the stratum above" (Weiss 1972: 170). It is no wonder that problems of living together in such a universe should take on cosmic proportions. Indians living in huts that are often rudimentary, with no second story, nevertheless picture in an extremely realistic fashion the nuisances that are the object of endless recriminations among neighbors in apartment houses: noise, leaks, balconies littered with orange peels and cigarette butts.

The Mundurucu believe that spirits "not specifically malevolent toward humans" live in the underworld. These spirits

> engage in fish-drugging expeditions. . . . Fish-drugging expeditions are always noisy affairs, but those of the Kokeriwat are so tempestuous that they create a huge wind, which is felt in the terrestrial world as the two- or three-day cold spell that strikes the Mundurucu country in June of every year. Conversely, Mundurucu *timbo*-fishing causes a cold spell in the underworld. [Murphy 1958: 20–21]

The Pipintu dwarfs of the Sanema Indians suffer much more from the presence of humans above them, whose litter rots their

117

heads and causes them to lose their hair (see p. 102). The theme of heads soiled with garbage and made bald is also found at the other end of the New World. In northwest North America it spreads across an area whose boundaries are difficult to assess, for it undergoes so many transformations that it often becomes difficult to identify with certainty. North American mythographers have given it the code name "anus-wiper." I studied and discussed this theme in *The Naked Man* (pp. 325–34) under other aspects than those I now intend to stress. In their Nez Percé and Kalapuya versions these anus-wiper myths seem to belong to a broader set (of which only a few traces remain in that area) in which there are four successive creations. At the end of the first one, according to the Kalapuya version, "the earth turned over. All the people [of the first mythic age] changed into stars" (Jacobs 1945: 174). Now, I have already pointed to a clear affinity between the Chaco myths of South America and the myths of northwest North America, and in the Chaco the theme of heads soiled with excrement and the theme of a world turned upside down are explicitly linked. According to the Ayoré, Sky and Earth used to live together, down on earth. But Sky got tired of the disgusting state of the earth; it was dirty because of humans, who urinated on it, and in Sky's face, too. Sky decided to separate from Earth and to look for a place where he would be more decently treated. He climbed up to where he is now. Earth remained below. For their part, the Toba say that "formerly the Earth occupied the place of the Sky, but the latter, tired of being soiled, changed places with the Earth" (Métraux 1946a: 24). For the Toba, shooting stars are excrement from fixed stars. In North America, the Ute also see shooting stars as the excrement of "dirty little star-gods" (Powell 1881: 27).

Conversely, nail clippings and other human waste are highly appreciated by the souls of the dead, according to the Tacana, by chthonian dwarfs, according to the Iroquois. It may be through rationalizing that an Iroquois informant accounted for this taste: chthonian dwarfs are good hunters, but animals spot them easily because of their smell and so avoid them; to prevent this, the dwarfs take baths in water in which they have steeped nail clippings, put into small pouches and given to them by humans as an offering. This way they take on a human smell and can get closer to their prey. But can't we also link this with the widespread habit that humans have—in America and elsewhere in the world—of carefully saving nails for use as decorations or talismans? For the Amazonian peoples, charms made of sloths' or small anteaters' nails give shamans the power of moving across long distances, bringing about rain or storms, and undergoing metamorphoses. Consequently, we can confirm, in this case, too, that chthonian dwarfs are to humans as humans are to tree-dwelling animals; and, at both ends of the human world, the people of underground dwarfs and the people of tree-dwelling animals are exact counterparts of each other.

The preceding considerations point to the prominent place of tree-dwelling animals in beliefs and representations. In a visible, tangible form, these animals illustrate the lot that falls to humans when they imagine other worlds above or below their own. They people the world Above with deities whose protection they expect; they try to gain their favor with prayers or offerings, to establish links of reciprocity with them. It nevertheless remains that gods live on high, the men down below. If gods are conceived of as live beings, men are no longer the sole residents in the cosmos, and their world will be reduced to the state of sewers or dumps, to be used by the residents "upstairs." The presence of tree-dwelling animals gives a certain reality to this imaginary relation. Taking the word etymologically, we can say that tree-dwelling animals constitute a hypostasis of the people of the world Above, for humans indeed live, eat, mate, and die "downstairs" from these tree-dwellers.

This position, which appears uncomfortable from both a logical and a moral standpoint, leads men to imagine a third world: that of chthonian dwarfs, over which humans enjoy the same vertical superiority as tree-dwelling animals do over them. Hence

119

also the great attention devoted to the animals' functions of elimination (and, *ipso facto,* ingestion), the various modalities of which,
according to the species, take on a philosophical value. Myths use
them as a foundation for a whole vocabulary and grammar of
communication between the strata.

From the very beginning of our research, we have met with
this vocabulary and this grammar, which generate all sorts of relations between humans and tree-dwelling animals. If the Goatsucker's farts are so violent that he becomes the mythical master
of all splitting, it is because his characteristic oral greediness
keeps him near to bursting all the time. And if the Sloth, once an
inveterate farter, now has a plugged anus, that is because his particular capacity for anal retention allows him to control himself.
Conversely, the Anteater, formerly deprived of an anus and forced
to excrete through his mouth, received from the cultural hero
Poronominaré, or one of his alter egos' the lower orifice he lacked,
thanks to which (as it is elsewhere said) he emits a stench that is
credited with magical virtues (see p. 99). This beneficial incontinence sets him in correlation with and opposition to another tree-
dweller, the Howler Monkey, to be studied presently. Bats, also
tree-dwellers, illustrate a third form of incontinence; according
to the Tucano-speaking Barasana, who live in the Uaupés River
Basin, they have been afflicted with diarrhea ever since they ate
the putrid corpse of the Moon, and they have to hang head down
to keep their whole body from emptying out.[1]

We have seen that a Tacana myth stressed the different defecating habits of the Howler Monkey and the Sloth. The one keeps
dropping his excrement from the top of trees; the other feels he
has to come down to relieve himself.

Howler monkey (in Brazil, *bugío, guariba, barbado*) is the
common name designating several species of the *Alouatta* genus,
a scientific name derived from a Carib word, *arawata,* which is
used to form the names of plants or animals that are completely

1. Interestingly, the aborigines of Queensland, in Australia, have the opposite
theory: that bats (fox bats) have no anus and must excrete through their mouths.

red—for instance, a venomous caterpillar, a hummingbird, a bee. Yet, not all species of howler monkeys have a reddish coat; some are black, and males and females can be of different colors within one species. The distinctive anatomical trait of the genus is a hyoid bone in the shape of a goblet. Myths interpret it as a pouch, a reservoir, as a large pit, or as a kitchen utensil that the animal has swallowed. This hollow bone acts as a resonating chamber; it amplifies the monkeys' cries, and these animals are all the easier to hear from a distance because they live in groups, and all scream at the same time.

Generally speaking, the myths give the howler monkeys a negative, if not sinister, connotation. The Tacana say that their throats stink. In Guiana they say that their cry is terrifying. According to the Yaruro, howler monkeys are descended from Indians who were transformed during the great flood. The Arawak of Guiana say that the red Howler Monkey once climbed a tree in order to escape a flood; he was so terrified that he started crying, as he still does today. Also when climbing a tree to avoid drowning, on the island where she had sought refuge, a woman pregnant with Poronominaré turned into a Howler Monkey, all skin and bones. She was rescued against her will, forced down from the tree by stones thrown at her. Later, her son was to live through his most dramatic adventures on the island "of the guariba," where he confronted the spirit of evil and had, as we know, a fight with the Sloth (see p. 88).

Throughout South America, people maintain that Howler Monkeys once were—even still are—cannibals. There is a permanent hostility between them and humans. All the attempts of a man and a Monkey woman to unite ended in failure, and these two races are now forever separated. There are several known versions of this myth. The Mundurucu version shows interesting parallels with the Jivaro Genesis story. Here is how it goes. The Monkey woman was abandoned by her husband while pregnant. She later married her son. All howler monkeys are descended from this incestuous relationship. The son was human through his father, simian through his mother; however, because the original couple

Fig. 6   The black howler monkey *Alouatta* (formerly *Mycetes*) *niger*
(After Brehm 1890: vol. 1, p. 205)

separated, and due to the subsequent incest, this mixed creature
went back to being an animal. Thus the race of men and that of
monkeys, instead of becoming one, took diverging paths. Let us
now return to a passage from the Jivaro myth: Mika, who embodies pottery, was abandoned by the Sloth, her husband, and committed incest with her son; their descendants were the first head-
hunters (see p. 73). We thus have, in the one case, a separation
between the human family and an animal family, which henceforth became two completely distinct genera; in the other case,
the human family is split internally into hostile groups, at war with
one another.

The myths set humans further apart from Howler Monkeys
than from Sloths, with whom they keep some affinity; the latter
may be enemies, but they still are manlike. Of course, there are
myths dealing with the aborted union between a man and a Sloth
woman (see p. 94), but the whole atmosphere is different; we

are not in the presence of a conflict between a man, representing his species, and a nation of Monkeys gathered into an alliance. Quite to the contrary, affairs between humans and Sloths are clandestine or at least private; they take place within a classic triangle made up of the two lovers and a brother, a mother, or an unlucky suitor, depending on the myth. And indeed, contrary to howler monkeys, who are social animals, the sloth is solitary.

*

As was implied in the Tacana myth in which a Sloth interacted with Howler Monkeys, the two species differ mainly in their defecating habits. In several respects, the howler monkey produces waste. First, metaphorically; for according to mythic thought, uproar is the figurative expression of rottenness (see *From Honey to Ashes,* p. 310). The monkey howls in the morning and in the evening, particularly at times when the weather is changing: "Guariba na serra, chuva na terra" ("Monkey howls far away, rain is on its way"). This peasants' saying is in keeping with both the Bororo belief that guaribas are spirits of the rain and with the Guiana Indians' belief that Howler Monkey spirits live in rivers and come up to the surface when it rains. According to naturalists, it is also a lowering of the temperature that prompts the sloth to defecate (see p. 91). Both animals function as barometers, the sloth by excreting, the monkey by howling—with its "stinking" throat.

The adjective "stinking," applied to the Howler Monkey's throat, brings us back to the literal meaning, for the howler monkey is indeed an incontinent animal that excretes copiously, frequently, and on any occasion. I once fed a guariba monkey for a time, while letting him run free (this proved fatal, for he was killed by a hunter). With clocklike regularity he would come three times a day to share our meals. But if I or my companions tried to approach him at other times, he would instantly produce an amazing amount of excrement; he would then roll it into balls with his hands and pelt us with these projectiles. Such incidents are no exception, for the author of a classic monograph on this animal reports similar incidents:

> Fecal matter may be released with reference to the observer. . . . An individual would slowly approach to a place directly above me, or as near-by as possible, and then would release excrement. . . . Seemingly, the dropping of branches and excrement is a kind of primitive instrumental act. [Carpenter 1934: 27]

We can now better understand why the Barasana Indians oppose the Howler Monkey to the Sloth, calling them, respectively, "open" and "closed." They also oppose the Howler Monkey and the Tapir because of certain opposite traits: a low-pitched, powerful voice versus a high-pitched but soft voice, oral incontinence versus oral continence, and anal indiscipline versus oral discipline. Indeed, the tapir (to be mentioned again later) also differs from the howler monkey in its defecating habits. It is said to be careful to defecate only in water, and if it is seized by a pressing need elsewhere, it will put its excrement in a basket and take it to the nearest river. Finally, the vocal characteristics of the howler monkey are opposed to those of the Sloth; the former howls, whereas the latter can do nothing but whistle softly, and that only at night (see p. 88).

The Carib of Guina have a myth in which Howler Monkeys take their revenge on a hunter by covering him with excrement. The Waiwai, Carib Indians of Guiana, have a celebration, called Shodewika, during which dancers in costumes imitate various animals:

> A flock of shïpïlï [howler monkeys] came dashing into the house. . . . They climbed rapidly up the poles of the house and the rafters, reaching the high cruciform platform. Here they began to eat the stored bananas, throwing the skins down on the heads of the dancers. Now and then they placed their posteriors outside the platform and let fall a banana skin as evidence of a "sumptuous" meal. [Fock 1963: 181]

Moreover, howler monkeys are not only incontinent; they also waste food, throwing away the equivalent of a good third of what they actually consume. According to the author of the monograph cited earlier, "Fruit or buds, the moment they are picked, seem to become less attractive than those still attached to stems; so the monkeys throw away the food they have picked and eat what is still in place" (Carpenter 1934: 37).

Starting from the Goatsucker—a bird, certainly, but one whose habits set him apart from his congeners—I showed that this bird connotes oral greediness in myths. Then we went to the Sloth, who, through a double inversion of terms, connotes anal retention. This connotation is expressed in three ways: either the Sloth does not excrete (he has not been able to since his anus was plugged), or he does, in which case he excretes *close to* the ground, or he descends *slowly* to the ground to excrete. In other words, connotations concerning the Sloth are established by myths and beliefs with respect to time or to space, or to both.

We have seen that the Sloth is opposed both spatially and temporally to the Howler Monkey, who defecates *high up* in the trees and *at any time*. The Howler Monkey is thus doubly qualified to connote anal incontinence. But there is more: as a noise-maker and waster of food, the Howler Monkey also connotes oral incontinence. Even if it were not expressly stated in the Poronominaré myth, one could come to the conclusion, through transcendental deduction, that the Sloth adds to his other functions the connotation of oral retention (he can only whistle softly).

Let us now return to the Oyampi myth and the episode that I intentionally left aside (see p. 114). When the Indian whose companion had been decapitated by the Sloths arrived in the underworld, he found the Sloths busy rubbing their bodies with the excrement of their victim, and he understood that, for these giant beasts, humans were like kinkajous. Compared with other myths that oppose humans to tree-dwelling animals, the strata of the universe are here shifted downward: instead of tree-dwelling animals smaller than humans and living above them, we find humans assimilated to kinkajous and thus smaller than giant tree-dwelling animals, the Sloths, who live below them. In these shifted strata, what kind of defecating behavior prevails between the various inhabitants? Following in the steps of mythic thought, one could expect to see one of two possible schemes: trading places, man should not defecate on the Sloth; or, through a process of mutual inversion, man should behave toward the Sloth in the same way as the Howler Monkey (the Sloth's opposite) behaves toward man: man should dirty the Sloth with his excrement.

Neither of these two possibilities is chosen by the Oyampi myth. Instead, it offers a striking illustration of the extra twist that always appears at the very last stage of a mythic transformation—one that I tried to schematize by what I called a "canonic formula" (see p. 57). In the case at hand we are actually dealing with a threefold twist: instead of being *passively* soiled by *living* creatures, the inhabitants of the underworld—in this case, giant Sloths—*actively* gather the excrement of a *dead* animal; they even rub their bodies with it. An action that would be *defilement* for men (since the excrement is human) becomes, for the Sloths, *anti-defilement:* the myth changes *excrement* into *ornament.* Ornaments, which formerly had no place in the system, have found an indirect way in: they became logically necessary in order to complete a cycle of transformations. In this system, ornaments, unlike excrement, are not a term but a function: the "anti-defilement" function of excrement. Within a different context, we saw the Ovenbird perform a similar function.

Thus a whole semantic field has gradually been spread before our eyes, arrived at in often unforeseen ways (but ways that are, as I have tried to show, consistent). It is a triangular field, with the Goatsucker, the Sloth, and the Howler Monkey occupying the corners. Other animals stand along the sides of this triangle, at various distances from the first three. Still others, whom we have met before, take places inside the triangle according to their degree of semantic proximity to or remoteness from the three animals who, from their strategic positions, dominate the whole field.

10

Excrement, Meteors, Jealousy, Dismembered Body

Excrement, meteors, jealousy, dismembered body: a set also found in North America. The Iroquois creation myth. The part played by dream interpretation. An introduction to the myths of southern California.

*

In a Tacana myth to which I have referred several times, a young Sloth explains to his mother that if he defecated from the top of a tree, his excrement would hit the ground like a comet, the earth would turn on its pivot, and everyone would die.

Comets, fireballs, and other igneous meteors play a quite important part in the myths of this part of America. The Cavina, who are neighbors of the Tacana and linguistically and culturally related to them, tell the story of an Indian who was married, while his two brothers were not. The elder bachelor kept sending the younger one to get manioc flour from their sister-in-law. No longer able to cope with all the work, she asked them for a new sieve. The older bachelor climbed a palm tree to get the leaves used in making this utensil. But, instead of palms, he threw down his legs, his entrails, his torso, and his arms. His head, which was all that was left, ordered the younger brother to put it on the path of the Tapir. When the animal appeared, the head leaped into the air, fell on the animal, and killed it. The younger brother ate it.

The head then ordered that it be placed on the spot where the village chief usually urinated. The chief wanted to show the head to his people. The head killed everybody, except for a little boy. It then had itself taken to a lake, where it disappeared. Sometimes it can be seen flying up into the sky and then falling back into the lake, like a fireball with a feathery tail. This is a bad omen, for a falling star predicts that someone will be stung by a venomous ant.

A few hundred miles to the northwest, still at the foot of the Andes, we find a Machiguengua myth whose hero suspected his wife of having an affair with his son by a previous marriage. He left on a trip to find a wife for the son and fell victim to a group of cannibals, who tore out his entrails; nevertheless, he managed to escape. Meanwhile, the unfaithful wife was preparing a poison for him. When he came back, the Indian begged her, in vain, to serve him a mixture of tubers, calabash pulp, and cotton thread to replace his intestines. Furious when she paid no attention, he wrecked the garden; then he took a bamboo cane, hit it with a stone, and set it aflame. He made himself a tail with it and turned into a comet. Sometimes he snatches up corpses and changes them into comets like himself (for a more detailed account, see M_{298} in *From Honey to Ashes*, pp. 315–16).

One man *dismembers* his own body, while another gets deprived of his *entrails;* the former *feeds* his brother with *meat,* while the latter *destroys* cultivated *plants,* and in both cases a comet issues from an individual who has been reduced to a part of himself. In Tacana myths, the comet results from the all-too-sudden separation between an individual (the Sloth) and a part of himself (excrement, which turns into a comet).

Let us now try an experiment "just to see." In two jumps—unequally daring—we will move first to Guiana, then to the Upper Missouri River. According to the Arawak, goatsuckers originated from the scattered brains of a supernatural spirit whose skull had been broken open by a clever Indian (see p. 43). In North America, the Pawnee trace meteors back to the death of an Indian who was killed by his enemies and devoured by wild beasts (the myth probably preserves the memory of the meteors that fell in huge numbers on November 13, 1833, in a spectacular shower that also stayed in the memories of the Dakota and Pima Indians). The gods ordered the beasts to put the body back together again, but they could not find the brain, which had been replaced with down. The Indian came back to life and became the chief of the people of meteors. In two points, thousands of miles apart, the scattered pieces of a brain generate, here meteors, there goatsuckers.

Let us quickly retrace our steps. We were led from the Goatsucker to the Sloth, from the Sloth to comets and meteors. Now, through the notion of a mutilated body, meteors take us back to the Goatsucker. Should this come as a surprise? Other features in these myths also take us back to our starting point. The myths seen just above, on the origin of igneous meteors, connect these meteors with oral greediness (or its reverse, anal retention, which is then thwarted) and with jealousy or marital strife. They are connected to oral greediness because the glutton in the Cavina myth appears as a doublet of the greedy sister in a Quechua myth (both crave flour) and of other starving or voracious characters in Goatsucker myths (see pp. 42–43, 62). On their part, jealousy and marital strife, aside from constituting the theme of the Machiguengua myth, send us back to similar situations we encountered, at the very beginning, in Jivaro myths and then in Karaja, Kraho, and Mundurucu myths (see pp. 14–15, 41–42).

The theme of excrement also finds a place in meteor myths, just as it already had in Goatsucker myths. It is the Sloth's excrement, dropped from on high, that is transformed into a comet; and before flying up into the sky like a fireball, the head, in order to make sure it will be discovered, goes to the very spot where the Cavina chief, like the Sloth, regularly relieves himself. Moreover, according to the Machiguengua myth, meteorites—excretion, it is true, rather than excrement—come from blood dripping from the head, changed into a meteor, as it soars across the sky.

*

We again find—and not without some surprise—the three key elements of the set—jealousy, excrement, and meteor—closely knit together in one of the greatest mythological systems in North America, that of the Iroquois Indians. We know several versions of their creation myth. The oldest ones, gathered by French Jesuits, date from the seventeenth century. More recent and detailed ones have been collected, translated, and published by researchers who were either half- or full-blooded Iroquois, mainly by J. N. B. Hewitt, whose mother was a Tuscarora. We know that the Iroquois were formerly a confederation of five, then six, "nations": the Cayuga, the Mohawk, the Oneida, the Onondaga, and the Seneca, who were then joined by the Tuscarora at the beginning of the eighteenth century. It would be impossible to examine here in detail all twenty-five or so known versions of the creation myth. The most complete one, told to Hewitt by Chief Gibson in Onondaga, takes up one hundred fifty quarto pages of the forty-third *Annual Report* of the Bureau of American Ethnology. I will give only the main outlines of the myth, occasionally drawing attention to significant variations.

The story starts at the time when the earth did not yet exist. In the world Below there was only water. In the sky, on a kind of island, lived supernatural beings, formed like humans, whose way of life prefigured what was to be the Indian way of life. Up there, in a village—which was undergoing a crisis (or, in some versions, was in a state of lack, as Propp would have put it)—a family was keeping two children, sometimes a brother and sister, in confinement. This was customary for children of high rank. They nevertheless visited each other secretly. Whether it was in consequence of these visits or due to events of a mystical order, the young lady became pregnant and gave birth to a daughter. Around the same time, her brother (in some versions, her maternal uncle) died, after insisting that his coffin be placed in the branches of a tree. (In the versions in which the uncle dies, the brother, called Séism, appears later in the story.)

The baby girl grew quickly but kept crying all the time. To calm her down, she was allowed long visits with the corpse, high in the tree. He would foretell her future and guide her conduct, and everything went according to his predictions. The girl was sent to another village to marry the chief. On her way there she had to elude the seductive tricks of her husband-to-be. When she arrived in the village, the chief, now her husband, put her on trial again and forced her to undress and cook corn soup in a huge pot. Soon her nude body was splashed from head to foot with the boiling liquid. Then, following the chief's orders, dreadful dogs licked her body with tongues so rough that she was covered with blood.

We might expect that this young necrophile (she kept company with a corpse), after bravely facing such sadism, would at last be out of trouble. However, she was not, for her husband was still jealous. He became ill, and all efforts to cure him failed. In desperation, he rounded up the population and begged them to guess what he had dreamt; otherwise he would die.

Let us sidestep for a moment. In a book in which I am trying to show that certain notions credited to psychoanalysis (oral and anal character and so on) were already inherent in mythic thought, I will not be straying from my topic if I dwell a little on the way the Iroquois and their neighbors thought about their dreams. We will see that here again they were far ahead of us when it comes to a good many of the notions that did not find expression in the Western world until Freud. Look how Father Ragueneau, a missionary among the Huron (who shared the Iroquois' views on the question) explained the local theories:

Aside from the desires we commonly have—free, or at least voluntary, desires coming from a prior knowledge of some good we see in the object of our desire—the Hurons think that our souls have other desires, both natural and hidden, so to speak; they say these come from the depths of the soul, not through knowledge but through a sort of motion of the soul toward certain objects. . . .

Now, they believe that the soul manifests these natural desires through dreams, which are like the words of the soul; so that, if its wishes are granted, it is satisfied; on the contrary, if it is not granted what it asked for, it shows its indignation, not only in refusing the body the well-being and happiness it wished to dispense, but often also in rebelling against it, causing various diseases and even death. . . .

Following these erroneous beliefs, most Hurons are intent on observing their dreams and giving to their souls

131

what they showed them in their sleep. For instance, if they saw a sword in their dream, they try to find it; if they dreamt they were having a festive meal, they have one when they wake up, if they can; and so on. And they call it *Ondinnonk,* a secret desire of the soul, manifested through dreams.

However, though we do not always openly declare our thoughts and inclinations, they will come to the knowledge of those who are said to see through to our hearts with some supernatural insight. In this same way the Hurons believe that some people are more clear-sighted than the average and can, so to speak, see through to the very depths of the soul, uncovering its natural and hidden desires, even though the soul had not manifested anything through dreams, or the dreamer had forgotten everything.

As we can see, the Indians even had psychoanalysts!

Now, in Ragueneau's terms, what plagued the Iroquois hero was indeed a "sickness of desire." In such cases, the only cure is to "guess what desires trouble the soul." Another missionary, Father de Quen, witnessed a scene identical to the one we saw in the myth: "An Indian had a dream, called all the leaders of the country, and told them he had had a dream which would not come true; but his own death would cause that of the whole nation; the earth would be turned upside down and shattered. . . . Then he asked them to guess his dream."

Let us come back to our myth. Here, too, the main dignitaries of the country gathered. One of them managed to guess the "word" in the dream, which was "tooth," "ordure," or "excrement," depending on the version. The last two words are translations of a single word in Onondaga and Seneca dialects, respectively, and "tooth" is the name for a liliaceous flower, the tiger lily or the dogtooth violet (*Erythronium*). A "tree of light," the most precious treasure in the village, bore these flowers, which shone on the celestial world; for in those days the sun did not exist. Other versions identify the tree of light as a wild apple tree (a rosaceous tree) or to a wild "cherry tree" (dogwood, a *cornus*). At any rate, Meteor, one of the chief's companions—precisely the one he suspected of being his wife's lover—guessed the hidden meaning of the dream: the tree had to be uprooted. Which was no sooner said than done. Soon there was a gaping hole where the roots had been. The chief, under the pretext of a picnic, led his pregnant wife to the spot and threw her into the hole. In a shorter version, the tree of light is replaced by a tree covered with ears of corn, the villagers' only staple. A young man, furious that the tree had been uprooted, kicked the woman into the hole. In this version, she was the sick one looking for a cure.

The young woman thus started on a long fall into the dark. Meteor, "who was supposed to have caused the jealousy of the Chief" in the Seneca version, had equipped her with a few items: a little firewood, a diminutive mortar and pestle, a small pot, etc. According to a version given by a Seneca chief, A. Parker, and confirmed by others among the same nation, the woman, as she fell, was enveloped by the light of a meteor, like a comet, terrifying the animals (inhabitants of the aquatic underworld), who, fearing they would be destroyed, created the earth to absorb the shock.[1]

Meteor had helped her because, as he told her, "Thy former husband accused me of the things for which he cast thee down" (Hewitt 1928: 481). He kept helping her through her fall. This character belongs to the race of the "Fire Dragons" or "Blue Panthers," whose nature confines them to the bottom of lakes. They are not hostile toward humans, but, were they to leave the water, they would set the universe ablaze. Why does the "word in the dream," guessed by this Meteor, designate sometimes the tree that is to be uprooted, sometimes ordure or excrement? Neither local informants nor the most knowledgeable commentators shed any light on the subject. Let me simply stress that these words, certainly heavy with meaning, appear in a context associating them with jealousy on the one hand, a meteor on the other. For if, going further—and probably beyond the limits set by any reasonable

---

1. For another version, see Converse 1908: 33.

method—we ventured to consolidate the Jivaro, Tacana, Machiguengua, and Iroquois traditions into a kind of metamyth (or, who knows, archemyth?) we would be led to conclude that an Iroquois heroine who for a while, through various rhetorical devices, was assimilated to a comet or a meteor; who fell through a hole in the celestial vault into water (excreted, in a sense, by her husband); and who finally, in her fall, threatened to destroy the animals of the world Below, can be compared at once with the excrement dropped too fast by the Sloth and with the Mother of Pottery of the Jivaro myths, who was also hurled from the sky after a scene with a jealous husband, and who left her mark on earth in the form of excrement (see p. 16).

This resemblance is augmented by some Seneca versions in which the woman introduces the first element of earth into the liquid world below (just like the Jivaro heroine, who brought potter's clay); for, in her fall, she had clung to the edges of the hole, and some dirt had remained under her nails. It is all the more tempting to establish these parallels because they are confirmed in a version collected by Father Sagard, another seventeenth-century missionary. According to this version, the heroine, in her subsequent adventures, plays a part similar to that of the Moon in Machiguengua and Campa myths. The heroine of the Huron and Iroquois myths, an evil creature, later to become the Moon, was supposed to govern death and be in charge of the souls of the dead: "Eataentsic [such is her name] takes care of souls; and because they think she causes men to die, they say she is evil" (Sagard 1636: vol. 2, p. 452). Father Brébeuf's remarks were similar. This is bound to recall the Machiguengua Moon god, who snatched corpses and ate them before sending them, in their former physical appearance, into the afterlife.

One detail—a minor one—could bring even more cohesion to the group of South American myths. The Moon god ate only the limbs of the corpses; he transformed their entrails into tapirs, which he fed to the same corpses, once he had returned them to their human form. This practice may shed a new light on the Tapir incident that seemed meaningless within the context of the Cavina myth (see p. 127). That incident would be more meaningful if the Tapir that was eaten by the brother of the dismembered Indian had also issued from entrails; in that myth the Indian's entrails dropped from a tree.

*

This attempt to consolidate myths from the two hemispheres into one system remains, I repeat, highly conjectural. I will thus go no further than this rough outline and leave it as a field of research open to others to complete and enrich. Boas said—and wrote— that he was convinced that several traits directly linked the Iroquois to the cultures of the Gulf of Mexico and South America— for instance, the structure of the language and the independent invention of the blowpipe (or its reappearance, which was attested no earlier than the eighteenth century). Jakobson and I once met with Boas, and I find an echo of our conversation in Jakobson's remark on the absence of labials in Seneca; this, he said, could be explained by the ancient practice of wearing lip-plugs— a trait that also suggests a southern origin.

These hypotheses are now being challenged, by Lounsbury among others. But if the similarities outlined here between Iroquois and sub-Andean myths could help in reviving them, one would be tempted to recognize in the Iroquois "tree of light," with its flowers like lilies (see p. 132), the ancient memory of a hallucinatory plant of the *Datura* genus (or rather *Brugmansia*, as it is a tree), whose flowers have a similar general aspect. Indeed, in their shamanic songs that are linked with the use of this plant, the Machiguengua say that the white flowers of the *Datura* give off such a bright light that the sun gets dimmer in its presence.

However, I will not venture such risky speculations; simply, a quick comparison attests that, in North and South America, a moral feeling—jealousy; a celestial phenomenon—meteors; and an organic substance—excrement, form, in certain myths, a well-articulated system.

To add support and scope to this demonstration, it remains to me to examine another area in North America—one whose myths exhibit the same system even more clearly than the Iroquois and Huron myths do. This area is southern California.

But first, one remark. The act of defecating consists in separating from the body something that formed an integral part of it. This anatomical disjunction finds its place in a series whose other terms are these: the disemboweled body, the dismembered body, the head severed from the body, and the skull deprived of its brain. We have seen that the myths systematically illustrate this series.

The myths of southern California also evolve within this semantic field, and, like those we have been considering, they give a prominent place to meteors and jealousy. Our sources will be peoples belonging to the Shoshonean and Yuman linguistic families: the Mohave, living in the interior, on the border between California and Arizona; then, going toward the coast, the Cahuilla and several groups collectively designated as "Mission Indians" because they fell under the domination of Spanish Franciscan missionaries in the eighteenth century. The distinctive names they were given bear witness to that domination: Luiseño, Diegueño, Juaneño, Gabrielino, and so on.

Some of these groups have almost disappeared. They were subjected to acculturation as early as the eighteenth century and were then contaminated or massacred during the nineteenth-century Gold Rush invasion. The other groups have seen their numbers drop to a few hundred individuals, if not a few dozen. All we have is a mutilated mythology, and the task of the comparatist is made even more complicated by the fact that this mythology shows highly original traits. It is tempting to see in it the vestiges of a very archaic stage—vestiges that might be evidence of one of the earliest migratory waves in the Americas. If such is the case, the parallels with South American mythical patterns would be all the more interesting. Let us add that plants of the *Datura* genus, or very closely related plants (Brugmansiae), are used for their narcotic and hallucinatory properties in two main areas in America. One covers central and southern California, with a few extensions eastward; the other is the sub-Andean zone that yielded most of the South American myths I have drawn from up to now.

Always obscure, often contradicting each other (and even self-contradictory), these California myths present such formidable problems of interpretation that one can scarcely comprehend them. I will roughly sort them into three groups of unequal importance. The first two deal with events described as relatively recent. The third goes back to the creation of the universe.

In one group of tales the main character is a cannibal monster called Takwish. A young Indian once fell victim to him. The boy's father, a great chief, resolved to avenge him. He visited Takwish and challenged him to an acrobatic dance contest, during which the ogre "broke his own bones, cut off his hair, threw it away, broke off his legs, and threw them away. Then he flew about with only body and head, and broke his head apart with his hands. . . . Then he put himself together again" (Kroeber 1906: 319). In the end he was killed and cremated by the Indians, but he came back to life in the shape of an igneous meteor or, more accurately, one of those lightning bolts or fireballs that apparently are often seen in North American skies. Out of curiosity, I consulted the *Scientific Event Alert Network Bulletin* of the Smithsonian Institution (vol. 9, nos. 2 and 3) and discovered that over a dozen igneous meteors were reported between February and March of 1984. One of the most famous authorities on the Indians of southern California, Constance Goddard DuBois, says that at the very beginning of the century a Luiseño Indian, who "with a great reluctance" had agreed to sing a sacred song for her, was so terrified by a lightning bolt that he refused to go any further. In this first group of myths, as in South America, the meteor (in the broadest sense of the term) stands within what could be called the semantic field of the dismembered body.

In the second group of myths, the heroes are twin brothers (though not of the same age), more or less directly descended

137

from the primordial couple, Sky and Earth. I will not retrace here their complicated adventures, which led to the death of one or both of them. They left a son and nephew called Chaup or Guiomar, who avenged his father and/or his uncle before turning into an igneous meteor. It will suffice to emphasize three points.

First, this group of myths always deals with meteors. There is, for instance, the Mohave version whose hero Ahta-tane (i.e., "Cane," a type of reed) only momentarily becomes a meteor, but he hurls, "like a meteor," his dead father's kneecap because the father's murderers were playing ball with it. In another episode the hero defeats an ogre called Meteor (I will come back to this). DuBois wrote: "The Dieguenos identified the being whose name on earth was Cuyahomarr [Guiomar], the wonder-working boy, and whose name in the sky is Chaup or Shiwiw, with the large meteoric fireball which is his physical manifestation" (DuBois 1908b: 125). The twins, father and uncle to this hero, also are meteors: "They shine like stars . . . ; their eyes shine like fire." A child sent out to spy on them reports: "There is something like stars in the house. They have eyes of fire, and I was afraid" (DuBois 1904b: 236). The child is so frightened that he thinks he is going to die.

Second, the theme of jealousy keeps recurring in the Mohave myth like a leitmotiv. The brothers were always jealous of each other. They fought over the eagles they killed to get feathers for their arrows, over the reeds they collected for making flutes, over the women they wanted to marry, and so on. The twins' mother was jealous of these women, and she managed to break up their marriages. One brother ended up killing the other out of jealousy. Later, their son or nephew arrived at the house of Meteor, the ogre, who did not receive him well: "No one comes to my house; I want to see no one come. I am stingy. I want no one to see my wives' faces. I am bad and want to kill any man who has been among my wives" (Kroeber 1948a: 13 n.62). Jealousy also ruled among this jealous man's wives; when he was killed, they quarreled over who should marry the murderer. In a Diegueno version, a woman who became pregnant under mysterious circumstances and gave birth to the twins suffered from her sister's jealousy.

Finally, the theme of dismemberment is present in these myths. In some Diegueño versions the hero's grandfather bets in succession all the parts of his grandson's body; elsewhere, the younger demiurge gambles and loses all his limbs and, finally, his heart. A whole semantic field thus takes shape again before us. It will come as no surprise (actually, it could almost have been deduced) that the first term in the series of the dismembered body—the separation of excrement (see p. 136)—appears in full view in the third group of myths: the creation myths.

The Diegueño versions sometimes deviate from the others, but they provide a transition from the first two groups to the third. At the beginning of time, they say, male water from Above and female earth from Below united. Their two sons first had to push the water higher up, so that it became the sky; then they made living beings from clay. One brother died and was cremated; the other went up to the sky, "[where] now, seen as ball-lightning, [he] carries away the spirits of people and so causes their death" (Curtis 1907–30: vol. 15, p. 123).

In other versions—Mohave, Luiseño, Cahuilla, and Cupeño— things and beings also originated from a primordial couple or from the conjugation of more abstract entities, who reproduced themselves in successive pairs, prior to the time when beings appeared as persons:

> In the very beginning there was nothing but darkness. . . .
> Sounds—humming or thunder—were heard at times.
> Red, white, blue, and brown colors came, all twisting together, to one point in the darkness. They were all acting together—twisting. They came together in one point to produce. The ball thus formed shook and whirled together into one substance, which became two embryos wrapped in this placenta. This was formed in space and darkness. These were born prematurely; everything

stopped, for they were stillborn. Then again all the lights whirled together, joined, and produced. This time the embryos came to full term—inside, the children talked to one another. [Strong 1929: 130–31]

Thus the creation progressively took shape. According to the Cahuilla and the Cupeño, it was quickly taken in charge by two demiurges, two competitors of unequal skill, Mukat and Temaïyauit. They constantly quarreled about which of them was the older, which worked more efficiently—a prototype of the quarrels between the jealous twins in the myths summarized above. In the end, the demiurges decided to part company. Temaïyauit opened up the earth and changed its surface in order to take the begins he had created down to the underworld:

> He tried to take earth and sky with him; a fierce wind blew and the earth shook all over, while the sky bent and swayed. Mukat put one knee on the ground, held one hand on all his creatures, and with the other held up the sky. He cried, "Hi! Hi! Hi!"—which is the way all people do now when the earthquake comes. In the struggle, all the mountains and canyons appeared on the earth's surface, stream beds were formed, and water came out and filled them. At last Temaïyauit disappeared below, all became quiet, and the earth stopped shaking; but its rough, uneven surface remains until today. [Ibid., p. 135]

So Mukat was left alone with all the things and beings he had created. From this point on, the southern California myths follow a parallel development. The Cahuilla myth, whose beginning we just saw, continues with Mukat as its hero. In other versions, Mukat is replaced by Matevilye (Mohave) or Wiyot (Luiseño), with a few changes: Matevilye and Wiyot appeared at the time of creation or immediately thereafter and are the educators of early mankind rather than demiurges. Also, Mukat's nature is definitely more ambiguous than theirs: he was a demiurge, a good creator, unlike his brother. However, later in the story, he plays an evil part: he brings about violent death by giving venomous fangs to the rattlesnake and bows and arrows to humans, teaching them how to make war on one another.

Despite their differences (see also pp. 151–52), these three characters made analogous mistakes and met with the same fate. Mukat made an obscene gesture at his sister, the Moon (Cahuilla, Cupeño). Matevilye did the same thing to his daughter, the Frog (Mohave). Wiyot, looking a charming young woman in the face, said to himself that her back was as scrawny as a frog's (Luiseño); she read his mind, and, like the other women, took offense at such ungraciousness; she won the animals over to her cause and talked them into avenging her.

They watched the god at night to find out where he secretly went to defecate. They discovered that he went to the ocean and climbed a pole or a scaffolding of logs planted in the water. Once up there, the god would relieve himself, and his excrement made a sound like thunder when it hit the water. One night the Frog girl, or another batrachian, kept watch, and when the god defecated, she swallowed the excrement before it hit the water or caught it and brought it back to the other conspirators, who scattered it in pieces, thus breaking up what had already been produced as separate pieces. Not hearing the usual sound, the god knew someone had taken his excrement. He became sick, knew that he was doomed, and died at last. His corpse was burned on a woodpile: this is the origin of cremation. But Coyote managed to steal the heart, which burned more slowly, and he ate it. Wiyot was transformed into the Moon (*moila*), and he comes back periodically to visit his creatures (Luiseño). From the ashes of Mukat (Wiyot's Cahuilla and Cupeño counterpart) cultivated plants arose.

11

California Demiurges as Jealous Potters

California demiurges or cultural heroes as jealous potters. Comparison
with sub-Andean myths. Moon and meteor. The arbitrary character of
the linguistic sign in mythical analysis. Symmetry between myths from
southern California and South American Sloth myths. Problems are
raised. Third application of the canonic formula.

*

According to the Diegueño creation myth, the demiurge (here
called Tuchaipa) extracted mud from the ground and made the
Indians with it; in the Cahuilla myth, Mukat created the first men,
"working slowly and carefully, modeling a fine body such as men
have now" (Strong 1929: 134). While the demiurge and his brother
were wondering whether men should be mortal, Mukat argued in
favor of death, because, if they came back to life,

> "the world [would] be too small," . . . . Then Temaïyauit
> [the bad demiurge] said, "We can then spread it wider."
> "Yes, but there will not be enough food for all of them,"
> answered Mukat. "They can eat earth," said Temaïyauit.
> "But they will then eat up all the earth," answered Mukat.
> Temïyauit replied, "No, for by our power it will be swell-
> ing again." [Ibid., p. 135]

As we see, the myths even conceived the idea of an expanding
universe.

Wiyot, the Luiseño cultural hero, teacher of mankind rather
than demiurge, first ruled over a world in which death was unknown and whose population, fed with clay, could grow indefi-
nitely. But, in dying, he took his knowledge with him. A council
had to be held to find out how the world, which had become
overpopulated, could survive. A decision was reached to divide

142

the primordial community into animal and vegetable species, each to be assigned its own habitat—on the ground, underground, in water, or in the air. Instead of there being a homogeneous population, feeding on earth, living in peace, and free to multiply, they decided who would eat whom; making the species antagonistic so that they would mutually limit their numbers. This amounted to a kind of cannibalism, for all living creatures were formerly one people, in which animals and plants were not distinguished, one from the other nor humans from animals: "And they killed . . . animals. . . . They killed acorns—which were people then—and killed everything that they now eat. For people turned into animals and seeds, acorns, and plants" (DuBois 1908b: 136–37). The Eagle, who was very wise and knowledgeable, tried to escape this tragic fate:

> So he went north, thinking that from there he could get entirely away from this world, reach its limits, and fly away; and he tried it everywhere but could not do it. He thought he could live forever and keep away from death; but there was death . . . wherever he went. Then he went east and did the same thing, and south and west the same. . . . He had to die. [Ibid., p. 137]

Burial rites were instituted in order to mark the border between the living and the dead.

Rites elsewhere also put into practice this philosophical interpretation of cannibalism. When an initiate died among the Juaneño, and probably among their neighbors also, an officiant called *takwé* cut off a piece of flesh from the corpse and ate it, or pretended to, in front of all the people assembled for the ceremony. He was highly dreaded and well remunerated. For the Indians this rite was connected with the episode in the creation myth during which Coyote stole and ate the heart of the dead god. This rite insured that the initiate's heart would go to the sky and become a star. The hearts and souls of noninitiates went to an underworld.

It used to be thought that the word *takwé* meant "eater," but this is now contested. Kroeber associated it with the word *tak-*

143

wish, "fireball," which is also the name of the cannibal monster, killed by the Indians, who comes back to life in the form of an igneous meteor (see p. 137). In the Cahuilla creation myth, a character by the name of Takwic, described as a "fireball demon," plays a key role in the episode in which the demiurge Mukat teaches humans how to shoot arrows at each other; in this scene, the men are tricked into this game by birds, who claim it is harmless (one of them is our old friend: "probably the nighthawk or the poorwill" [Strong 1929: 288]). The men soon realize their mistake: the "survivors saw their dead comrades and began to cry loudly" (ibid., p. 137).

In a preceding episode, Moon, the only woman among all of Mukat's creatures, divided the population into exogamous halves, gave them animal names, and "taught the coyote people to sing against the wildcat people as though they were singing enemy songs [and] to run, jump, wrestle, and throw stones and balls of mud at each other" (ibid., p. 136). In other words, Moon instituted a social order based on antagonism, in which each camp was animated by a hostility that foreshadowed, "in a game," what was later to become the rule between foreign groups.

Let us recall that in this set of myths the demiurge or cultural hero can have two types of relations with the moon. For the Luiseño, Wiyot, the teacher of mankind, turns into the moon after his death and regularly comes back in this form to visit humans. His Cahuilla counterpart, Mukat, was a demiurge. He created the moon by extracting it from his heart; later on he caused the vanishing of Lady Moon, the teacher of early mankind. When he died and his corpse was cremated, tobacco arose from his heart, squashes from his stomach, watermelons from his pupils, corn from his teeth, wheat from his lice eggs, beans from his semen, etc. Therefore, in one case, Mukat alive draws the moon from his body; in the other, symmetrical, instance, Wiyot dead is reincarnated in the moon. And mankind gains: in the one case, the moon in the sky; in the other, cultivated plants on earth.

*

Where are these remarks leading us? They put us on the track of striking analogies between the California themes and those we encountered, far from there, in South America, in the myths of sub-Andean peoples. Like the Indians of southern California, the Machiguengua—whom we have already encountered, along with their Campa neighbors and relatives, also settled at the foot of the Andes—saw creation as the result of a conflict between a good and a bad demiurge. Like them, they believed in "comet demons," whom they called *kachiboréni* (see p. 128). Like them, finally, they thought that, in the beginning, men fed on earth. True, they made one distinction on this point that introduced a reverse symmetry with the Luiseño myth: for the Luiseño, humans ate white clay but not red clay, which was used only for pottery; for the Machiguengua, early men ate "a red earth similar to that used to make pots . . . , a kind of clay they kneaded and cooked in coals [and] swallowed like hens; for they had no teeth with which to chew" (Garcia). As for their part, the Campa say that humans, in the beginning, ate pieces of termite nests.

According to a Machiguengua myth, the Moon god once stole into the hut where a young girl, menstruating for the first time, was secluded. He brought her cultivated plants as a gift. Later, he offended her, or another girl in the same condition. They retaliated by spraying him with menstrual blood or saliva, which left spots on the moon. In another version the spots came from the dismembered corpse of Moon's wife, pieces of which stuck to his face. In fact, all versions say that the wife died and that, following this, Moon became a cannibal god.

Both in California and among the Machiguengua, then, Moon—or another character more or less directly assimilated to this celestial body—is a sexual offender. Actually, neither Mukat nor Wiyot was ever a cannibal. But by dying without leaving their knowledge to their creatures, by taking this knowledge into their graves, they became responsible for the metaphorical cannibalism that was to prevail on earth; for, from then on, creatures who had been all alike, all of one race, were condemned to eat one another. The ritual cannibalism of the *takwé* commemorates this revolution, and, in the myth, a character bearing this name helped the god institute, if not cannibalism, at least war (see p. 144).

We come to the same conclusion regarding the Moon character, whether it appears in the Machiguengua or California myths: Moon is ambivalent, oscillating between two poles. On the one hand, he or she is a teacher and benefactor (a benefactress for the Luiseño); on the other, he or she is responsible for war, death, and, more or less directly, cannibalism. In the first case, Moon appears as a luminary with a protective and civilizing role. Under its second aspect, Moon, male or female, becomes closer to the cannibal meteor, to the point of becoming one with him. Witness the creation myth of the Dieguèño, in which the demiurge's brother, Chakopa or Tuchaipa, went blind and rose up to the sky, like Wiyot. He can still be seen there today, but, unlike Wiyot, who became the moon, he is "a lightning bolt [that] carries away the spirits of the people and so causes their death" (Curtis 1907–30: vol. 15, pp. 122–23).

Let us briefly come back to the Jivaro, whose myths we have already consolidated with the Machiguengua's. They see "fire rings" and "fireballs" as one of the tangible manifestations of *arutam*, "ancestral spirits." When Goatsucker exhumed the Moon, buried by the Sloth, and let her bolt from the hole straight up to the sky, did he not transform her into a reversed meteor? The Machiguengua, for their part, say that, before the sky became the moon's permanent dwelling place, only the Sloth shone weakly in the sky at night. According to the Shipaia of the Xingu, who in the past had a solid reputation as cannibals, Moon was an incestuous brother whose sister was trying to meet him in the sky, to which he had escaped; he hurled her down into space, and she turned first into a meteor, then into a tapir. Finally, in Machiguengua myths, the cannibal Moon god, who roasted and ate the limbs of the dead, transformed the rest of their bodies into tapirs. We will deal later with the relation between the tapir and the moon (see p. 168).

In these myths from the Americas, moon and meteors are commutable, as well as the moon and the head severed from the body—which, as we saw, sometimes becomes a meteor. Severed head, meteor, and moon constitute a system whose first two terms have a negative connotation, whereas the third one oscillates between a positive and a negative connotation. Given that the myths attribute to the Moon goddess (or, more often, god) the role of organizer of the cosmos, how could it be otherwise? Wild or venomous beasts, diseases, war, death—all have their place in the universe. Whoever tolerated them, created them even, cannot be entirely good.

This ambivalence can also be explained by reasons of a formal order, as I pointed out in *The Origin of Table Manners* (pp. 127–29). I then wrote that, even when it does not change sexes, the moon, often an androgyne or hermaphrodite, provides a ready theme for a mythology of ambiguity. This ambiguity stems from the fact that celestial bodies return at regular intervals—every year, month, or day, depending on each case, and, with respect to this, the moon is opposed to the seasonal constellations because of its monthly instead of yearly phases, whereas its absence or presence, in alternation with the sun, reflects the shortest kind of periodicity: that of day and night.

Apropos of that analysis, I was somewhat ingenuously accused of a contradiction. Did I not say, in the same sentence, (*The Origin of Table Manners,* p. 195) that the sun and the moon can each "signify anything" but that the sun can do so only on condition that it is "a beneficent father or a cannibalistic monster" and that the moon must be either at once "a legislator and a trickster" or "a sterile, virgin girl, or a hermaphroditic personage, or an impotent or dissolute man"? According to my critic, I was at one and the same time reaffirming the principle of the arbitrary character of linguistic signs and giving these very signs concrete contents.

Now, my critic's argument continues, these contents are derived from the specificities of the two great luminaries:

> The sun has a daily and an annual cycle. While the sun is not subject to change itself, but is either shining or not shining, the moon is waxing and waning. The sun is ei-

ther there or not there, and only a very short period of transition exists at sunrise and sunset. The moon is never completely there or completely not there, and there is a short period of transition at the full moon and the new moon. The mode of existence of the sun expresses contrasts, an opposition between being and not-being; the mode of existence of the moon expresses transition and mediation, always moving between being and not-being. [Oosten 1983: 144]

There could be no better condensation of the analyses made in the course of the four volumes of *Mythologiques*. But is it true, as the author claims, that the principle of the arbitrary character of the linguistic sign is at the same time asserted and betrayed? Three points need to be made concerning this issue.

In the first place, saying, as I always have, that the meaning of mythemes resides in the way they are combined is not equivalent to applying to mythemes the Saussurean principle of the arbitrary character of the linguistic sign, about which I myself have expressed some reservations (*Structural Anthropology*, pp. 81–97). The principle of the arbitrary character of the linguistic sign concerns words and concepts in their respective relationships with signifiers and physical objects. I, on the contrary, have stressed that if one wants to establish a parallel between structural linguistics and the structural analysis of myths, the correspondence is established not between mytheme and word but between mytheme and phoneme (*The View from Afar*, pp. 144–46). Now, if it is true that the phoneme, without signifying anything in itself, serves the function of differentiating significations, it does not follow that a phoneme in a given language can serve this function anywhere and in any circumstance. Its use is bound by constraints that are determined by its position at the beginning, the middle, or the end of a word, by its compatibility or incompatibility with the phoneme that immediately precedes or follows it. The constraints I was alluding to in a figurative way are of the same kind. They pertain to what I would call, in my own terms, the armature of the myth.

Second, the relations of correlation and opposition between the sun and the moon, also noted by my critic, in no way constitute objective properties, immediately perceptible by the senses. These properties are drawn from experience, through abstraction, in which the understanding is at work. They consist in logical relations that, by reason of their formal nature, can accept a wide variety of different contents. I was only offering a few examples of such contents.

Third, these relations of correlation and opposition are those that were devised and applied within one family of Amerindian myths among others. They correspond to one particular way in which the mythemes sun and moon were used to form a system of significations. One should not go further and grant them a general application. In America and elsewhere, other families of myths choose other relationships: they may oppose sun and moon, but on different bases; they may oppose them, separately or together, to other celestial bodies or even to objects of an altogether different order. The principle that the signification of mythemes always hinges on their position is not compromised by the fact that one family of myths attributes to the sun and the moon relative semantic positions that allow them to convey specific significations. Rather, this is a way of confirming the principle by illustrating, concretely, one of its applications.

In the case at hand, the point to be remembered is this: according as one views it under one or the other aspect, the moon evokes differing forms of periodicity, the one daily, the other monthly, and neither of these involves changes comparable to those of the seasonal cycle. At the very most, the moon, exclusively associated with a short, serial periodicity, merges with meteors, which have no regular periodicity but are frequent enough, as I said, to constitute a series. In *From Honey to Ashes* I summarized and discussed a Machiguengua myth (M_{299}; pp. 320–24) in which the human wife of the Moon god died in giving birth to her fourth child. Her mother insulted her son-in-law, telling him that, now that he had killed his wife, all he had to do was eat her corpse—which he did. Since then he has become not only a cannibal but a necrophage. In commenting on this myth, Mme Cazevitz-Renard made a very insightful comment: "If Moon proved a good husband in giving his wife four children, he lacked moderation in having her conceive every year, . . . not every three or four years" (Casevitz 1977: 131). The moon's short periodicity accounts for its cannibalism and its "meteoric" affinities.

Despite its periodicity, and because it is alternately new and full, the moon takes on a character of discontinuity that has led several Amerindian peoples to consider each of its aspects as a separate being. Such was the case with the ancient Tupi and, to a lesser degree, the Araucan, whose myths gave an important place to a meteoric deity, a cannibal, portent of sickness and death—a good reminder of the fact that the Araucan, also a sub-Andean people, belong to a set of cultures we keep meeting in the course of our investigations.

We now need to come back to an aspect of the system that I have already touched on (see pp. 139, 142). The Moon god who feeds his creatures on earth or clay or who teaches mankind to replace it with a new diet, based on cultivated plants, is a potter. When the young recluse in Machiguengua myths presented Moon with the baked earth that humans ate, the god explained that it was not an edible substance; it should be used to make pots, vases, and other vessels in which they would cook manioc, the nutritious tuber of a plant that was in his sole possession and would henceforth be the main food of mankind.

Indians of southern California believe that early men were made of clay—a Mesopotamian type of belief, so to speak. According to the Cahuilla, the demiurge Mukat modeled them carefully; he then put them out to bake in the sun. Depending on the degree of their exposure to the heat, some became black, others red, while others yet, with little exposure, remained white; this is how the human races were formed. Wiyot, the Luiseño cultural hero, taught pottery to humans, among other arts.

The lunar god or hero also has a jealous nature. He is prone to persecuting his creatures. These traits are particularly apparent in the demiurge Mukat. He insisted that his creatures be mortal. Pretending that it was a game, he incited them to kill each other: "This is the way Mukat tricked and deceived his people" (Strong 1929: 138). Revolted by this, several of his creatures united against him: "Mukat thus finally incurred the ill-will of mankind, because he caused quarreling and fighting" (ibid., p. 369). Even Wiyot, the wise teacher of mankind, who "educated his people, watched over them, provided for their needs, and called them his children" (ibid., p. 269), behaved so perversely that they resolved to kill him.

Father Geronimo Boscana, a Franciscan missionary who catechized the Indians in the beginning of the nineteenth century, drew a very dark portrait of Wiyot. Appearing at first as pacific, good, and generous, a few years later he proved a fierce monster, a cruel despot, occasionally a murderer; his subjects grew to hate him, and finally, in desperation, they decided to do away with him. Waterman has challenged this report, saying that Boscana's prejudice as a Catholic priest had led him to paint a disparaging portrait of this indigenous deity. For my part, I would be inclined to share Father Boscana's views, for his portrait of Wiyot coincides with those found in myths concerning the demiurge Mukat (substituted for Wiyot in Cahuilla myths) and his Serrano counterpart, Kukikat (humans decided to take their revenge on him because he had split them into nations speaking different languages and at war with each other). According to the Maricopa, who speak a Yuman language, like the Mohave, the demiurge, furious at humans because they had abused his favorite snake, exposed them to violent death (either by the bites of venomous snakes or in wars). A frog caused his death by swallowing the vomit he was dropping from atop a pole (vomit here replacing excrement).

Wiyot's creatures would have had no reason for wanting to kill him had he not behaved hatefully toward them. It is true that Wiyot appears as a more benevolent character in myths collected around the turn of this century, but, in opposition to Waterman's thesis, I would tend to interpret this as the effect of a gradual Christianization of the deity.

Like the South American myths with which we began our investigation, those of southern California associate pottery with jealousy. The theme of excrement also reappears, within a plot that is a mirror image of the South American myths presenting the same theme.

The Tacana Sloth has to descend from his tree to defecate on the ground; otherwise his excrement would change into a comet. In perfect symmetry, Mukat and Wiyot are in the habit of climbing to the top of a pole to defecate, and, from there, their excrement, crashing into the ocean, makes the sound of thunder. When he does not hear the usual noise (for a frog, sitting at the foot of the pole, snatched the excrement before it hit the water) Mukat (or Wiyot) realizes that a spell has been cast on him. In most versions, the frog swallows the excrement, and the god, becoming sick, understands that he is doomed. Again in a symmetrical fashion: if the excrement of the Tacana Sloth were to fall from his tree and hit the ground, it would cause the loss, not of himself, but of all mankind—the mankind that in the California myths tries, on the contrary, to preserve itself by snatching away the god's excrement before it hits the water.

The link established by myths between excrement and jealousy is reinforced when we note that among the Mohave (whose cultural hero Matavilye replaces Wiyot, the Luiseño hero) the magical substances used as talismans are said to be "madly jealous" of those who possess them. From the psychoanalytic perspective of his study, George Devereux believes that these substances can be assimilated to excrement. According to Mohave myths, excrement, an eminently magical substance was used in the very first act of sorcery, and the Cahuilla are reported to bury their excrement carefully for fear it might be put to some magical use.

Because of its poor thermal regulation, the sloth is restricted to a forested zone in South and Central America with a rather limited temperature range; this zone extends from the northern part of the Brazilian state of Rio Grande do Sul to Honduras. We will thus not expect to encounter the sloth in California. However the goat-sucker, connected in myths to the sloth through correlation and opposition, is a native of California and could be present in myths there (see p. 144). In a Luiseño myth, two rival groups were trying to climb a greased pole. They were the People of the West and the People of the Mountain. The winner dropped baskets full of food from the top of the pole, and everyone fought over the food. After one of these events, the Mountain People noticed a "bird with a big mouth" among them (probably a nighthawk or a poorwill) and exclaimed: " 'It is your turn now to eat!' . . . So he opened his mouth, and they poured everything into it, and he gulped it all down. So the mountain people won" (Strong 1929: 288).

How can we account for the fact that, in an area of the New World where there could be no conception of the sloth, the part played by this animal in South American myths is present as the photo-graphic negative of its South American counterpart? It may be that mythic thought, taken by the kind of fancy we attribute to Nature, by chance conferred the same appearance on completely unre-lated objects. Still, nothing prevents us from giving free rein to our imagination, even concerning a nonexistent problem. Leaving the beaten track sometimes leads to unsuspected realities, thanks to which research can take a new turn. Let us sidetrack for a while, then, and ask: If the problem were real, how could we solve it?

In the past few years, the first settlement of America has been moved back to a much earlier date than was formerly thought. In-stead of ten thousand or twelve thousand years, which used to be the accepted figure, some are now talking of one to two hundred thousand years. Given the present state of our knowledge, thirty to forty thousand years seem to be a reasonable evaluation, and some authorized opinions stretch it to seventy thousand. In this remote past, was the geographic distribution of the sloth much greater? We know that, much later on in the Americas, man shared his world with a megafauna (which he probably exterminated), including giant sloths, *Mylodon* and *Megatherium,* which originated in South America but were also present in North America. However, those animals were too heavy to climb trees, from which they could have dropped their excrement, and we have no fossils attesting to an area of distribution of tree-dwelling sloths that is wider than their present-day distribution.

Since we are getting no answer from animals, let us turn to men. Even though they crossed over from Asia to America on dry land, where the Bering Strait is today, nothing tells us that, during the course of thousands of years, populations always migrated from north to south. There may have been movements in the opposite direction, like those, well attested, that proceeded from the Amazon to the Caribbean islands and thence to the southeastern United States. Besides, the rule of hygiene attributed to the god in the myths of southern California (climbing a pole at night to defecate) belongs to the realm of the imaginary, whereas the sloth's habit is real. In view of this observation, we could see in the California myths a secondary elaboration, produced by people who wanted to maintain or reproduce their traditional mythic schemes in their new, more northern environment. I have shown elsewhere (see *The Origin of Table Manners,* pp. 253–59) how an animal that is absent in a new environment can nevertheless retain a metaphysical existence in mythic imagination. I was actually dealing with much shorter distances then. The traits attributed to an animal in a given environment can also be transferred to another animal living at a great distance from the first. South American Indians claim that all anteaters are female. The Creek of the southeastern United States entertain the same belief about the opossum (see pp. 100, 110), and in Canada the Tsimshian say the same of the beaver.

We might consider yet another hypothesis. A mythic scheme could have been elaborated in the abstract in North America, could then have moved down as such to South America, and could there have met with an unexpected realization: its incarnation in the habits of one specific animal.

These two hypotheses will certainly remain gratuitous. In favor of the first, it could be stressed that the habits of the California demiurge and those of the Sloth (playing the part of an anti-demiurge in South American myths) are connected through a transformation. The habits attributed to the Sloth have an empirical basis, while those attributed to the deity, of course, do not. The passage in *The Origin of Table Manners,* quoted above, also went on to show that, if a species is absent in a given environment but remains present in myths, it is then projected into "another world," where the semantic functions the myths assigned to it elsewhere—when it was an animal in the real world—are systematically reversed.

Whatever becomes of these speculations, we have reached one firm conclusion: the California god is to be placed within a set of transformations whose other stages up to now have been identified as the severed head changed into the moon or a meteor; excrement detached from the body and changed into a meteor; and a supernatural personage separated from his excrement and changed into the moon. One idea, well attested in the Americas, seems to underlie these transformations: that excrement is a substance charged with the life-force of its producer. However, when one starts to compare what can, from a strictly logical standpoint, be called the initial and final stages, a remark I have often made comes to mind: at the end of the series, we do not have a single transformation to add to the preceding ones, but two simultaneous transformations. Indeed, the last stage puts a double twist on the first: excrement in the final position transforms the head in the initial position, and it does not "function" in the same way, if I may say so. Whether by the act of the subject or by a third party, the head is forcibly severed from its own body. Such is not the case with excrement, which is naturally destined to be separated. The Sloth, defecating at *long* intervals, leaves its excrement at a *short* distance from his body. Conversely, the California gods Mukat and Wiyot leave their excrement at a *great* distance but defe-

155

cate every night—at *short* intervals. In these actions, they are all accomplishing a natural function, the periodic separation of excrement from their bodies. Therefore, the spell cast on the California god cannot result *from the fact that the excrement is separated from its own body;* it must result *from the fact that it is intercepted by another body* (whether swallowed or dispersed by the frog, it is exposed to the same danger). In the initial stage of the transformation, the head *severed from its own body* turns into the moon or a meteor. In the final stage of the same transformation, excrement takes the place of the head only insofar as, *attached to another body,* it reverses the head's function. Applying the canonic formula of mythic transformations (see pp. 57, 126), we arrive at the following formula:

$$\frac{F_{moon}}{(head)} : \frac{F_{meteor}}{(excrement)} :: \frac{F_{meteor}}{(moon)} : \frac{F_{head\,-\,1}}{(excrement)}$$

It will be noted[1] that the first member in the equivalence essentially corresponds to South American myths, the second member to the California myths. To justify the first term of the second member,

$$F_{meteor(moon)},$$

See the discussion on pages 149–50, above.

1. Also, the formula appears here under one of its transformations:

$$F_{x_{(a)}} : F_{y_{(b)}} :: F_{y_{(x)}} : F_{a\,-\,1_{(b)}}$$

This is legitimate as long as the initial conditions are met: one of the terms must be replaced by its reverse, and there must be an inversion between a term value and a function value.

12
Myths in the Form of Klein's Bottle

Myths in the form of Klein's bottle. Blowpipes, smoking pipes, and other tubes. Psychoanalytic interpretations; discussion. The semantic field of body openings. Anal greediness and oral incontinence and retention. Theory of the Tapir. Fourth and fifth applications of the canonic formula.

*

We must now add a third hypothesis to the two I have put forward to account for the structural analogies in the California and sub-Andean myths. In both North and South America, myths could be the concrete expression of a scheme reflecting certain mental patterns—a scheme sufficiently abstract to have been conceived of anywhere at all, without recourse to experience or observation. Even if this scheme, once formed, had never encountered the sloth in the forests of tropical America, thus missing the chance of passing from the abstract to the figurative, it would have borrowed other images or it would have done without them.

What could this scheme be? All the American myths I have compared have essentially two traits in common. First, they establish a logical primacy of the moon over the sun and even a historical primacy when they claim that the moon was created before the sun. Second, all these myths can be described as being, to put it briefly, in the form of Klein's bottle. Now, what does this mean?

First, one remark. Though present elsewhere, the image of the tube or pipe appears in these myths with unequaled frequency. In the Jivaro Genesis it is used at least twice. In order to punish his mother, the Moon, for not preventing the incest between his wife and his son, Uñushi, the Sloth, shoved her into a hole and buried her there; then Goatsucker, who was in love with Moon, came to her help. He made a horn from the shell of a large water snail, crept into the hollow trunk of a fallen palm tree, and blew into his instrument. On hearing this call, Moon burst out of her grave, shot

157

through the trunk like a meteorite, pushing Goatsucker before her, and flew straight up to the sky. Later, Sun decided to punish his incestuous grandson. He stuffed him into the hollow trunk of a palm tree and blew into it, as into a blowpipe, while slowly spinning it. Ahimbi, the guilty grandson, emerged from the other end transformed into a boa and was then tied up by his grandfather and left at the bottom of the river rapids (see pp. 72–74).

Likewise, in the Amazonian myth of Poronominaré—also a lunar myth (see p. 88)—the hero manages to escape through the soul of his blowpipe, leaving the house of a deceived husband who is trying to kill him with explosive farts. In short, a pipe saves him from another pipe. In a later episode, Poronominaré's adversary is the Sloth (as we know, this animal can be compared to a plugged pipe). The Sloth throws him from the top of a tree. He plunges, like a meteorite, through the earth (which becomes a pipe in this circumstance) and arrives in the underworld. With the help of the Cicadas, he comes back up, using the soul of his blowpipe as an elevator shaft. Then he throws the Sloth, in turn, into the underworld. At the beginning and end of the myth, two personages are pierced, so to speak: the hero's sister or female companion, who has no vagina, has one bored into her by a fish, and the Anteater is given an anus, whereas, before, he was reduced to defecating through his mouth.

It would be tempting to imitate the myths and see in these episodes (and in part of the Waiwai myth mentioned on p. 94) an imagery inspired by the use of the blowpipe. Indeed, we are at the heart of the area in which this weapon is found. Used for hunting, it is ten to sixteen feet long and is efficient only when made with extreme precision. Stirling, Nimuendaju, and Bianchi, among other observers, have given detailed descriptions of the fabrication process of the pipe and of the curare with which the darts must be poisoned as soon as the game reaches a certain size. It is not surprising, then, that the blowpipe should be so prominent in the representations created by its users. Still, the blowpipe presents problems. In Peru it is almost certainly of pre-Columbian origin, but it seems that it was then used without poison and only for

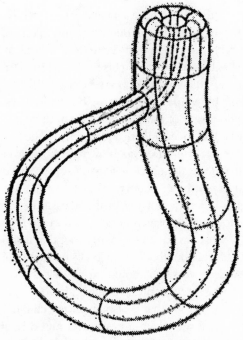

Fig. 7   Klein's bottle

hunting small birds. On the other hand, in the piedmont of the Andes and beyond, the missionaries and conquerors who reached this zone in the sixteenth century either made no mention of the blowpipe or left accounts too vague to be relied on. The Jivaro, then, who make blowpipes with a high degree of perfection, may have discovered this weapon only toward the end of the sixteenth century or even later. We know that in other areas it was introduced even more recently. If it is confirmed that the blowpipe appeared at a relatively late period in tropical America, we will be at a loss to account for its prominent place in mythical imagery—all the more so because a very similar imagery is found in the California myths, and there are no documents attesting the use of the blowpipe in California (in North America, it was present only in the southeastern United States, and it was used there without poison).

159

A Jivaro group, the Shuar, have a myth that provides a transition between the two hemispheres. It describes the childhood of Etsa, the sun-to-be, who was raised by an ogre (not without an ulterior motive). Once, as he was practicing his hunting skills, Etsa heard a turtledove cooing in a close thicket. The dove ordered this Siegfried to stick his blowpipe deep into the bush and then come to him through the inside of the pipe. From him the child learned that his mother had been killed and eaten by the ogre. Back home, Etsa saw that the ogre was blowing a horn made of his mother's skull and that the ogre's wife was using an eye extracted from the skull to polish her pottery.

With a slightly different plot, this myth can easily be recognized as one of the most famous of all American myths (see *From Honey to Ashes,* M_{264}). What is surprising, then, is not that it should also be found in California but that the analogies between the California and sub-Andean versions should be so striking as to make them appear to be exact replicas. I have already introduced a Mohave myth (see p. 138) that is also about the childhood of an orphaned hero who was given a home and raised by the murderers of his father. He heard the whole story from an insect that had landed on his lips, and these lips are actually the opening of a tube constituted by his own body; for his name is Cane, and, as we shall see, the myth very concretely assimilates him to a hollow stalk. Cane discovered, thanks to the insect, that his father's murderers were playing ball with their victim's kneecap, which thus plays a part similar to that of the eye in the Shuar myth.

A few hundred miles northwest of the Mohave, in Owens Valley, the Mono relate the adventures of two cultural heroes, named Wolf and Coyote, in myths belonging to the same cycle as the Mohave's Cane myth and the myths that the Mission Indians tell about the hero Chaup or Guiomar. Wolf and Coyote were looking for wives: "So they prepared to go to Tovowa, where the women lived. The husbands of the women were hunting. From his house to the women's house Topi [Wolf] extended a long tube, and through it he and his companion passed" (Curtis 1907–30, vol. 15, pp. 124–25). When facing a similar problem, Chaup/Guiomar (who, let us not forget, was an igneous meteor) flew in through the smoke hole in the roof or dug a tunnel to get into the hut.

Now, the characters in the Mohave and Cahuilla myths are not limited to the use of tubes or hollow stalks. They are changed from internal bodies into external envelopes, from contained into container, and thus become tubes themselves by means of a transformation that, as I said, evokes the image of Klein's bottle. The Mohave hero named Cane could at will change into the plant bearing the same name. During his adventures he died and came back to life. One of the women watching over him told the others that he fed exclusively on tobacco. They brought him some; he put it straight into his mouth and asked for more. "Then the youngest sister gave him a cane as long as a hand, filled with tobacco. The boy smoked it. He did not smoke it long: he sucked once and swallowed the smoke. . . . The whole cane was burned up except the end. He chewed that up and spat it out" (Kroeber 1948a: 12). Later, the hero stayed with Kwayû, the cannibal meteor, and when he asked him for tobacco, his host said: "You are too young to smoke, but I will give you tobacco. You do not know how to smoke a cane, for the Mohave smoke clay pipes." The boy answered: "I do know how to do that, for that is my name [I am Cane]" (Kroeber 1948a: 13). So Kwayû gave him two canes filled with tobacco. The hero smoked one and saved the other. One is tempted to say he "smoked himself."

In the Cahuilla creation myth, when the demiurges emerged from darkness and wanted to "blow—aah! away the dark" (Strong 1929: 131), each drew a pipe and tobacco from his heart in order to dissipate the surrounding darkness with smoke. But the pipes were solid cylinders, and they had to bore a hole in each one with their whiskers. First the hole was too wide, and the tobacco fell out; then they made it the right size. After the pipes and tobacco, the demiurges drew from their bodies the sun, light, "the center pole of the world," and all living creatures. Each of their bodies thus appears as a hollow container from which a solid container emerged (the pipe they could not use) and then the contents it was destined to receive (the tobacco): the container had to be made hollow (they bore a hole in it) before it could properly accommodate its contents. The rest of the story conforms to the same dialectic: a hole had to be drilled into the earth in order for the first dead to reach the netherworld. And when Mukat, one of the demiurges, climbed to the top of a pole, or a scaffold, to defecate into the ocean, he himself was assimilated to a pipe, for the myth calls his excrement "his tobacco, . . . which he eats and drops down" (Strong 1929: 139).

Authors following in the footsteps of psychoanalytic theory, such as Erikson, Roheim, and Posinsky, or who were marked by it, like Kroeber, who practiced this discipline for a time, having attributed an oral-anal or wholly anal character to a few societies in central California, in particular to the Yurok, to whom several studies along these lines were devoted. According to Erikson, "the Yurok's identification of world and body focus on the *alimentary* zone, in the sense of 'the tubular food-carrying passage extending from the mouth to the anus'" (Erikson 1943: 297). In this statement Erikson comes very close to the myths I am discussing, though these myths come from an area much further south than Yurok territory. We are indeed dealing with widely different societies, and we cannot extend to all of them the specific characteristics of Yurok culture and personality on which Erikson's analysis is based, namely, a particular kind of mother-child relationship, control over bodily functions, distinctive attitudes about eating, eliminating waste matter, acquiring wealth, and so on. Rather, we are in the presence of a single logical and philosophical problem faced in similar ways by different societies.

If it were otherwise, how could we account for the recurrence of one and the same scheme throughout both hemispheres and among cultures totally foreign to one another in all other respects? The notion of a tube or pipe, illustrated in South America by the blowpipe and in North America by the smoking pipe, is the starting point of a transformation in three stages: (1) the hero's body enters a tube that contains him; (2) a tube formerly contained in the hero's body emerges from it; (3) the hero's body becomes a tube—something either goes in or comes out of it. The tube is first extrinsic, then intrinsic; the hero's body is first contained, them becomes a container. We can represent this in the following formula:

$$\frac{\underset{\text{(body)}}{contained}}{\overset{F}{}} : \frac{\underset{\text{(tube)}}{container}}{\overset{F}{}} :: \frac{\underset{\text{(tube)}}{contained}}{\overset{F}{}} : \frac{\underset{\text{(container)}}{body - 1}}{\overset{F}{}}$$

In other words, the contained body is to the containing tube as the contained tube is to a container that is no longer a body but is itself a tube.

What we must first fix our attention on is thus not specifically the blowpipe or the smoking pipe (they are used in many other ways in American myths), nor will we concentrate on the Goatsucker, the Sloth, or the Howler Monkey, which are simply empirical realizations of an underlying formal structure. Likewise, oral greediness and anal retention and incontinence are only the markers of certain aspects of this structure. As I pointed out at the very beginning of this study, there is a wide range of potential combinations within the semantic field constituted by natural tubes and their openings. These openings can be at the front or back, above or below: mouth, nose, ears, vagina, anus, etc. Each can perform three different functions: closed; open to receive; open to eject. The myths under study here illustrate only a few of these combinations. However, one could easily find other myths or groups of myths to illustrate the remaining possibilities.

Various personages can be cited as examples of anal greediness. The Kagaba, for instance, describe a supernatural being named Taimu as having teeth in both his mouth and his anus and using either orifice indiscriminately when it eats; several mythologies attribute the same talent to the Tapir. The Barasana of the Uaupés region identify their shamans with tapirs and with howler monkeys because of their healing techniques, which consist of sucking or blowing. Howler monkeys blow, whereas tapirs are of the "suck-in" type. In a reversal of childbirth the Tapir tries to suck newborn babies into his anus with a flute (another realization of the tube) because he is jealous of those about to turn from spirits into humans. The Tapir and the Howler Monkeys once got into an argument over this issue. The Monkeys eventually stole the Tapir's loud voice and left him with his present-day whine. A Mundurucu myth (see *The Origin of Table Manners,* M_{402}) relates the adventures of a young boy led astray in the forest by his maternal uncle, who had turned into a Tapir; believing the animal to be dead, the boy stuck his arm into its anus in order to remove its entrails. The Urubu have a similar tale in which the Tapir breaks the arm of an Indian who was submitting him to the same treatment. Finally, in the two Americas, in myths of the Chippewa and the Tupi, there is a Trickster god or a cultural hero who pretends to be dead in order to capture a vulture, and when the bird is about to devour his rectum, the Tapir contracts his sphincter, trapping the bird's head.

It would be pointless to dwell on vaginal greediness, for it is abundantly illustrated by the *vagina dentata* theme and by others associated with the sexual greediness of women in both North and South America (see, for instance, the Barasana female demiurge and the Apache Vulva woman). As for oral incontinence, it is represented in many myths, among them those in which one or several characters cannot refrain from talking or laughing (see pp. 44, 53). As they became familiar with white people, the Indians apparently discovered an animal species that used speech in an immoderate fashion; witness the way the Menominee of the Great Lakes parodied the way the white trader spoke to one of them: "All right, Indian, all right, all right, all right! Bring it, bring it, bring it! I'll give you credit, I will, I will, I will!" In short, "White men are wordy" (Bloomfield 1928: 268–69). According to Boas, "In the Tsimshian language the term for 'to play' means to talk to no purpose; and doing anything 'to no purpose' is contemptible to the Indian" (Boas 1890: 815). The same is true in South America, where "The Bororo call civilized people *kidoe kidoe,* 'parakeet, parakeet,' because, like these birds, they talk too much" (Albisetti-Venturelli 1962–76: vol. 1, p. 717; Viertler 1979: 815). The white man thus has his place in the native bestiary side by side with the Goatsucker, the Howler Monkey, the Tapir, and many other animals. In return, white observers have often mentioned oral retention, "a fierce reluctance to speak except when absolutely necessary," as a behavior typical of American Indians (Basso 1970: 213).

In North America, in the Puget Sound area, it has been noted that some personages appearing in ritual formulas, sacred songs, or myths systematically convert all voiced occlusive consonants into nasals. The reason for this could be similar to the one that prompts the Cuiva shamans in Colombia to operate behind a screen and nasalize their incantations; according to them, "It is very dangerous for the mouth to open a direct contact between the throat and the outside" (Ortiz-Gomez 1983: 227). Nasality thus appears as a form of oral retention.

Other examples of oral retention or incontinence can be drawn from myths that lend distinctive verbal behaviors to certain supernatural beings. For instance, the Amazonian demon by the name of Jurupari belches and farts and complains or sings at the top of his lungs. In Suya myths, cannibal monsters have an odd, slurred way of speaking. Boré, the Yanomami's Master of Bananas, lisps. In North America, a supernatural character in Nootka myths changes all sibilant consonants into lateral consonants (*s* into *l,* etc.); in myths of the neighboring Kwakiutl tribe, another supernatural character does just the reverse. In Wishram myths, Bluejay starts all his words with *ts!-.* The Kutenai say that Coyote is unable to pronounce the letter *s.* The Haida Wealth woman stutters, and so does the Kwakiutl ogress named Dzonoqwa. For the Cree, Wolverine mutters between his lips. These are but a few examples, and, to move to other parts of the world, we can cite Kitsune, the Japanese Fox, who cannot utter complete words. A comparative study, covering the whole world, would be endless.

Let us be content with these few American examples. They give us sufficient proof that myths apply all the potential stages of an interesting combinatorics of body openings. This does not mean that in each myth or group of myths in this family all of the stages of this combinatorics will necessarily be present. Among those we have just examined, only anal greediness as embodied by the Tapir can find a place—though a secondary one—next to the three stages that were, so to speak, selected by the myths discussed in this book: oral greediness and anal retention and incontinence.

In chapter 8 I suggested that we see the Anteater as a combinative variant of the Sloth. This now needs to be qualified, for the Anteater stands between the Sloth and the Tapir and can thus be substituted for either. I have already noted that, according to Goeje, the Carib name for the great anteater is related to the name for the sloth (see p. 98). According to Goeje, the Carib words for "tapir," *waria* or *waila,* are used as stems in the words designating the anteater: *warisi, *wariš-ima.* Also, among the Carib of Guiana, Tikokë, a spirit who sometimes takes on the appearance of an anteater, sucks the blood of his human victims with a flute; thus, like the Tapir in other tribes, he is an aspiring demon.

The Tapir and the Anteater differ in other respects. The former aspirates through his anus; the latter excretes through his mouth (see p. 158). Anteaters are supposed to be of one sex only, to lead solitary lives, and to reproduce themselves on their own; on the other hand, in Indian thought the Tapir stands as a symbol of sexual appetite—and we will see why. (Apropos of this belief, Goeje suggests a relationship between the Tupi words *tapiira,* "tapir," and *t-apia,* "scrotum.") Besides this, the Tapir seems to stand at a greater distance from the Sloth than the Anteater does. For the Indians, the excreting habits of the Sloth and the Tapir are exact opposites. As we have seen, the Sloth moves downwards in order to leave his excrement on the ground—always at the same spot. The Tapir, by contrast, is supposed to walk under water, taking his excrement with him in a basket—thus, along a horizontal axis; but in fact this animal, though it does excrete in water and on river banks, also at times does so away from water and even up in the hills.

More generally speaking, in South American myths the Tapir

appears as a self-centered and gluttonous character but also as a regular seducer of married women, who succumb whenever they encounter him. Moreover, the whole set of myths we are examining establishes a connection, even an equivalence, between the Tapir and the meteor.

South American Indians divide celestial bodies into two categories. The first includes the sun, the moon, Venus, the constellations, and stars having names; the second includes the nameless stars and also erratic bodies or phenomena, such as meteors and comets. This opposition finds a perfect illustration in myths establishing a contrast between "the star of the Sloth" (called *kupirisi yumañ* by the Carib of Guiana), which sinks to the horizon at the start of the long dry season (this represents the animal's coming down to the ground once a year to relieve himself) and the devastating comet that will, according to the Tacana, issue from the Sloth's excrement if he is harassed, prevented from coming down from his tree, and so forced to defecate from above, thus violating the ideal rule of periodical regularity. The most aberrant of the nameless celestial bodies are the comets and meteors; their behavior is as scandalous in the cosmic realm as the Tapir's is in the social realm, where he starves people and seduces women. Besides, as an abortionist (see p. 163), the Tapir manifests an anal greediness that is symmetrical with the vaginal greediness of the women who are crazy about him. Also, his anal greediness is radically opposed to anal retention and incontinence, much more so than these two terms are opposed to each other; for incontinence and retention are contrary, not contradictory, terms.

Against the analysis just outlined, one might perhaps invoke an important group of myths in which the Tapir, the seducer, flies up to the sky and becomes a constellation—generally, the Hyades. Now, besides the fact that this interpretation has been contested by Lehman-Nitsche, we could also oppose it with the following argument: the Pleiades and Orion form a major oppositional pair (see *The Raw and the Cooked,* pp. 220–28); placed in between the two, the Hyades may appear to be a supernumerary constellation, a kind of intruder, like the seducer who intrudes on a married pair.[1] Above all, the ambiguity of the Tapir's position in the astronomical realm reflects the ambiguity already noted in myths in which the moon is preeminent over the sun. These myths attribute opposite characters to the lunar god or hero, alternatively or simultaneously: he brings order and civilization to the world, but he also seduces virgins, is jealous and treacherous, and is sometimes a cannibal. The moon oscillates between the two categories of celestial bodies, belonging sometimes with those bearing a name, sometimes with the meteors (see pp. 146–47). The Tapir is also marked by ambiguity: with his big penis, he gives more satisfaction to women than their husbands do; but he also starves the Indians, for he is master of the food tree and keeps its location secret (for more detail, see *From Honey to Ashes,* pp. 296–305).

Let us now examine another characteristic of the Tapir. The Tumupasa, who are close neighbors of the Tacana, say that the Tapir's wife eats the moon every month, when it is waning; then she vomits it, and the moon starts waxing again. Once, lacking patience, the Tapir copulated with his wife before she had time to regurgitate the moon, and he has had a big penis and three testicles ever since (see *The Origin of Table Manners,* p. 83). As a result, the Tapir disrupted—or almost disrupted—the cosmic order; for this rash action of his also endowed him with the physical means to disrupt the social order that requires women to remain true to their husbands, resisting the seductions of nature.

An Ayoré myth runs along the same lines. The Tapir and the Moon god once competed for the favors of humans. The Tapir promised that if men obeyed him they would grow nice and fat. Moon promised, in exchange for their allegiance, to make them come back to life like him. The ancestors chose to go with the Tapir because they envied his corpulence. That is why humans die and never come back to life. What is more, the informant added,

1. We could see this as an astronomical pathology parallel to the pathological state of the marriage relationship found in the same myths (see *From Honey to Ashes,* p. 303).

they were cheated by the Tapir, for there are today as many thin Indians as fat ones. In another version Moon was the father of the Ayoré. Once Tapir challenged him to a race and won; so now, instead of going up to the sky to be with Moon when they die, Indians go down to the underworld—a muddy, murky world, without honey. We have already met with a Machiguengua myth about a girl kept in confinement on reaching puberty (see p. 150). The Moon god visited her in secret and taught her, and her parents as well, the art of pottery and the cultivating of gardens. A reverse variant of this myth says that a demon prematurely freed a pubescent girl from her confinement, and she emerged from her hut changed into a tapir.

In all these instances the Tapir is opposed to the Moon in a conflict for or against periodicity: the regular succession of the moon's phases, the resurrection of the dead according to that same rhythm, and observance of the prescribed duration of taboos.

Given the fact that the Tapir and the Moon are antagonistic terms, we are now able to solve one specific problem. In what could be called the American Vulgate, the Sun and the Moon were once incestuous siblings. The girl went up to the sky and became the Sun; she had left a mark on her brother's face or body in order to identify her mysterious lover. He was transformed into the Moon and has been pursuing her in vain ever since. However, in a Shipaia myth, cited above (see p. 146), this scheme is altered: the brother still becomes the Moon, but his sister turns first into a Meteor, then into a Tapir.

What does this Shipaia myth make of the sun? Its sex cannot be determined, first, for the simple reason that it does not appear in the story and, second, because the two sexual poles are occupied—one by the brother, the other by the sister. So the sun, if it has a sex in Shipaia mythology, must be on one side or the other, and we cannot tell which one it is.

Let us make an experiment to see whether the canonic formula (see pp. 57, 126, 156, 163) will enable us to deduce the sex of the sun. First, we know that in the American Vulgate the moon is given a male function and the sun a female function. Second, we can draw the following hypothesis from our preceding considerations: the Meteor and the Tapir (results of the transformations of the Shipaia heroine) appear in the myths as *terms,* while holding the *function* of a reversed moon. To this point, we still know nothing about the Shipaia conception of the sun. The formula appears as follows:

$$\frac{F}{male} \atop (moon) \quad : \quad \frac{F}{female} \atop (sun) \quad :: \quad ? \quad : \quad \frac{F}{moon - 1} \atop (female)$$

If we continue to apply the formula, we will automatically obtain the missing part in the second member:

$$\frac{F}{male} \atop (sun)$$

This means that if, as we have just seen, there is a Shipaia myth in which the sun is absent and the woman (who elsewhere becomes the sun) changes into an anti-moon, then there must also be a Shipaia myth in which the sun appears as an anti-woman—in other words, a man. There is indeed such a myth. According to the Shipaia, the sun as we know it today is actually the youngest son of a former sun, also a male, whom men had to bury deep in the earth because he was a cannibal. (The myth undergoes an interesting development: the sun is diminished and loses his cannibalistic character, while elsewhere—in Machiguengua myths, for example—the moon becomes a cannibal when it is "meteorized.") Consequently, the masculine nature of the sun in Shipaia mythology, and the "reversed-moon" function of the pair meteor + tapir in the set of myths to which the Shipaia ones belong, reciprocally validate each other.

13

The Nature of Mythic Thought

The nature of mythic thought: a plurality of codes. Place of the psycho-organic code. Orality and anality. The alimentary cycle of food and the technical cycle of vessels. The dialectic of container and contents. Conservatism and jealousy in families of potters. Women and the exogamy of pots. Vaginal retention. Along the north Pacific coast; back to the blowpipe and Amazonia.

*

Every myth confronts a problem, and it deals with it by showing that it is analogous to other problems, or else it deals with several problems simultaneously and shows that they are analogous to one another. No real object ever corresponds to this set of images, which mirror each other. More exactly, the object draws its substance from the invariant properties that mythic thought manages to identify when it sets a number of statements side by side. To simplify matters considerably, we could say that a myth is a system of logical operations defined by the "it's when . . ." or "it's like . . ." method. A solution that is not a real solution to a specific problem is a way of relieving intellectual uneasiness and even existential anxiety when an anomaly, contradiction, or scandal is presented as the manifestation of a structure of order that can be perceived more clearly in aspects of reality that are less disturbing to the mind and the emotions.

Mythic thought thus operates in a unique way, using several codes. Each code brings out latent properties in a given realm of experience, allowing a comparison with other realms—in short, a *translation* from realm to realm. Imagine a text, difficult to understand in one language, translated into several languages; the combined meaning of all the different versions may prove richer and more profound than the partial, mutilated meaning drawn from each individual version.

This is not to say that each myth brings into play all possible codes or even all the codes inventoried in the set of myths to which it belongs. A myth appears as a system of equations in which the symbols, never clearly perceived, are approximated by means of concrete values chosen to produce the illusion that the underlying equations are solvable. Such choices are guided by an unconscious finality, but they are made among arbitrary and contingent elements, the products of history, so that the initial choice remains as impossible to explain as the choice of the set of phonemes that come to make up a particular language. Moreover, the choice of a certain code over all the codes offered by a given environment, history, and culture is a function of the problems that a specific myth or set of myths is attempting to solve. We shall not expect to find just any code operating anywhere.

There is more. Each code constitutes a kind of deciphering grid applied to empirical data; but the myth, which always uses several codes at once, keeps only parts of each grid, and, combining these with parts taken from other grids, it creates a kind of metacode, which becomes its distinctive tool. Among all the commutations I have tried to inventory, two kinds are used extensively in the myths examined to this point: those illustrating what today would be called oral character and anal character, which are also prominent in psychoanalytic theory. We will now take some time out to examine this convergence between psychoanalytic and mythic thought.

Let us return to a problem that was posed at the beginning of this book. Some of the myths associated themes that to us seemed completely unrelated. Plots primarily motivated by marital jealousy chose a Goatsucker for a hero or heroine and connected this Goatsucker physically or logically with the Sloth, who "originated in jealousy" and was also jealous of his excrement. Through the Sloth we were introduced to the image of the comet or meteor. In South America it issued from the excrement over which the Sloth had lost his jealous control. For the Iroquois, the comet or meteor was the immediate cause of the marital jealousy that prompted a husband to eject his wife through a hole, as if she were his excrement. Jealousy can be defined either as a feeling emanating from the desire to hold on to something or someone that is being taken away from you or as the desire for something or someone you do not possess. We can say, then, that jealousy tends to support or create a state of conjunction whenever there is a state or threat of disjunction. All subsequent developments, however varied their themes, pertain to different modalities of disjunction, whose immutable nature is to break up formerly united terms by putting distance between them—a distance sometimes large, sometimes relatively small.

If, for the sake of convenience, we agree to treat the various stages examined in this book as stages in a transformation that spread through the New World, from Bolivia and Peru all the way to California, it may seem that what this disjunction affects in the first stage is a wife while, in the final stage, it is excrement. But, from the very beginning, we have noticed a link between these two terms. In the Jivaro myth on the origin of pottery, two husbands, tired of quarreling over the same wife, climbed up to the sky and respectively became the Sun and the Moon. Their wife followed them but fell back to earth, where either her body, turned into clay, or the clay she was carrying in a basket, or even her excrement, dropped in fright while she was falling, became potters' clay. This last version comes from the Achuar, whose territory borders the Jivaro's, and whose dialect belongs to the same linguistic family.

At the other end of the area we are investigating, in California, we find the same passage from clay to excrement among the Serrano, the Cahuilla, and the Chemehuevi. This last tribe is related to the former in the same way as the Achuar are to the Jivaro: they are close neighbors and members of the same linguistic family, in this case the Shoshonean. According to the Cahuilla and the Serrano, the demiurge modeled the first men from clay (see p. 142). The Chemehuevi say that the demiurge made their own ancestors and those of the Mohave out of his excrement.

173

Psychoanalysts would certainly have no trouble explaining the presence of the same element in two areas thousands of miles apart (they would find it more difficult to account for its absence in the intervening area). This passage from clay to excrement would be sufficiently explained for them by all sorts of ideas about early childhood. We will stay away, however, from all-purpose interpretations. The myths we have singled out share a specific armature, best represented by the image of Klein's bottle. They offer a unique pattern, follow an original development, which we cannot overlook: we cannot restrict ourselves to using child psychology, even if it were universal, as an explanatory tool; its value is weakened by the fact that the myths we are trying to interpret were not produced by mankind in general but by specific Indian tribes.

In order to understand the theme of dwarfs who, having neither mouths nor anuses, fed on the smell of food (see pp. 101–19), one could also invoke some psychic constant; for this theme has been attested since antiquity (Pliny described the same kind of creatures in his *Natural History*, book 7, chap. 1), and it is found today in so many different places that it can be said to belong to a universal folklore. It is probably the ancient trace of a Paleolithic theme that had time to go around the world before historical civilizations appeared.

However, I was dealing only with American myths, and when I linked the theme of the dwarfs with tree-dwelling animals, I was consciously avoiding any consideration bearing on the issue of origins. The question at hand was to see how a well-defined group of cultures had shaped the theme and integrated it into a context that included both empirical observation and the ideas and opinions that made up their world view. In short, my concern was not with the question of the psychological or historical sources of this theme; rather, I wanted to show how a particular culture, or group of cultures, connected it to all of the other themes.

*

The myths we are examining at the moment give a prominent place to clay and excrement. For the Mission Indians of California and the Machiguengua of South America, early men fed on clay; in the myths of southern California, excrement, eaten by the Frog, caused the death of the demiurge and the passage from the original mankind to men as they now are. Clay and excrement coincide with the starting and finishing points of two cycles, namely, the technological and the physiological. Clay, by the way, is not, strictly speaking, nonfood: geophagy, the eating of earth, has existed throughout the world since antiquity. The Greeks ingested a certain kind of clay as a medical treatment; in North America, the Pomo mixed red clay into the dough of their acorn bread; geophagy still occurs in rural areas in the southern United States (Frate 1984); and, finally, women potters among the Indians of Mexico "presumably tasted or bit their paste to determine texture or other qualities deemed essential to successful firing" (Foster 1955: 28).

We have not touched on the essential point, however. Potter's clay undergoes extraction from the earth, then modeling, and then firing to become a container designed to receive a content: food. Food itself undergoes the same treatment, but in reverse: it is first placed in a clay container, then cooked, then processed in the body through the operation of digestion, and finally is ejected in the shape of excrement:

$$\left\{ \begin{array}{l} \text{clay} \rightarrow \text{extraction} \rightarrow \text{modeling} \rightarrow \text{firing} \rightarrow \text{container} \\ \text{excrement} \leftarrow \text{ejection} \leftarrow \text{digestion} \leftarrow \text{cooking} \leftarrow \text{food} \end{array} \right\}$$

For the equivalence between the physiological process of digestion and a cultural process, I refer the reader to *The Origin of Table Manners*. There is one difference, though: in that book and the other three in the *Mythologiques* series, dealing with the issue of the origin of cooking fire, I established a correspondence between digestion and cooking:

During digestion the organism temporarily retains food before eliminating it in a processed form. Digestion therefore has a mediatory function, comparable to that of cooking, which suspends another natural process leading from rawness to rottenness. In this sense, it may be said that digestion offers an anticipatory model of culture. [*The Origin of Table Manners,* p. 476]

This reflection led to a group of myths that, like those examined here, operate through a set of commutations: a heroine *"goes through* an obstacle while she is *full"*; another one *"adheres* while she is *hollow."* They are two illustrations of a combinatorics of body openings that we have encountered in other myths in earlier chapters.

However—and this is the reason for the difference—these myths and those examined in the *Mythologiques* do not constitute redundant sets. Both deal with the passage from nature to culture, from raw to cooked; but one set stresses cooking fire, while the other stresses pottery, whose culinary use presupposes the existence of the cooking hearth. The second set is therefore dependent on the first or, rather, it prolongs the first into a different register, the way a harmonic is produced on a violin. A cooking art based on the primitive method of directly exposing food to the fire brings forth the image of another art, a more elaborate one—removed one step further, so to speak. Kroeber pointed to the fact that "pottery and agriculture are definitely associated in the Mohave mind, their myths telling how the god Matsamho thought farm food incomplete until vessels were provided to cook and eat it in" (Kroeber 1925: 736; for an analogous link in South American myths, see above, p. 82). We thus see a transition from myths on the origin of cooking fire to myths on the origin of pottery, the latter often being mere transformations of the former.

The lesson taught in these myths is that earth must no longer be what men eat but must instead be cooked, like food, in order to enable men to cook what they eat. In the state of nature, earth was food; in its cooked form it becomes a vessel—that is to say, a cultural product. As I indicated in *The Naked Man* (p. 619) and examined in more detail in chapter 11 of the present book, this transformation shifts the emphasis from the conquest of celestial fire by earthlings to the gifts of clay and the mysterious art of pottery made to earthlings by supernatural beings at once aquatic and chthonian. The event no longer occurs along an earth/sky axis; instead, the axis has the earth at one end, water and the underworld at the other.

In South America (among the Machiguengua and the Campa) and in southern California this shift is accompanied by a shift within the cosmic realm. The moon is moved away from the category of periodical bodies and brought closer to the erratic bodies because of its doubly irregular character: it is present or absent, depending on the night of the month, and, even when it is present, its appearance is always changing.

Finally, at the same time as the function of fire becomes double (it cooks food or cooks pots in which food will be cooked) there emerges a dialectic of internal and external, of inside and outside: clay, congruent to excrement *contained* in the body, is used to make pots *containing* food, which will be *contained* in the body until the body, relieving itself, ceases to be the *container* of excrement.

Every art imposes form on matter, but, among the so-called arts of civilization, pottery is probably the one in which the transformation is the most direct, involving the smallest number of intermediate stages between the raw material and the product, which comes from the craftsman's hands already formed, even before it undergoes firing.

Clay extracted from the earth is also the "crudest" of all raw materials known and used by man. With its coarse appearance and its total lack of organization, it confronts man's sight and touch, even his understanding, with its primacy and the massive presence of its shapelessness. "In the beginning, the earth was without form and void," as the Bible says, and it is not without reason that other mythologies compare the work of the creator to that of the potter. But imposing a form on matter does not mean simply imposing a discipline. The raw material, pulled out of the limitless range of potentialities, is lessened by the fact that, of all these potentialities, only a few will be realized: all demiurges, from Prometheus to Mukat, have jealous natures.

In the case of pottery, the restrictions imposed on the raw material are the source of other restrictions: as a container the waterproof vase will keep shapeless liquids within its walls, and it will keep tiny solids, such as grains of wheat, from being scattered and lost. On a small scale, the potter is another demiurge; she, too, is jealous, she also imposes constraints on free matter. Once this matter has been modeled and then fixed in an immutable shape by the process of firing, it restrains in its turn: it "culturalizes" vegetable and animal substances that were still in the state of nature. But that is not all; for though the art of pottery narrows, in the most radical way, the gap between matter and form, its results are uncertain and subject to many risks, and this does not fail to affect the mind of those who practice it.

Foster gives the following explanation of the conservatism of Mexican families of potters:

> [The] reason lies in the nature of the productive process itself, which places a premium on strict adherence to tried and proven ways as a means of avoiding economic catastrophe. Pottery-making is a tricky business at best, and there are literally hundreds of points at which a slight variation in materials or process will adversely affect the result. A slight difference in raw materials, in glazes, in paints, in firing temperatures—any of these may mean that a week's or a month's labor is in vain. Hence, economic security lies in duplicating to the best of the potter's ability the materials and processes he knows from experience are least likely to lead to failure. A premium is placed on hewing to a straight and narrow productive

path. Straying very far from one side to the other is apt to mean economic tragedy. . . . This breeds a basic conservatism, a caution about all new things, that carries over into the potter's outlook on life itself. [Foster 1965: 49–50]

Howry has made a similar observation:

> In learning to make ceramics, the child so rigorously imitates the instructor that the peculiarities of the instructor are passed along. . . . The young and old potter alike derive style and technological facility from the household in which they live. [Consequently,] the knowledge of ceramic techniques is considered a private matter and discussed only within the family. [Howry 1978: 247]

It might be objected that, in the parts of Mexico in which these observations were made, pottery is the work of men and women who take their pots to be sold in markets. However, so-called primitive cultures of tropical American have been the object of similar comments. An observer of the Cashinawa, for instance, says:

> Clay is obtained from the banks of the small streams near the village. Not all clays can be used; only a few locations near each village are thought to have clay of the appropriate quality. (One of the considerations in the selection of a new village site is the availability of a good clay supply.) Each clay deposit is controlled but not owned by one woman or the women of a single household, who have exclusive rights of access. [Kensinger et al. 1975: 55]

Over fifty years ago, Nordenskiöld made particular mention of the conservatism of Indian potters of the Bolivian Chaco: in decorating pots, they remained very close to traditional designs and refused to venture on unexplored paths.

In their book, *The Early Formative Period of Coastal Ecuador,* Meggers, Evans, and Estrada comment on the lack of receptivity on the part of modern Papago potters to potentially acculturative influences. Several women were shown films of pottery-making by New Mexico Pueblo Indians, as well as a variety of archeological materials in the museum, and although they expressed great interest and asked numerous questions, they made no effort to incorporate any of the techniques or motifs of decoration into their own work. [Meggers et al. 1965: 82–83]

Other investigators make the following similar observation:

What is most interesting is that Papago potters who have been "trained" in traditional Papago pottery techniques adhere to those techniques even when shown others. . . . Papago pottery changes, to be sure, and there is an extensive allowable range of forms, clays, tempers, firing fuels, and so on. But the changes, like the range in techniques and materials, all occur within a framework that is distinctively Papago and beyond whose bounds no true Papago pottery will go. [Fontana et al. 1962: 171–72]

There certainly have been some innovative potters. In 1895 it occurred to one that she could copy the fourteenth-century ceramics coming from the archeological excavations in Hopi country, at Sikyatki. But she followed her models so blindly that it is now almost impossible to tell her pieces and those of her imitators from the authentic ones.

I have noted (see p. 22) that Indians of the Americas not only consider woman to be the efficient cause of the clay pot but establish a symbolic identification between the two. This may very well be a universal tendency; it is attested by breast-decorated vases of protohistorical Europe. In America it may shed light on the nature of the link between pottery and marital jealousy, a leitmotiv that has been our guiding thread throughout this book. We find such a connection in the Uaupés area, among tribes that speak mutually unintelligible dialects but follow a rule of intertribal marriage. This exogamy is also applied to potters' clay:

> Among the Desana, only women manufacture pottery, and good plastic clay must be fetched by them from certain spots that lie outside their territory but within either Pira-Tapuya or Tukano territory. Similarly, Pira-Tapuya women gather clay in Desana or Tukano territory, while Tukano women obtain theirs from Desana or Pira-Tapuya territory. [Reichel-Dolmatoff 1978: 281]

Along the same lines, these exogamous groups are said to "cook" their brides before the marriage exchange; also, the various steps of pottery-making are given a male or female sexual connotation:

> A woman's body is a cooking-pot. . . . Each vessel is . . . placed upside down over one of the three short tubular poststands of clay, [each of which] represents one of the exogamic units: Desana, Pira-Tapuya, and Tukano, whose men are "cooking" the woman/vessel. The entire image finds its idiomatic expression in the designation . . . "big pot" for women in an advanced state of pregnancy; an alternative expression is . . . "to become pot-shaped." [Ibid., p. 282]

We are led back to the image of Klein's bottle: woman, the efficient cause of pottery, is transformed into her product; she was physically exterior, she is now morally integrated with it. The metonymy uniting woman and pot has been turned into a metaphor. And doesn't Pandora, herself modeled from clay, become one with her jar? She may not be a jealous potter, but her pottery is marked by jealousy, for it contains all the plagues that will afflict mankind.

Let us go back for a moment to a theme mentioned above. Many American myths present woman in general or certain women as the very image of vaginal greediness or retention: they devour their partner's sex during coitus (a theme well known under the name of *vagina dentata*), or they hold their partner prisoner between their thighs, as in the California myths M_{292d-g} in *From Honey to Ashes* and *The Naked Man*. Though pottery is found only sporadically in California and is of a rudimentary kind (it is replaced by baskets woven with the highest degree of perfection and sufficiently waterproof to be used for culinary purposes), these vaginally retentive California women, pending a *top → bottom* transformation, behave as "jealous potters," congruent with the Goatsucker, the symbol of oral greediness. This is yet another path—one that I am only pointing to here—that would lead us back to our starting point.

The character illustrating vaginal retention in the California myths is a Skate woman. Like their South American counterparts, the Indians who tell these myths compare the Skate (a fish) to female genitals; the body of the fish represents the uterus, while the tail is the vagina. A body—whole and solid—is here equated with one of its parts—a hollow one—again through the transformations *external → internal* and *content → container*. I showed in *The Naked Man* (pp. 557–59) that in North America the Skate sometimes changes into a Butterfly. Another Butterfly with the same characteristics is found in the Amazon Basin: in the creation myth of the Tukuna Indians, a Butterfly (*Morphos menelaus*) suddenly closed his wings around the demiurge's stomach (= contained container), which had been dropped by his sons; these sons had formerly retrieved the stomach from inside the throat (= containing content) of a cannibal female jaguar. We thus have a transformation whose first and final stages are: *penis captivus → gaster captivus*. A hole had to be burned in the Butterfly's wings in order to free the stomach.

Again in *The Naked Man* (p. 43) I compared Tukuna myths with others that, nearly perfect replicas, come from regions north of California. In California proper the chronicle of the demiurge's son(s) offers no less striking similarities with the Tukuna myths. The Tukuna heroes were prisoners of the ogres who had murdered their mother; they managed to escape, like the Amazonian hero Poronominaré, through a hollow tube: their blowpipe. The story unfolds along the same lines in Amazonia and California, except for the nature of the tube.

The characteristic role of the tube (a hollow pipe or cane or reed in California, a blowpipe in South America) is also evident in Tukuna myths on the origin of ritual musical instruments (M_{181} and M_{182} in *The Raw and the Cooked*). The instruments were first painted red by the cultural hero. One of his companions, who disapproved of this choice, showed him where to find superimposed beds of clay of various colors. The hero was not to touch the clay with his hands; instead, he was to thrust his blowpipe into the ground to obtain samples of each color, similar to the core samples taken by prospectors and geologists. Then he was to empty the pipe with a stick and paint the instruments with a mixture of all these kinds of clay. Women who looked at the sacred instruments thus painted would die.

We have seen that the Tukuna represent the Master of Potters' Clay as an aquatic monster (see pp. 25, 29). He kept a jealous watch over his clay and once ate up a woman who had come to extract clay while she was in an advanced stage of pregnancy. It is said that if a pregnant woman touches clay or even comes near it while the potter woman is working, the coils will not stick together and the pots set out to dry will fall to pieces. The Master of Clay often takes the shape of the Rainbow of the West. The ritual instruments of rainbow-painted clay are brought out and used principally in the long, rigorous, and intricate puberty rites of Tukuna girls.

All these elements together lead to the following conclusion: multicolored paint (probably presenting a gradual range of colors due to the extraction technique) represents the rainbow, which becomes a major hazard for young women, especially in connection with their pottery-making activity. Potters' clay is usually *in the rainbow* (dependent on the Rainbow, its Master); by an unexpected use of the blowpipe—which we can now explain—the rainbow now finds itself *in clay* in the form of multicolored paint put *on* instruments; and the main instrument is a kind of megaphone *containing* the voice of a demon. This perspective brings pottery back to the foreground and justifies the choice of Klein's bottle as an image representing the function of tubes or pipes in the myths of the Americas.

14

A Jivaro Version of *Totem and Taboo*

A Jivaro version of *Totem and Taboo*. Criticism of the principles of psychoanalytical interpretation. Two conceptions of the symbol. Freud and Jung. Freud's thought as authentic mythic thought. His views on the relationship between psychoanalysis and the social sciences. The nature of metaphor. Sexual impulse or logical exigency? The reciprocal relativity of codes: the example of Japanese scripts. Sophocles and Labiche: a comparative approach. What "signifying" means.

*

Freud gave the following subtitle to *Totem and Taboo:* "Some Points of Agreement between the Mental Lives of Savages and Neurotics." In the preceding pages I have set out to show instead that there are points on which the mental lives of savages and psychoanalysts coincide. At almost every step we have encountered perfectly explicit notions and categories—such as oral character and anal character—that psychoanalysts will no longer be able to claim they have discovered. All they have done is to rediscover them.

Better yet: it is *Totem and Taboo* in its entirety that, well ahead of Freud, the Jivaro Indians anticipated in the myth that for them plays the part of a Genesis: societies arose when the primitive horde split into hostile clans after the murder of the father whose wife had committed incest with their son. From a psychological point of view the Jivaro myth offers an even richer and more subtle plot than *Totem and Taboo*.

Let us outline the plot again. While his father, Uñushi, was away on a long trip, Ahimbi, the Snake, slept with his mother, Mika, the Clay Pot. It is as if these two offenders—the snake and the vase—symbolized, respectively, the male and the female genitals, naturally destined to unite, notwithstanding the social rules that would restrain their freedom. And the patriarch—their father and grandfather—actually banished them. They remained vagrants and had many children. When the deceived husband returned and discovered his misfortune, his wrath was directed not against the offenders but against his own mother, whom he accused of having encouraged their crime. It would be tempting to say that he held her responsible for his own incentuous desire for *her* and that his son's crime was the enactment of his own secret wish. The offspring of the incestuous couple wanted to avenge their grandmother, so they beheaded their mother's husband in *Totem and Taboo* style. This triggered a series of conflicts. Mika killed her children, who had murdered her husband; her incestuous son then sided against her, and, from that point on, the three camps—the father's, the mother's, and the son's—engaged in a merciless fight. This is how Society came about.

Psychoanalytical theory cannot be credited with uncovering the latent meaning of myths. Myths were its precursors in this. The Jivaro Indians' theory on the origin of society may well be similar to Freud's—indeed, they did not wait for him to announce it. How wise are the Americans in calling psychoanalysts "head-shrinkers," thus spontaneously associating them with the Jivaro!

Therefore, Freud cannot be credited with knowing what myths say better than the myths themselves do. Myths don't need any help when it comes to reasoning like a psychoanalyst. Freud's merit lies elsewhere; it is of the same order as the merit I have recognized in Max Müller's achievements (see *The Naked Man*, p. 44). Each of these great minds deciphered one of the codes—Müller, the code of astronomy; Freud, the psycho-organic code—that myths have always known how to use. But each of them made two mistakes.

First, they tried to decipher myths by means of a single and exclusive code, while a myth will always put several codes in play, and it is from this layering of codes, one on top of another, that rules of interpretation derive. The signification of a myth is always global; it cannot be reduced to the interpretation provided by one particular code. No language—astronomical, sexual, or other—conveys the "better," meaning. As I pointed out in *The Raw and the Cooked* (p. 240):

The truth of the myth does not lie in any special content. It consists in logical relations which are devoid of content or, more precisely, whose invariant properties exhaust their operative value, since comparable relations can be established among the elements of a larger number of different contents.

There is no more truth in one code than in any other. The essence of the myth (or its message, if one wants to call it that) is founded on the property inherent in all codes: that of being mutually convertible.

The second mistake lies in the belief that, among all the codes available to myths, one particular code is obligatorily employed. A myth always uses several codes, but it does not follow that all conceivable codes, or all the codes identified by comparative analysis, are simultaneously at work in all myths. One could certainly draw up a list of all the codes that mythic thought uses—or could use—and such a list would be helpful to mythologists in the same way as the periodic table of elements is helpful to chemists. But each myth or family of myths makes a choice among all these codes. The few at work in a specific myth are in no way representative of all of the inventoried codes and are not necessarily the same ones as another myth or family of myths would have selected for its own particular use.

In this book I have concentrated on one family of myths in which the psycho-organic code—the sexual code, if you will (but I will come back to that)—is pressed into service, along with others: the technological, the zoological, the cosmological, etc. One would be wrong to assume from this that the psycho-organic code will have the same operational value in any other myth or family of myths, which may use entirely different codes.

*

The following problem was raised by Freud in Lecture X of his *General Introduction to Psychoanalysis:* "Even if there were no dream-censorship, we should still find it difficult to interpret dreams, for we should then be confronted with the task of translating the symbolic language of dreams into the language of waking life" (Freud 1935: 150). In other words, the essence of dreams lies in the fact that they are coded. But how can it be that we have access to this code, that "we arrive . . . at constant substitutions for a series of dream-elements, just as in popular books on dreams we find translations for everything that occurs in dreams," even though, "when we employ the method of free association, such constant substitutions for dream-elements never make their appearance"? (ibid., p. 134). Fifteen years later, in his *New Introductory Lectures on Psycho-Analysis,* Freud, still preoccupied by the problem, formulated it in the same terms: the contents of dreams "are to be taken as symbols for something else. . . . Since we know how to translate these symbols, while the dreamer does not . . . , the sense of the dream is immediately clear to us . . . , while the dreamer himself is still puzzled by it" (Freud 1933: 23).

Here psychoanalysis and structural analysis diverge on an essential point. Throughout his works, Freud oscillates—and in fact never succeeded in choosing—between two conceptions of the symbol: realist and relative. A realist conception would attribute one and only one signification to each symbol. These significations could all be listed in a dictionary, which, as Freud suggested, would differ little from a "dream book," except for its greater size. The second conception admits that the signification of a symbol varies with each particular case, and, to discover the signification, it has recourse to the method of free association. So, in an elementary and unsophisticated fashion, it recognizes that the symbol draws its signification from the context, from the way it relates to other symbols, which themselves, in turn, find their meaning only in relation to it. This second conception can yield positive results, provided the simplistic method of free association finds its due place within a global attempt at understanding the individual by reconstructing his personal history and the history of his family his social environment, his culture, and so on. One would thus seek to understand an individual in the way an ethnographer seeks to understand a society.

So, though Freud had taken the first steps in this direction, he went no further; instead, hoping to discover an absolute signification for symbols, he seems to have turned more and more to everyday language, etymology, and philology (at times building on some significant mistakes made in these fields, as Benveniste has pointed out). Freud's purpose in this was identical to Jung's; they differed only in that Jung proceeded with great haste, while Freud lingered in the backwaters of scholarly research and the arduous pursuit of what he called "the original myth":

> Consequently [in a search for the absolute meaning of symbols] I hold that the surface versions of myths cannot be used uncritically for comparison with our psychoanalytical findings. We must find our way back to their latent, original forms by a comparative method that eliminates the distortions they have undergone in the course of their history. [Freud-Jung 1974: 472]

Freud is quite right in opposing his method to Jung's, for, "in his recent mythological studies, [Jung . . .] uses any mythological material whatsoever . . . without selection. . . . Now, mythological material can be used in this way only when it appears in its original form and not in its derivatives" (Nunberg and Federn 1962– n74: vol. 3, p. 335).

This criticism is quite pertinent—and intriguing, too, for it can also be applied to its author. Under the pretense of going back to the original myth, all Freud did—all he ever did—was to produce a modern version even more recent than the ones Jung used, which he condemned for their inauthenticity. Psychoanalysis has never been able to prove that its interpretations recreate myths in their original form—if only for the simple reason that the original form (provided this notion means anything) is and remains forever elusive. However far back we may go, a myth is known only as something that has been heard and repeated.

In starting off on a search for the original form, and in believing that he has found it, the psychoanalyst finds in the myth only what he himself has introduced into it, as Freud himself has candidly confessed: "The material has been transmitted to us in a state that does not permit us to make use of it for the solution of our problems. On the contrary, it must first be subjected to psychoanalytic elucidation" (Nunberg and Federn 1962–74: III, 335). In a letter to Jung about the writing of *Totem and Taboo* and his difficulties, he sadly admitted, "Besides, my interest is diminished by the conviction that I am already in possession of the truths I am trying to prove" (Freud-Jung 1974: 472). One could hardly say it better.

In a way, though, Freud is unfair to himself. His greatness lies partly in a gift he possesses in the highest degree: he can think the way myths do. Considering that the snake can take on a male or female connotation, he wrote: "This does not, however, mean that the symbol has two significations; it is simply employed in the inverse sense" (Nunberg and Federn 1962–74: III, 335). He also wrote that in dreams we often find "the procedure of reversal, of turning into the opposite, of inverting relationships" (Freud 1964: XXII, 188). Still, working in an indirect way, Freud here reaches a key notion: that of transformation, which is at the root of all his analyses. According to him, in order to understand the biblical myth of Genesis or the Greek myth of Prometheus, one needs to invert them. Eve becomès the mother who gives birth to Adam, and man, rather than woman, fecundates his spouse by giving her seeds (a pomegranate) to eat. The myth of Prometheus also becomes clearer if the fennel stalk containing fire becomes, through inversion, a penis, that is, a tube carrying water (urine), allowing men to destroy fire (instead of obtaining it). Likewise, by an inversion of container into content, the actual theme of the legend of the Labyrinth turns out to be an anal birth: the winding paths of the maze represent the intestines, and Ariadne's thread is the umbilical cord.

These are excellent variants. They way they relate to the myths they are based on is quite similar to the relationship the ethnologist observes between the myths of one population and those of another, which, in borrowing the myths, has inverted the terms or has transposed them into a new code. One can easily imagine the neighbors of the ancient Hebrews telling the myth of Adam and Eve in the Freudian fashion, or Hesiod's Boeotian contemporaries similarly giving their own version of the Promethean myth. The trouble is that they did not. But it is in part thanks to Freud that these myths are still present in our spiritual heritage. The Oedipus myth, to cite but one example, has retained its vividness, still has an impact on us, because of Freud's new interpretations of it and the interest they have aroused among all groups and levels of our society. That is why, as I said thirty years ago, we must not hesitate to place Freud after Sophocles among our sources for the Oedipus myth. The variants elaborated by Freud obey the laws of mythic thought; they respect the same constraints and apply the same transformational rules.

Freud himself was aware of this affinity between mythic thought and his own. I mentioned above (pp. 187–88) that throughout his life he was haunted by the same question: "How do we profess to arrive at the meaning of these dream-symbols, about which the dreamer himself can give us little or no information?" (Freud 1935: 141). If such a difficulty exists, it comes from Freud's strange conception of the way this information reaches the analyst: "Just as in primitive, grammarless speech, only the raw material of thought is expressed, and the abstract is merged again in the concrete from which it sprang" (Freud 1933: 32–33). The ethnologist and linguist will certainly be startled by the notion that primitive languages are grammarless; but, leaving that aside, we can see that Freud actually touched on the crux of the problem when he wrote: "The dream seems to be an abridged extract from the associations, which has been put together in accordance with rules which we have not yet understood" (ibid., p. 22). These rules are precisely those of a grammar he considered from the start to be nonexistent, as we have just seen.

In order to avoid this dead end, Freud makes a strategic move:

> We derive our knowledge [of the meaning of dream-symbols] from widely different sources: from fairy tales and myths, jokes and witticisms, from folklore, i.e., from what we know of the manners and customs, sayings and songs, of different peoples, and from poetic and colloquial usage of language. Everywhere in these various fields the same symbolism occurs, and in many of them we can understand it without being taught anything about it. [Freud 1935: 141]

It is true that in all languages there are more or less exactly matching expressions, based on similarities or contrasts that might be thought to issue from assonances or homophonies that are specific to each language but in fact are the emanation, in popular language, of thoughts that draw their substance from the very roots of the mind. Freud could have propped up his theory better by quoting from chapter three of Rousseau's *Essay on the Origin of Languages:* "Figurative language came first; literal meaning was discovered last. Men first spoke only in poetry; it was a long time before they invented reasoning."

But if we accept Freud's solution, can we consider psychoanalysis as anything more than a branch of comparative anthropology applied to the study of individual minds? Freud himself acknowledged more than once the dependence of psychoanalysis on the social sciences and the humanities: "The province of symbolism is extraordinarily wise: dream-symbolism is only a small part of it. . . . Psycho-analytic work is so closely intertwined with so many branches of science, the investigation of which gives promise of the most valuable conclusions: with mythology, philology, folk-lore, folk psychology, and the study of religion" (Freud 1935: 149–50). However, this recognition proved so embarrassing that he hastened to add: "In its relation with all these other subjects, psycho-analysis has in the first instance given rather than received" (ibid., p. 150)—a claim supported only by the assertion that "the mental life of the human individual yields, under psychoanalytical investigation, explanations which solve many a riddle in the life of the masses of mankind or at any rate can show these problems in their true light" (ibid.). But the whole lecture from which these quotations are drawn rests on the very opposite of this premise, namely, that various facts that are relevant to the mental life of the individual—facts for which he himself can find no explanation—can be understood only by relating them to "the life of the masses of mankind." Precisely.

His *New Introductory Lectures,* written later than the *General Introduction,* show more caution on this issue. They cast a cloud over the whole debate, simply saying that "any confirmation we could get from other sources, from philology, folklore, mythology or ritual, was particularly welcome" and that "very often pictures and situations appear in the manifest content of the dream which remind one of well-known themes from fairy stories, legends and myths" (Freud 1933: 38–39). But precedence is no longer an issue.

In *The Raw and the Cooked* (p. 338) I myself pointed out that the interpretation of myths from distant regions, myths that appear extremely obscure at first, is sometimes similar to the very obvious analogies we make in our native tongue, whatever it may be. But to understand the phenomenon we need to define symbolism as more than mere comparison. Neither figurative language nor its most common means of expression, metaphor, can be reduced to a transfer of meaning from one term to another. For these terms do not start out jumbled together in an indiscriminate mass; they are not contained in a common pool from which one could draw, at will, just any term and associate it or oppose it to just any other. Meaning is transferred not from term to term but from code to code—that is, from a category or class of terms to another category or class. It would be especially wrong to assume that one of these classes or categories naturally pertains to literal meaning, the other to figurative meaning; for these functions are interchangeable and relative to each other. As in the sex life of snails, the function of each class, literal or figurative, starts out as un-determined; then, according to the role that it will be called upon to play in a global structure of signification, it induces the opposite function in the other class.

In order to show that dream work translates abstract ideas into visual images, Freud cites an observation made by Silberer: "I think that I intend to smooth out an uneven passage in an essay I am writing. Visual image: I see myself planing a piece of wood" (Freud 1933: 37). However, the image of a writer sitting at his desk and bending over his manuscript to cross out a word would be no less visual than the image of the carpenter. This example is remarkable (note that it bears no trace of repression or sexuality), not because of the passage from the abstract to the concrete, but because an expression that in waking life is used in a figurative way is metaphorically transposed by the discourse of the dream into its literal meaning. It might be objected that the adjective "uneven," properly speaking, can refer only to a material surface, but in everyday life none of us thinks in the categories of the grammarian. To the writer, the work of the carpenter is an image of his own work, just as the writer's work might remind a carpenter of his own activity. A metaphor always works both ways; if I may use a rough simile, it is like a two-way street. In switching terms that belong to different codes, the metaphor rests on an intuition that these terms connote the same semantic field when seen from a more global perspective. The metaphor restores this semantic field, notwithstanding the efforts made by analytic thought to subdivide it. In Silberer's dream the metaphor does not replace an abstract element with a concrete one. Like all metaphors, it restores the full meaning of a notion that, whether used in its literal or its figurative meaning, is bound to be impoverished in everyday language. In other words, the metaphorical process is a regression effected by the savage mind, a momentary suppression of the synecdoches that are the operative mode of the domesticated mind. Vico, and Rousseau after him, were well aware of this. They came short in only one thing: they saw figurative or metaphorical language as issuing directly from passions and feelings. (Voltaire held the same belief, saying that metaphor, when it comes naturally, pertains to passions, whereas comparisons pertain solely to the mind.) They failed to see that it is, rather, the primitive apprehension of a global structure of signification—and *that* is an act of the understanding.

*

Vico, Rousseau, and Voltaire were on the wrong track, and Freud followed them in claiming that, for dream symbols, there is an unlimited number of signifiers, while the signifieds remain always the same—matters concerning sexuality. What was Freud's real stand on this issue? There is no doubt that any true disciple could provide a brilliant demonstration that, in his *New Introductory Lectures,* Freud was not contradicting himself when he repudiated a few formulas "which we have never put forward, such as the thesis that all dreams are of a sexual nature" (Freud 1933: 17), and then declared, only a few pages later, "Our work of interpretation uncovers what one might call the raw material, which often enough may be regarded as sexual" (ibid., p. 39); or, again, when he broadened his conception of sexuality, defining it as an "unconscious impulse, . . . the real motive force of the dream" (ibid., p. 35), and when he reproached Pfister for disputing "the splitting up of the sex instinct into its component parts" (Freud 1963: 62); for, as he had clearly stated in the *New Introductory Lectures,* "It is one of the tasks of psycho-analysis to lift the veil of amnesia which shrouds the earliest years of childhood and to bring the expressions of infantile sexual life which are hidden behind it into conscious memory" (Freud 1933: 44), adding that "all imperishable and unrealisable desires that provide the energy for the formation of dreams throughout one's whole life are bound up with the same childish experiences" (ibid.)—these childish experiences being of a sexual nature, as he has just stated. Besides, dream formation is not the only thing at stake: "The world of myths and fairy tales first

195

became intelligible through the understanding of children's sexual life. . . . That has been achieved as a beneficial by-product of psychoanalytical studies" (Freud 1950: 60).

Such statements, oscillating between explicitness and ambiguity, leave one puzzled. It is not that sexuality is shocking to a mythographer: the tales told by American Indians and other peoples have put him into the swing of things, so to speak. But isn't it becoming increasingly clear that, even though dreams that can be interpreted as emanating from repressed sexual desires do indeed constitute a real, even an important, category of dreams, they remain just that: one special category among others? The dreamer uses a much more complex material in elaborating his dream. He doubtless draws on conscious or repressed desires; but he also vaguely perceives noises around him, his movements may be restrained by the presence of a foreign object in the bed, he may be physically indisposed, he may be worried about his work or his career, etc. Freud agrees that "the condition of repose without stimuli . . . is threatened . . . in a chance fashion by external stimuli during sleep, by interests of the day before which have not yet abated, and . . . by the unsatisfied repressed impulses, which are ready to seize on any opportunity for expression" (Freud 1933: 28). For him, however, these stimuli and interests constitute raw materials used by the repressed impulses to code a message that remains their property from start to finish. Couldn't one rather say that all these disparate elements are offered to the dreamer's subconscious as the scattered pieces of a puzzle and that, since their heterogeneity is intellectually discomforting, the subconscious will be obliged in the dream (dream-work also being a form of "bricolage"), by piecing them together into a syntagmatic sequence, to give them, if not coherence (certainly not all dreams are coherent), at least some sort of organized framework? According to Freud, "the real motive force of the dream always finds its outlet in a wish-fulfillment" (Freud 1933: 35). But wish-fulfillment presupposes desire, which is one of the most obscure notions in the whole field of psychology, and there are other motives at play, upstream from desire, so to speak: appetites and needs; and the universal need motivating dream-work is, contrary to what Freud sometimes appeared to think (see above, p. 191), a need to impose a grammatical order on a mass of random elements.

It is not my purpose here to replace sexual symbolism with a symbolism of a linguistic or philosophical nature; that would bring us dangerously close to Jung, who, as Freud rightly pointed out, "attempted to give to the facts of analysis a fresh interpretation of an abstract, impersonal, and ahistorical character" (Freud 1948: 96). We will not attempt to find the "true" signification of myths or dreams. Myths, and perhaps also dreams, bring a variety of symbols into play, none of which signifies anything by itself. They acquire a signification only to the degree that relations are established among them. Their signification is not absolute; it hinges on their position.

To make a simplistic comparison, the analysis of myths is faced with something reminiscent of Japanese script or, rather, scripts. Japanese uses two syllabaries, which differ only in the way they are written; it also uses, in addition, a set of ideograms derived from Chinese. These scripts are not independent but complementary. Each of the two *kana* syllabaries gives an unambiguous phonetic rendition of words but an ambiguous semantic one because of the great number of homonyms in Japanese; for example, the words *kan, kô,* and *shô* are each given no less than fifteen homonyms in a dictionary of everyday language. The Chinese characters, or *kanji,* work in the opposite way: most include a key or root that indicates the semantic field to which the transcribed word or words belong, whether in their noun or verbal forms. In Japanese one character can refer to more than ten words that are semantically related but sometimes completely different phonetically. The sound of the word is indicated by one or more *kana,* written above or next to the *kanji;* the meaning is mainly provided by the *kanji.* Japanese writing thus uses two codes at once (and even three, though nowadays one of the two syllabaries tends to be reserved for the transcription of foreign words not yet integrated into the language). The meaning of a text cannot be drawn from one or the other code, since each of them, taken alone, leaves ambiguities; it is the combination of the two that provides complete understanding. Myths work in a similar way, except that a greater number of codes are brought into play.

If the sexual code were the sole key to the decipherment of the Oedipus myth, how could one account for the pleasure we take in reading or listening to *The Italian Straw Hat*[1]—a pleasure of a different kind, but just as great? Indeed, Sophocles' tragedy and Labiche's comedy are one and the same play, for the same part is played by Uncle Vézinet, who is deaf, and Tiresias, who is blind. Tiresias says everything and no one believes him. Vézinet tries to say everything—they won't let him. Because of their physical handicaps, these two are regarded as not fully dependable interlocutors, and their statements are given no credit, although, had they been interpreted correctly, they would have brought the plot to an end before it had even begun. In both cases, it is because the solution they offered was ignored that a crisis erupted between in-laws: in the one case, between the hero and his brother-in-law, whom he accuses of scheming against him; in the other, be-

---

1. *The Italian Straw Hat* was written in 1851 by Eugène Labiche (1815–88), the author of many of the most popular and amusing light comedies of the nineteenth-century French stage. Typically, his plays are based on an improbable incident that develops into an imbroglio. In *The Italian Straw Hat* the plot goes as follows: Jules Fadinard is about to marry Hélène Nonancourt. On his way to the wedding he rides through a park, where his horse sees a straw hat sitting on a hedge and eats it. The hat belonged to Anaïs de Beauperthuis, who was in the park with her lover, a lieutenant, and cannot go home to her husband without her hat: her honor is at stake. The lieutenant is furious and makes Fadinard take them to his house, where the couple intends to hide until Fadinard finds a new hat. The whole party is there for the wedding, and poor Fadinard goes on a desperate search through the whole town—from the town hall to a milliner's to Anaïs' husband's house—to no avail, such hats being extremely rare. Throughout the play, amidst the general confusion, old Uncle Vezinet, who is deaf, tries to call attention to a present he has brought for the bride. In the end it turns out that this present is an Italian straw hat. All's well that ends well.—Trans.

tween the hero and his father-in-law, who accuses him of failing in his duty.

The similarity runs deeper. The same problems are posed by both plays, and both attempt to solve them in exactly the same way. In *Oedipus Rex* the initial problem is to find out who killed Laius; anyone who fulfills the stated requirements will do. In *The Italian Straw Hat* the initial problem is to find a hat identical to a hat that has vanished; any hat will do, provided it meets the requirements. But halfway through the plays this initial problem is put aside. In Sophocles, the search for a murderer progressively gives way to a much more interesting discovery: the assassin they have been looking for is the very person searching for the assassin. Likewise in Labiche: the search for a hat identical to the first is gradually replaced by the discovery that the hat they have been looking for is none other than the hat that was destroyed.

The two dramatists could have stopped at that. But both introduce a new development in the plot by bringing to the surface a problem that, as I said, had been there from the beginning, implied by the original problem though not clearly formulated. The question at hand in both plays has to do with marriage rules and the social status of the couple. Through the hints given by Tiresias, *Oedipus Rex* raises the issue of the real public identity of Oedipus and its relation to his assumed public identity; the former is opposed to, the latter conforms to, the social norms—they are contradictory. The starting point for *The Italian Straw Hat*—its prime motive, I should say—is the presence under the same roof of two couples of opposite public identity: one is a young married (or about-to-be-married) couple; the other, an illegitimate, scandalous couple (for had it not been socially unacceptable for a young bourgeois couple to share a house with an adulterous pair, Fadinard would not have set out on a search for the hat, and there would have been no play).

In order to relate these antithetical elements to each other and bring them to the point where they will become merged, the two plays follow the same threefold development. The three stages in *Oedipus Rex* are as follows: (1) Oedipus learns from his wife, Jocasta, the circumstances in which Laius was murdered, and he organizes his search accordingly; (2) Oedipus learns from the messenger that he is not the son of Polybus and Merope but an abandoned child; (3) Oedipus learns from the servant that this child was the son of Laius and Jocasta—that is, himself. Now for *The Italian Straw Hat:* (1) Fadinard learns from a milliner, a former lady-love, about the existence of a hat identical to the one he is looking for, and he organizes his search accordingly; (2) Fadinard learns from the owner of the hat that she has given it away; (3) in his meeting with the servant, Fadinard understands that the hat he has been looking for is the one that was eaten up.

Also in both plays, with each step made toward the solution of the problem, the characters surrounding the hero take a step in the opposite direction. Jocasta, first, and then the messenger are on two occasions sure that they can prove—each time more convincingly—that the problem does not exist. Throughout the play, the guests at Fadinard's wedding think they are going through all the stages of a real wedding: the town hall, the restaurant, the newlywed's house. At the end of his two opposite courses of action, Oedipus' two public identities become superimposed, and we understand how they can coincide despite their initial incompatibility. Likewise at the conclusion of a twofold course of action, the incompatibility that had appeared at the outset in Labiche's play disappears when Anaïs de Beauperthuis, the adulterous woman of the beginning, takes on the appearance of a faithful wife wrongly suspected: in the eyes of society she becomes homologous to the character of Hélène, the pure and innocent bride, and ceases to be her opposite.

In both plays these results were achieved when someone made up his mind to discover the hidden thing (in the one play, an object, in the other, a person), whose existence had been known or suspected from the start. In Labiche it is the present from Uncle Vézinet (nobody until the end cared to open the box, though the uncle was dying to reveal what was in it and kept dropping hints); in Sophocles it is the servant (who holds the key to the mystery), whose existence was known from the start but who was summoned only as a last resort. The two plots progress along parallel paths, with dramatic twists devised by the authors to delay the outcome.

Therefore, the sexual coding cannot account for the interest we take in the Greek tragedy or for the fascination with which we watch its plot unfold. Take another look at *Oedipus Rex:* a point of constitutional law is at the crux of the whole matter (Who can hold power legitimately: the queen's brother, or her husband?); it is a detective story[2] whose puzzle is progressively solved in the course of a public trial—a genre currently illustrated, with an elegant economy of means, in Earle Stanley Gardner's novels. The interest we take in Sophocles' tragedy and Labiche's comedy comes, despite their different contents, from the specific properties of the armature they share. In a sense, one could say that *Oedipus Rex* and *The Italian Straw Hat* are expanded metaphors of each other. And their plots, which are strictly parallel, throw into relief the very nature of metaphor; for metaphor, by establishing links between terms or series of terms, subsumes them under a wider semantic field, whose deep structure (let alone its unity) could never have been revealed by each of its terms, or series of terms, considered in isolation.

*

This playful exercise in structural analysis should not be taken too seriously. It is only a game, though not as gratuitous as it may seem, for it helps us understand that our interest in widely different plots is awakened less by their content than by their form.

2. As Vernant has remarked, the whole play is a kind of detective story that Oedipus has to solve (Vernant and Vidal-Naquet 1981: 91). The idea is not new. It was made as early as the first detective story, whose inventor was, as we know, Emile Gaboriau (1832–73). In an article following that writer's death, Francisque Sarcey praised him for having brought about the renewal of "a kind of story found throughout the centuries, from *Zadig* to the legend of Oedipus written by Sophocles, which seems to me to be the prototype" (Sarcey, quoted in Bonniot 1985: 332).

Some Hellenists have come to the same conclusion in their study of *Oedipus Rex*, though they proceed from totally different perspectives: "It takes the form of a purely operational schema of reversal, a rule of ambiguous logic. But the tragedy gives content to the form," writes J.-P. Vernant (1981: 110). In a book about Sophocles, J. Lacarrière suggests that the Greeks may have sought to discover "the secret laws that reveal the Tragic itself," that is, a tragic approach about which "we can wonder if it is not an attempt to find, in the fate of men, the same symmetry as the one that Greek science and philosophy found in the cosmic order" (Lacarrière 1960: 103, 108).

What, then, is this scheme (or form, or symmetry)? It is, as I just said, the one that would later be popularized by thousands of detective novels, though in them the scheme is applied to such monotonous material that is appears stripped, reduced to an immediately perceptible framework, one that makes the genre appealing even to an uneducated public. The scheme however, remains the same: it consists of a set of rules aimed at bringing coherence to elements that are at first presented as incompatible or even contradictory. We have an initial set and a final one, both made up of terms (the characters) and relations (the functions attributed to them by the plot); various operations—superposition, substitution, translation, rotation, inversion—will result in establishing a correspondence between the two sets so that each element in one will be an image of one element in the other; each operation in one direction is compensated by its counterpart in the other, so that the final set is also a closed system. Everything will remain the same, and everything will be different. The result is intellectually satisfying in proportion to the complexity of the operations and to the ingenuity required in manipulating them. In sum, the intellectual pleasure derived from such exercises lies in the fact that they make the presence of invariance felt beneath the most improbable transformations.

I will perhaps be charged with reducing the life of the mind to an abstract game, replacing the human soul and its passions with a clinical formula. I do not contest the existence of impulses, emotions, or the tumultuous realm of affectivity, but I do not accord primacy to these torrential forces; they irrupt upon a structure already in place, formed by the architecture of the mind. If we were to ignore these mental constraints, we would regress to the illusions of a naive empiricism, with one difference: the mind would appear passive before internal rather than external stimuli, a *tabula rasa* transposed from the realm of cognition to that of emotional life. A primitive schematism is always there to impose a form on the turmoil of emotions. In its most spontaneous impulses, affectivity tries to break through obstacles that also act as landmarks: these mental obstacles restrain affectivity while leading it along a limited number of possible paths, each with required halting-places.

Oedipus Rex no doubt takes precedence over *The Italian Straw Hat* by reason of its great age, and one could argue that the two plots are not really parallel. Someone will say that all that Labiche did was to pick a worn-out scheme—invented by Sophocles—from the garbage cans of a literary tradition that had already used it time and time again. Granted, it would come as no surprise if Labiche had remembered *Oedipus Rex* from his studies, which were rigorous enough to get him into law school. But in using this mold for such incongruous matter, he would nevertheless have demonstrated that, already in Sophocles, the mold was more important than the content. And can one go so far as to say that the presence of the same canonic triangle in both plays is also the result of deliberate imitation? At the apex of the triangle stands a character, of important social standing, who holds the key to the riddle—Tiresias, who is aware that he holds it; Vézinet, who is not. The two corners at the base of the triangle are occupied by two menial persons: a messenger and a servant in *Oedipus;* a footman and a chambermaid in *The Straw Hat.* The two important characters have an internal knowledge of the solution of the riddle, an esoteric knowledge in a way, conscious in the one case, unconscious in the other (and even this difference fades before the fact that Tiresias draws his knowledge from supernatural inspiration). On the other hand, the servants' knowledge can, strictly speaking, be defined as exoteric: it is obtained from the outside; it results from their positions on the edges of the field of dramatic action— Corinth and Thebes in *Oedipus,* the Fadinard and Beauperthuis homes in *The Italian Straw Hat*—and the truth springs from the fact that these characters once had been, and in the end again become, spatially contiguous. Finally, in both cases, a tangible proof is produced at the opportune moment: swollen feet, a fragment of the hat, confirm an identity that had remained secret and that comes to be revealed by the comings and goings (that is, in a down-to-earth way, literally and figuratively speaking) of two servants (socially impaired characters to whom nobody had paid attention), and each member of *this* pair is opposed to a physically impaired character (one blind, the other deaf) who had an informed knowledge of this identity but was never heeded by his peers. We cannot exclude *a priori* the theory that there were memories of Sophocles in Labiche; but the matter he deals with is so different, while the formal correspondence is so precise and so detailed, that we are more inclined to think that one scheme, once it was established, always unfolded in the same way, engendering here and there identical configurations.

This parallel between a sublime tragedy and a farcical piece of entertainment, separated by a lapse of some two thousand three hundred years, will perhaps be rejected in the end. But aren't myths also timeless? And didn't those that were brought together in this book belong to genres that went from the course of heavenly bodies to organic functions, from the creation of the world to the making of pots, from the world of the gods to that of animals, from cosmic disorder to marital strife? Let us also bear in mind the fact that American Indians consider as highly sacred stories that to us are vulgar, if not obscene or scatological.

I was therefore following the example of these myths, faithful to the lessons of mythic thought, when I confronted comedy with tragedy, legendary heroes with vaudeville characters; for each of these genres provides a grid that allows us to decipher messages—a task that neither, alone, could accomplish.

Is this not always the case when it comes to questions of signification? We know that the meaning of a word is doubly determined: by the words that precede or follow it in the sentence and by the words that could be substituted for it to convey the same idea. Sequences of the first type are called syntagmatic chains by linguists; they are articulated in time. The second type are called paradigmatic sets; they are made up of words that could be mobilized at the moment a speaker chooses one in preference to others that he might also have used.

Now, what are the processes involved in defining a word, in shifting it into a figurative sense, and in choosing a symbol to represent the notion it stands for? Defining a word is replacing it with another word or phrase drawn from the same paradigmatic set. Using a metaphor is taking a word or phrase from one syntagmatic chain and placing it in another syntagmatic chain. The symbol, for its part, is an entity that entertains within a given conceptual realm the same syntagmatic relations with its context as, within a different conceptual realm, the thing symbolized has with its context. Symbolic thought thus brings together into the same paradigmatic set homologous terms each of which belongs to its own syntagmatic chain.

But the signification, or added signification, that one is aiming at does not belong per se to the new word, the new syntagmatic chain, or the new paradigmatic set. Signification is the product of the relations established between them and the other word, chain, or set, which they supplement rather than replace, so that they will enrich or nuance the semantic field to which they belong or will define its limits more precisely. Signifying is nothing but establishing a relation between terms. Even rigorous lexicographers, aware of the dangers of circular definitions, know that, in their efforts to avoid them, they often do no more than widen the ,circle. Definitions are bound to be circular: words are defined by other words that are ultimately defined by the very words they were defining. The vocabulary of a given language may be made up of tens or hundreds of thousands of words; nevertheless, ideally at least, at a given point in time it constitutes a closed system.

Thus the reciprocity of perspectives that I have seen as the specific character of mythic thought can claim a much wider range of applications. It is inherent in the workings of the mind every time it tries to delve into meaning. The only difference lies in the dimensions of the semantic units to which the mind applies itself. Free from the concern of anchoring itself to an outside, absolute reference, independent of all context, mythic thought should not thereby be opposed to analytical reason. With an authority that cannot be denied, it arises from the depths of time, setting before us a magnifying mirror that reflects, in the massive form of concrete images, certain mechanisms by which the exercise of thought is ruled.

December 1983–April 1985

Appendix
Tribes, Peoples, Linguistic Families

*

Achomawi
Achuar
Aguaruna
Ainu
Algonquians
Apache
Arapaho
Araucan
Arawak
Arikara
Ashluslay
Assihiboine
Athapaskan
Ayoré
Aztec

Barasana
Baré
Bella Coola
Blackfoot
Bororo

Cahuilla
Caingang Coroado
Campa
Canelo
Carib
Cashinawa
Catio
Cavina
Cayapa
Cayuga
Chamula

Chane
Chemehuevi
Cherokee
Chinook
Chippewa
Chon
Choroti
Coeur d'Alene
Colorado
Cree
Creek
Cuiva
Cupeño

Dakota
Delaware
Desana
Diegueño

Flathead

Gabrielino
Gé
Gros Ventre
Guarani
Guarayo
Guiana Indians

Haida
Hidatsa
Hixkaryana
Hopi
Huamachuco
Huron

Ipurina
Iroquois

Jicaque
Jivaro
Juaneño

Kagaba
Kalapuya
Kalina
Karaja
Kayapo
Kickapoo
Klamath
Koasati

Kraho
Kutenai
Kwaikiutl

Lengua
Lipan Apache
Luiseño

Machiguenga
Maidu
Makiritaré
Malecite
Mandan
Maricopa
Mataco
Maya
Mbaya
Menominee
Micmac
"Mission Indians"
Mocovi
Modoc
Mohave
Mohawk
Mohegan-Pequot
Mojo
Mono
Motilon
Mundurucu

Nez-Percé
Nootka

Ofaina: see Tanimuka
Oglala Dakota

Ojibwa
Omaha
Oneida
Onondaga
Oyampi

Pano
Parintintin
Pawnee
Penobscot
Pima
Pira-Tapuya
Ponca
Pueblo

Quechua
Quiche Maya

Salish
Saliva
Sanema
Seneca
Serrano
Sikuani
Siouan
Shipaia
Shoshonean
St Francis
Surara
Suya

Tacana
Tanimuka
Tapirape
Taulipang
Tehuelche
Tembe
Tenetehara
Timbira
Toba
Trumai
Tsimshian
Tucano
Tukuna
Tumereha
Tumupasa
Tupi
Tzotzil

Umutina
Urubu
Ute

Waiwai
Wanabaki
Warau
Waura
Wayapi: see Oyampi
Wishram
Wyandot

Yagua
Yalbiri
Yanomami
Yaruro
Yuman
Yupa
Yurok
Yurucaré

Zuñi

References

*

(Numbers in the righthand column denote pages in the present text on which sources are cited. Sources not page-referenced to the text were consulted but are not specifically cited.)

Introduction

Sébillot 1895; Belmont 1984
Sébillot 1895: art. "Cordonniers," p. 11
Medawar and Medawar 1983: 100
Montaigne, bk. III, ch. XI   4
Soustelle 1979: 114–15, 168
Morley 1946: 230–31; J. Eric S. Thompson 1970: 243–46;
    Sablott and Rathje 1975; Soustelle 1982: 170
McIlwraith 1948: I, 361
Buicker 1973: 19
Lévi-Strauss 1966
Magaña 1982a, b; Frickel 1953: 271–72 and nn. 4, 5
Fock 1963: 56–71
Tastevin 1926: 163   7
Alvarez 1939: 156
Becher 1959: 106
Reichel-Dolmatoff 1978: 271, 285–86   8
Radcliffe-Brown 1948: 311–12
Seeger 1977: 358; 1981: 92–93, 119   8
Ortiz-Gomez 1983: 143–44, 216
Meggitt 1962: 49
Posener 1959: art. "vases"
Héritier and Izard 1958: 23
Maquet 1961: 10

211

References

Sales 1981: 53
Léger 1981: 259–71
Aston 1896: I, 119–22
Lévi-Strauss 1984: 109–11   13

Chapter 1 A Jivaro Myth

Karsten 1935: 519–20; Farabee 1922: 124–25   15
Karsten 1935: 521, 522
Guallart 1958: 92
Pellizzaro 1982: 53–89
Descola 1984: 91–92, 272   16
Stirling 1938: 123   17
Guallart 1958. *See also* bibliographies in Pellizzaro, Rueda
Stirling 1938: 124–28   17
Berlin 1977
Sauer 1950: VI, 505   18
Karsten 1935: 141, 138   19
Descola 1984: 190
Casevitz-Renard 1972: 249
Garcia 1935–37: vol. 17, 223, 226; (vol. 18, 170)   20
Guallart 1958: 8, 33; Descola 1984: 165
Descola 1984: 166; Pellizzaro n.d.: 117–22
Stirling 1938: 122
Stirling 1938: 73, 95, 126, n. 37
Karsten 1923: 12; 1935: 100, 492   22
Pellizzaro 1978: 86–89

Chapter 2 Pottery, a "Jealous Art"

Lévi-Strauss 1973
Karsten 1935: 99–100   23
Stirling 1938: 94   23
Orbigny 1844: III, 94
Duviols 1974–76: 176–77
Foster 1965: 46   24
Garcia 1935–37: vol. 17, 223   24
Duviols 1974–76: 176–77
Nimuendaju 1946a: III, 723–24
Chaumeil 1983: 188 n. 34   25
Tastevin 1925: 172–206   25

Harner 1977: 69; Rueda 1983: 89–91
Schomburgk 1922: I, 203. Cf. Lévi-Strauss 1976b   27
Penteado Coelho 1984: 12–13
Huxley 1956: 247
Briffault 1927: I, 466–67
Nicklin 1979: 436–58
Hissink and Hahn 1961: 227–28
Pellizzaro 1978: 121
E. von Hildebrand 1976: 181–87   27
Walker 1917: 141 n. 1.
Speck 1935: 83
J. O. Dorsey 1888: 77; 1890: 217
Bowers 1965: 165–66, 373–74, 375, 389–92
Cushing 1887: 510 f.
Stevenson 1905: 373–77; Parsons 1916: 523–24
Chapman 1967: 209–11   32
Skinner 1921: 285–86   32
Neill 1884: 251

Chapter 3 Goatsucker Myths in South America

Lehmann-Nitsche 1927, 1928, 1930
Léry 1975: 156–57
Nimuendaju 1952: 116–18
Goeje 1943: 11, 21, 54, 124
Reichel-Dolmatoff 1968: 166
Musters 1872: 203
Humboldt, in Brehm n.d.: II, 571; Brehm 1891: 233–39;
Roth 1915: 161–62   36
Descola 1984: 100
Azara 1803: II, 527–29   36
Rodrigues 1890: 151–52
Verissimo 1886: 62
Orico 1929: 67–70
Schultz and Chiara: 128–30
Lehmann-Nitsche 1927; Roth 1915: 371
Ahlbrinck 1956: art. "woka"
Banner 1957: 59
Recinos 1950: 147 and n. 17; Edmonson 1971: 119–20
Couto de Magalhães 1940: 170
Civrieux 1980: 52–54

213

Rivet and Rochereau 1929: 82, 89
Weiss 1975: 260; Vega 1737: ch. XXVIII, 332–33
Ahlbrinck 1956: art. "woka"
Amorim 1928: 319–39
Teschauer 1925: 69–78   39
Lehmann-Nitsche 1930: 268–72   40
Stirling 1938: 124
Nordenskiöld 1924: 291–92
Wavrin 1937: 635. Cf. Lévi-Strauss 1978
Goeje 1943:54
Murphy 1958: 121; Kruse 1946–49: 655
Lévi-Strauss 1978: M_{110}; Wagley and Galvão 1949:
   140–42
Batchelor 1901: 185–87
Lehmann-Nitsche 1928, 1930   42
Banner 1957: 59–60
Nimuendaju 1946b: 179–81
Roth 1915: 161–62, 175–76, 274, 371
Nimuendaju 1952: 131
Lévi-Strauss 1969b
Bernand-Muñoz 1977: 70–82; Wagner 1967: 17, 101–3
Lehmann-Nitsche 1930: 253
Wagner 1967: 17–19, 117
Bernand-Muñoz 1977: 230–32
Wagner 1967: 19–20

Chapter 4 Potters' Kilns and Cooking Fire

Métraux 1946b: 213–14, 367–68   49
Métraux 1944
Brehm 1891: 541   51
Banner 1957: 59; Ahlbrinck 1956: art. "woka"
Ihering 1940: art. "João de Barro"   52
Métraux 1946a: 33–36
Métraux 1939: 10–11   53
Barabas and Bartolomé 1979: 126–28
Karsten 1967: 107
Ewers 1945: 289–99
Métraux 1943: 19
Greenberg 1956; Suárez 1973

Abreu 1914: 489, 494, 275–76
Brehm 1891: 540   56

Chapter 5 Goatsucker Myths in North America

Bent 1964; Brasher 1962: II, 393–400
Robbins et al. 1966
Schaeffer 1950: 42; Teale 1965
Beckwith 1938: 14, 293
Speck 1921: 362–63; 1935: 24–25
Skinner and Satterlee 1915: 442
J. O. Dorsey 1895: 500
Witthoft 1946: 379
Converse 1908: 174, 181, 183
Michelson 1927: 107, 111, 115
Stephen 1936: 307 n. 1, 470; Cushing 1920: 161
Powell 1881: 25
Dixon 1912: 192–97; 1908: 163–65   62
Gatschet 1890: I, 502, II, 234; Barker 1963a, b
Ray 1963: 46–47
Curtin 1912: 186–90
Ahenakew 1929: 335–37; Beckwith 1930: 387–89; 1938:
    292–93; G. A. Dorsey 1906: 446–47; 1904: 146–47;
    Dorsey and Kroeber 1903: 69–70; Grinnell 1892: 165;
    Jones 1915: 13, 130; Josselin de Jong 1914: 15–18;
    Kroeber 1901: 260–64; 1907: 69–70; Rand 1894:
    316–17; Reichard 1947: 143–44; Wissler and Duvall
    1908: 24–25; etc. *See also* S. Thompson 1929: 300
Schaeffer 1950: 42
Kroeber 1901: 260–64
Audubon 1868: I 121   67
Speck 1946: 256; Fenton 1953: 202
Lowie 1909: 120, 108–9
Wissler and Duvall 1908: 24–25, 37
Nunes Pereira 1945: 117
Riggs 1890: 422; Wallis 1923: 66, 57
Opler 1941: 195 (300–301; 1946: 125–31)   68
McDermott 1901: 245
Goeje 1943: 54   69
Bryce Boyer 1979: 226

References

Chapter 6 Oral Greediness and Anal Retention

Buffon 1763: XIII, 38–48; Brehm 1890: 644–57; Grassé
    1955: XVII, 11: 1182–1266
Stirling 1938: 124–29
Karsten 1935: 519–20; Pellizzaro 1982: 53–89; Rueda
    1983: 59–60
Stirling 1938: 72–73; Karsten 1935: 98; Harner 1962: 266
Pellizzaro 1980a: 195
Goeje 1943: 47
J. E. Thompson n.d.; Métraux 1931: 151; 1946b: 367
Pellizzaro n.d.: 16; Guallart 1958: 61
Pellizzaro 1982: 70–71; Karsten 1935: 526
Stirling 1938: 129
Karsten 1935: 222; Guallart 1958: 92
Pellizzaro 1982: 59   74
Wavrin 1937: 601
Ehrenreich 1948: 129
M. von Hildebrand 1975: 356–57; 1979: 269–77
Schultz 1964: 230–32
Albisetti and Venturelli 1962–76: II 1139–67   82
Nimuendaju 1952: 123–24

Chapter 7 The Sloth as Cosmological Symbol

Hissink and Hahn 1961: 39–40
Descola 1984: 165, 269–70
Guallart 1958: 33
Ihering 1940: art. "Preguiça"
Ahlbrinck 1956: art. "Kupírisi"; Hugh Jones 1979: 196   87
Chaumeil 1982: 53 n. 16; 1983: 150
Weiss 1975: 270, 570
Amorim 1928: 138–45   88
Oviedo y Valdes, in Britton 1941: 14
Beebe 1926: 35–37   90
Ulloa, in Britton 1941: 15   90
Schomburgk 1922: I, 110–11
Wagley and Galvão 1949: 159
Enders 1940: 7   90
Britton 1941: 195–96, 32   91
Krieg 1939: 291; 1961: 20–23   91
Pellizzaro 1980b: 32   92

216

Roth 1915: 369
Monod-Becquelin 1975: 168 n. 141
Craydall 1964: 188
Beebe 1926: 37–39; Goffart 1971: 111–26
Thevet 1878: ch. LII   92
Oviedo y Valdes, in Britton 1941: 14   92
Léry 1975: ch. X   92
Gillin 1936: 203–4
Murphy 1958: 121; Wagley and Galvão 1949: 155
Hartt 1952
Goeje 1943: 72
Roth 1915: 204
Murphy 1958: 124–25; Kruse 1946–49: 631
Fock 1963: 65–67; Derbyshire 1965: 28–43
Hissink and Hahn 1961: 287
Fock 1963: 57, 70 n. 39
Murphy 1958: 121; Amorim 1928: 145
Spruce 1908: II, 454. Cf. Lévi-Strauss 1973   95

Chapter 8 In Quest of Zoemes

Goffart 1971: 1–20
Lévi-Strauss 1981   97
Enders 1935: 490
Ihering 1940: art. "Tamanduá"
Goeje 1946: 47   98
Seeger 1981: 96–98; Roth 1915: 274
Hugh Jones 1979: 268; Pellizzaro 1980a: 192–94;
    Goeje 1943: 23
Rodrigues 1899: 54; Stradelli 1890: 669 f.
Goffart 1971: 2, 90; Van Tyne 1929
Lévi-Strauss 1969b
Enders 1935: 494   99
Hissink and Hahn 1961: 165–76, 406–15;
    Amorim 1928: 145; Borba 1908: 22   100
Enders 1935: 494; Civrieux 1980: 104–5
Hissink and Hahn 1961: 286, 295; Amorim 1928: 235 n. 8
Borba 1908: 25
Cadogan 1959: 84; Schaden 1963
Cardus 1886: 369; Nino 1912: 37; Wallace 1889: 314
Hissink and Hahn 1961: 167
Hissink and Hahn 1961: 124–25, 351–55

References

Hissink and Hahn 1961: 39
Bórmida and Siffredi 1969–70: 236, 225;
  Suarez 1973; Ritchie Key 1978a, b, c
Karsten 1935: 125–26, 513–16; Guallart 1958: 88;
  Harner 1962: 269; Berlin 1977; Garcia-Rendueles
  1978; Pellizzaro 1978; Descola 1984: 267 f.
Chaumeil 1983: 163, 172–74; Rivet and Rochereau
  1929: 82; Barrett 1925: II, 360–81
Nimuendaju 1952: 119
Wilbert 1962: 864–66; 1974: 86–90   103
Wilbert 1963: 234. Cf. Goeje 1943: 129
Harner 1962: 266
Opler 1940: 45–46
Sapir and Spier 1930: 279; E. D. Jacobs 1959: 7, 9;
  M. Jacobs 1959: I, 101; Haeberlin 1924: 429;
  Adamson 1934: 81–83
J. O. Dorsey 1888: 237; 1895: 421
Dorsey and Kroeber: 122–23
Barbeau 1915: 112
Speck 1928: 261–62
Witthoft and Hadlock 1946; Gatschet 1888: 237
Teit 1930: 180   105
Hissink and Hahn 1961: 88–89; Chaumeil 1982: 53 n. 16
Wagley 1940: 257–58
Roth 1915: 127; Wilbert 1970: 424–31; Goeje 1943: 128
Opler 1940: 46
Andrade 1931: 61
Barbeau 1915: 111
Cornplanter 1938: 46–57
Lévi-Strauss 1971: 497
Hewitt 1928: 801, 808–9; Curtin and Hewitt 1911: 616, 622
Stradelli 1929: 362; Orico 1937: 21; Camara Cascudo
  1962: I, 11
La Barre 1980: 78
Beebe 1926: 66   107
Enders 1935: 423
Huxley 1956: 227   108
Derbyshire 1965: 105
Weiss 1975: 265
Civrieux 1980: 127–31, 184
Weiss 1975: 389–90, 397
Petrullo 1939: 237

218

Nimuendaju 1952: 123–24; Ortiz-Gomes 1983: 202–5
Murphy 1958: 118; Kruse 1946–49: 628–30
Swanton 1929: 200 n. 3
Mooney 1900: 265, 449
Sahagun 1950–53: bk. VI, pt. VII, ch. 28; bk. XI, ch. 1;
  cf. Seler 1961: IV, 506–13   110
Caso and Bernal 1952: ch. X
Goeje 1943: 72
Lévi-Strauss 1969b   111
Amorim 1928: 134
Colbacchini 1919: 114–15; 1925: 179–80
Laughlin 1977: 76–77, 259
Barrett 1925: 360–81
Laughlin 1977: 2
Whiffen 1915: 225–26   113
Wavrin 1937: 515–16, 620   114
Grenand 1980: 322–24, 39–40, 42   114
Descola 1984: 267 f.
Laughlin 1977: 76
Hocart 1929: 47; Boas 1894: 153–82   115
Grain 1957: 91–92; Curtin and Hewitt 1911: 616;
  Hewitt 1928: 801
Hissink and Hahn 1961: 88–89

Chapter 9 Levels of the World

Weiss 1972: 170; 1975: 256
Murphy 1958: 21   117
Phinney 1934: 88–112; Jacobs 1945: 173–78
Jacobs 1945: 174   118
Bormida 1918: 3–4
Métraux (1939: 9); 1946a: 24–25   118
Powell 1881: 27   118
Hissink and Hahn 1961: 162–63
Converse 1908: 105 n. 1; Parker 1912a: 119;
  Cornplanter 1938: 54
Hissink and Hahn 1961: 406–7
Hugh Jones 1979: 274
Ratcliffe 1963: 28
Hissink and Hahn 1961: 39–40
Ihering 1940: art. "Bugio"; Ahlbrinck 1956: arts.
  "api", "arawata"

References

Hissink and Hahn 1961: 440–42
Brett 1880: 130–32
Petrullo 1939: 235
Brett 1880: 131
Stradelli 1929: 758; Amorim 1928: 142–44
Wilbert 1970: 466–68; Roth 1915: 231, 292–93;
  Lévi-Strauss 1969b; 1973
Murphy 1958: 118; Frikel 1953: 267–69;
Roth 1915: 150–51; Wilbert 1970: 364–76
Albisetti and Venturelli 1962–76: I, 371
Goeje 1943: 47
Carpenter 1934: 27   124
Hugh Jones 1979: 123, 175
Wallace 1889: 154; Enders 1935: 484 f.
Roth 1915: 211
Fock 1963: 181   124
Carpenter 1934: 37   125

Chapter 10 Excrement, Meteors, Jealousy

Nordenskiöld 1924: 294–95
Garcia 1935–37: vol. 18, 8, 9; 1942: 233–34
G. A. Dorsey 1906: 61–62; Mallery 1887: 136–39;
  1894: 722 f.; Russell 1908: 38, 47
Swanton 1938
Hewitt 1928: 453–611; cf. Smith 1884; Hewitt 1903;
  Curtin and Hewitt 1911; Cornplanter 1938
Ragueneau, de Quen, in Jésuites 1972: vol. 4, p. 70, 73;
  vol. 5, p. 26 (years 1648, 1656)   131
Curtin and Hewitt 1911: 460
Parker 1912b; Hewitt 1903: 282
Cornplanter 1938: 19   132
Converse 1908: 33   133
Hewitt 1928: 481   133
Curtin and Hewitt 1911: 336–37, 341, 798, 804–6
Hewitt 1903: 172, 222; 1928: 629
Fenton 1962: 292
Sagard 1636: II, 452; Brébeuf, in Jésuites 1972:
  vol. 1, p. 34 (year 1635)   134
Boas 1940: 334, cf. Lévi-Strauss 1978
Jakobson and Waugh 1979: 127
Lounsbury 1978: 336

Baer 1978; 1979: 128–29
Lockwood 1979; Naranjo 1979
Kroeber 1906: 319; Boscana 1978: 180–85;
    Curtis 1907–30: XV, 101   137
DuBois 1908b: 76 n. 6
DuBois 1904b; Kroeber 1948a: 4–23; DuBois 1906: 145–64
DuBois 1908b: 125–26; 1904b: 236–37; 1906: 155   138
Kroeber 1948: 13 n. 62
DuBois 1906: 158; 1908a: 230
Curtis 1907–30: XV, 122–23; DuBois 1901   139
Strong 1929: 130–31, 268–70   140
Strong 1929: 135   140
Bourke 1889; Curtis 1907–30: II, 56; Kroeber 1925: 770;
    Devereux 1961: 286–87 and *passim;*
    DuBois 1904a, 1906, 1908b
Kroeber 1906: 314–16; Curtis 1907–30: XV, 109–21;
    Strong 1929: 130–43, 268–70; DuBois 1904a;
    Kroeber 1925: 637, 678, 692, 714, 770–71, 788–92;
    Bean 1972: *passim*

Chapter 11 California Demiurges

Strong 1929: 134, 135   142
DuBois 1908b; White 1957   143
DuBois 1908b: 136–37   143
Kroeber 1925: 642–44; Strong 1929: 300–301
Harrington, in Boscana 1978: 185
Strong 1929: 136, 137, 142   144
Garcia 1935–37: vol. 17, pp. 223–24; vol. 18, p. 135   145
Harrington, in Boscana 1978: 125
Garcia 1935–37: vol. 18, p. 3; 1942: 230;
    Pereira 1942: 240–41; Cenitagoya 1943: 192
Weiss 1975: 369
Curtis 1907–30: XV, 122–23   146
Naranjo 1979: 127
Stirling 1938: 128
Cenitagoya 1943: 196
Nimuendaju 1919–20: 1010–11
Garcia 1935–37: vol. 18, pp. 230–33. Cf. Lévi-Strauss 1973
Oosten 1983: 144   148
Casevitz 1977: 131   150
Couto de Magalhães 1940: 171

References

Latcham 1924: 384–85, 567–68
Pereira 1942: 240–43
Strong 1929: 134, 136; DuBois 1904a: 185
Strong 1929: 138, 269   151
DuBois 1904a: 55
Boscana 1978: 32
Waterman 1909: 48
Kroeber 1925: 619; Curtis 1907–30; II, 86
Curtis 1907–30: XV, 119–20; Strong 1929: 139
Devereux 1961: 203, 206, 210; Bean 1972: 81
Goffart 1971
Strong 1929: 288   153
Moratto 1984; Chartkoff 1984; MacNeish 1978, 1982
Boas 1916: 141

Chapter 12 Myths in the Form of Klein's Bottle

Stirling 1938: 80–85; Nimuendaju 1952: 27–30;
    Bianchi 1976   158
Speck 1938; Riley 1952
Pellizzaro n.d.: 36–37
Kroeber 1948a: 8–10
Curtis 1907–30: XV, 124–25; DuBois 1904b: 237;
    1906: 155   160
Kroeber 1948a: 12–13   161
Strong 1929: 131–32, 139 n. 317   161
Erikson 1943; Posinsky 1957; Kroeber 1948b: 617–18   162
Erikson 1943: 297
Preuss 1919–26: 194–99
Hugh Jones 1979: 121–24, 141, 197, 285
Murphy 1958: 95–102; Huxley 1956: 80
Barnouw 1955: 344; Lévi-Strauss 1969b
Hugh Jones 1979: 280–81; Lévi-Strauss 1973;
    Goodwin 1939: 38
Bloomfield 1928: 268–69   164
Boas 1890: 815   164
Albisetti and Venturelli 1962–76: I, 717; Viertler 1979: 26   164
Basso 1970: 213–30   165
Thompson and Thompson 1972: 448
Ortiz-Gomes 1983: 227   165
Hugh Jones 1979: 305–6; cf. Biocca 1966: I, 230;
    Saake 1958: 273

Seeger 1981: 210
Biocca 1966: II, 218
Sapir 1910: 471; 1968: 186–87
Boas 1940: 479
Boas and Hunt 1902: III, 88; Swanton 1905–9: 95
Skinner 1916: 343
Hearn 1901: I, 331
Goeje 1943: 51, 103; Enders: 484 f.; Wallace 1889: 154   166
Ahlbrinck 1956: art. "kupírisi"
Lehmann-Nitsche 1922
Hissink and Hahn 1961: 157, 163
Bórmida 1978: 5–6; Wagner 1967: 56, 126
Garcia 1935–37: vol. 18, pp. 6, 10; 1942: 232; 1943: 186
Nimuendaju 1919–20: 1010–11

Chapter 13 The Nature of Mythic Thought

Kroeber 1908a: 240
Frate 1984
Foster 1955: 28   175
Kroeber 1925: 736
Foster 1965: 49–50   179
Howry 1978: 247   179
Kensinger et al. 1975: 55   179
Nordenskiöld 1920: 148
Bunzel 1929; Fewkes 1919: 218; Linné 1945: 33
Gimbutas 1981: 26–31   180
Reichel-Dolmatoff 1978: 281–82   181
Gifford 1928
Nimuendaju 1952: 122–23, 132–33, 77–78, 134, 46

Chapter 14 A Jivaro Version of Totem and Taboo

Freud 1962   185
Stirling 1938: 124–29
Lévi-Strauss 1981: 44   186
Lévi-Strauss 1969b: 240   187
Freud 1935: 150, 134   188
Freud 1933: 23   188
Benveniste 1966: I, chap. vii
Freud-Jung 1974: 472   189
Nunberg and Federn 1962–74: III, 335   189

References

Freud-Jung 1974: 472   190
Nunberg and Federn 1962–74: III, 335   190
Freud 1964: XXII, 188 and passim
Freud-Jung 1974: 473
Freud 1935: 141   191
Freud 1933: 32–33, 22   191
Freud 1935: 141   192
Freud 1935: 149–50   192
Freud 1933: 38–39   193
Lévi-Strauss 1969b: 338   193
Freud 1933: 37   194
Voltaire 1764: 294–95
Freud 1933: 17   195
Freud 1933: 39, 35   195
Freud 1963: 62   195
Freud 1933: 44   195
Freud 1950: 60   196
Freud 1933: 28   196
Freud 1933: 35   196
Freud 1948: 96   197
Labiche 1892–94: I, 1–132   198
Sophocles 1959: 11–76   198
Vernant 1981: 110   202
Sarcey, in Bonniot 1985: 332
Lacarrière 1960: 103, 108
Lévi-Strauss 1981   204

Abbreviations

*

Bibliography

*

Abreu, J. Capistrano de
 1914 *Rã-txa hu-ni-ku-ĩ: A lingua dos Caxinauás.* Rio de Janeiro.
Adamson, Th.
 1934 *Folk-Tales of the Coast Salish.* MAFLS, vol. 17. New York.
Ahenakew, E.
 1929 "Cree Trickster Tales." *JAFL,* vol. 42
Ahlbrinck, W.
 1956 *Encyclopaedie der Karaiben.* (VKAWA, n.s. vol. 21, no. 1,
    1931.) French translation by D. van Herwijnen. Mimeogr.
    Paris.
Albisetti, C. e Venturelli, A. J.
 1962–76 *Enciclopédia Boróro.* 3 vols. Campo Grande.
Alvarez, J.
 1939 "Mitologia, tradiciones y creencias religiosas de los sal-
    vages Huarayos." *Actes du 27ᵉ Congrès Intern. des Améri-
    canistes,* vol. 2. Lima.
Amorim, A. B. de
 1928 "Lendas em Nheêngatu e em Portuguez." *Revista do In-
    stituto historico e geographico brasileiro,* vol. 154.
Andrade, M. J.
 1931 *Quileute Texts.* CUCA, vol. 12. New York.
Aston, W. G., ed.
 1896 *Nihongi: Chronicles of Japan from the Earliest Times to
    A.D. 697.* Transactions and Proceedings of the Japan So-
    ciety. 2 vols. London.
Audubon, J. J
 1868 *Scènes de la nature dans les États-Unis et le Nord de
    l'Amérique, trad. par E. Bazin.* 2 vols. Paris: Sauton.

227

Azara, F. de
    1803   *Apuntiamentos para la historia natural de los pájaros*
                 del Paraguay y Rio de la Plata. Madrid.
Baer, G.
    1978   "The Matsigenka View of the Religious Dimension of
                 Light." Paper read at the 10th International Congress of
                 Anthropol. and Ethnol. Sciences. Multigraph. Madras.
    1979   "Religion y chamanismo de los Matsigenka." *Amazonia*
                 Peruana-Chamanismo, vol. 2, no. 4. Lima.
Banner, H.
    1957   "Mitos dos indios Kayapo." *Revista de Antropologia,* vol.
                 5, no. 1. São Paulo.
Barabas, A. M., and Bartolomé, M. A.
    1979   "Un Testimonio mítico de los Mataco." *JSA,* vol. 66. Paris.
Barbeau, M.
    1915   *Huron and Wyandot Mythology.* Geological Survey of
                 Canada, Memoir 80, Anthropology Series no. 11. Ottawa.
Barker, M. A. R.
    1936a   *Klamath Texts.* University of California Publications in
                 Linguistics, no. 30.
    1936b   *Klamath Dictionary.* Id., no. 31
Barnouw, V.
    1955   "Interpretation of a Chippewa Origin Legend [3]." *JAFL,*
                 vol. 68.
Barrett, S. A.
    1925   *The Cayapa Indians of Ecuador.* INM, no. 40. 2 vols.
                 New York.
Basso, K. H.
    1970   "To Give Up on Words": Silence in Western Apache Cul-
                 ture." *SWJA,* vol. 26, no. 3.
Batchelor, J.
    1901   *The Ainu and Their Folklore.* London.
Bean, L. J.
    1972   *Mukat's People: The Cahuilla Indians of Southern Cali-*
                 fornia. University of California Press.
Becher, H.
    1959   "Algumas notas sôbre a religião e a mitologia dos Su-
                 rára." *RMP,* n.s. vol. 11. São Paulo.
Beckwith, M. W.
    1930   "Mythology of the Oglala Dakota." *JAFL,* vol. 43.
    1938   *Mandan-Hidatsa Myths and Ceremonies.* MAFLS, vol. 32.
                 New York.

Beebe, W.
1926   "The Three-Toed Sloth." *Zoologica,* vol. 3, no. 1. New York.

Belmont, N.
1984   "Mythologie des métiers: À propos de 'Légendes et curiosités des métiers' de Paul Sébillot." *Ethnologie française,* vol. 14, no. 1. Paris.

Bent, A. C.
1964   *Life Histories of North American Cuckoos, Goatsuckers, Hummingbirds, and Their Allies.* 2 vols. New York: Dover.

Benveniste, E.
1966   *Problèmes de linguistique générale.* 2 vols. Paris: Gallimard.

Berlin, B.
1977   "Bases empíricas de la cosmologia aguaruna jíbaro, Amazonas, Peru." *Studies in Aguaruna Jívaro Ethnobiology.* Report n. 3. University of California, Berkeley.

Bernand-Muñoz, C.
1977   *Les Ayoré du Chaco septentrional: Étude critique à partir des notes de Lucien Sebag.* Paris and the Hague: Mouton.

Bianchi, C.
1976   *Armas.* Mundo Shuar. Series C, no. 6. Sucua.

Biocca, H.
1966   *Viaggi tra gli Indi: Alto rio Negro-alto Orinoco.* 4 vols. Consiglio Nazionale delle Ricerche. Rome.

Bloomfield, L.
1928   *Menomini Texts.* PAES, no. 12. New York.

Boas, F.
1890   "First General Report on the Indians of British Columbia." *Reports of the British Association for the Advancement of Science, 59th Meeting.* London.
1894   *Chinook Texts.* BBAE, no. 20.
1916   *Tsimshian Mythology.* ARBAE, no. 31.
1940   *Race, Language and Culture.* New York: Macmillan.

Boas, F., and Hunt, G.
1902   *Kwakiutl Texts.* MAMNH, no. 5. New York.

Bonniot, R.
1985   *Emile Gaboriau ou la naissance du roman policier.* Paris: Vrin.

Borba, T. M.
1908   *Actualidade Indigena.* Coritiba.

Bormida, M.
1978   "Ayoreo Myths." *Latin American Studies,* vol. 2, no. 1.
Bormida, M., and Siffredi, A.
1969–70   "Mitología de los Tehuelches meridionales." *Runa,* vol.
            12, parts 1–2. Buenos Aires.
Boscana, G.
1978   *Chinigchinich.* Translated by A. Robinson. Annotations by
            J. P. Harrington. Banning: Malki Museum Press.
Bourke, J. G.
1889   "Notes on the Cosmogony and Theogony of the Mojave
            Indians." *JAFL,* vol. 2.
Bowers, A. W.
1965   *Hidatsa Social and Ceremonial Organization.* BBAE,
            no. 194.
Brasher, R.
1962   *Birds and Trees of North America.* 4 vols. New York:
            Rowman & Littlefield.
Brehm, A. E.
1890   *Brehms Tierleben: Säugetiere.* Vol. 2. Leipzig and Vienna:
            Bibliographisches Institut.
1891   *Die Vögel.* 2 vols. Leipzig and Vienna: Bibliographisches
            Institut.
n.d.   *La Vie des animaux illustrée: Les Oiseaux.* 2 vols. Paris:
            Baillère et Fils.
Brett, W. H.
1880   *Legends and Myths of the Aboriginal Indians of British
            Guiana.* London.
Briffault, R.
1927   *The Mothers.* 3 vols. New York: Macmillan.
Britton, W. S.
1941   "Form and Function in the Sloth." *Quarterly Review of
            Biology,* vol. 16, nos. 1 and 2.
Bryce Boyer, L.
1979   "Stone as a Symbol in Apache Folklore." In R. H. Hook,
            ed., *Fantasy and Symbol: Studies in Anthropological In-
            terpretation.* London and New York: Academic Press.
Buffon, G. L. L. de
1763   *Histoire naturelle générale et particulière.* Paris.
Buicker, V. R.
1973   *Ritual Humor in Highland Chiapas.* University of Texas
            Press.

Bunzel, R. L.
1929   *The Pueblo Potter: A Study of Creative Imagination in Primitive Art.* New York: AMS Press.

Cadogan, L.
1959   *Ayvu Rapyta: Textos míticos de los Mbyá-Guarani del Guairá.* São Paulo.

Câmara Cascudo, L. da
1962   *Dicionário do Folclore Brasileiro.* 2 vols. Rio de Janeiro.

Cardus, J.
1886   *Las Misiones Franciscanas entre los infieles de Bolivia.* Barcelona.

Carpenter, C. R.
1934   "A Field Study of the Behavior and Social Relations of Howling Monkeys." *Comparative Psychology Monographs,* vol. 10, no. 2.

Casevitz, F.-M.
1977   "Du Proche au loin : Etude du fonctionnement des systèmes de la parenté et de l'alliance matsiguenga." *Actes du 42ᵉ Congrès intern. des américanistes,* vol. 2. Paris.

Casevitz-Renard, F.-M.
1972   "Les Matsiguenga." *JSA,* vol. 61. Paris.

Caso, A., and Bernal, I.
1952   *Urnas de Oaxaca.* Mexico City: Instituto Nacional de Antropologia e Historia.

Cenitagoya, V. de
1943   *Los Machiguengas.* Lima: Sanmarti.

Chapman, A.
1967   *Les Enfants de la mort: Mythologie des Jicaques.* Paris: Ecole pratique des hautes études. (Multigraph.)

Chartkoff, J. L., and Chartkoff, K. K.
1984   *The Archaeology of California.* Stanford: Stanford University Press.

Chaumeil, J.-P.
1982   "Représentation du monde d'un chamane Yagua." *L'Ethnographie,* vol. 78.

1983   *Voir, savoir, pouvoir: Le chamanisme chez les Yagua du Nord-Est péruvien.* Paris: Ecole des Hautes Etudes en Sciences Sociales.

Civrieux, M. de
1980   *Watunna: An Orinoco Creation Cycle.* Edited and translated by D. M. Guss. San Francisco: North Point Press.

Colbacchini, A.
1919   *A Tribu dos Boróros.* Rio de Janeiro.
1925   *I Boróros Orientali "Orarimugudoge" del Matto Grosso,
          Brasile.* Contributi scientifici delle Missioni Salesiane del
          Venerabile Don Bosco. Torino, s.d.
Colbacchini, A., and Albisetti, C.
1942   *Os Boróros Orientais.* São Paulo and Rio de Janeiro.
Converse, H. M.
1908   *Myths and Legends of the New York State Iroquois.* New
          York State Museum Bulletin, no. 125. Albany.
Cornplanter, J.
1938   *Legends of the Longhouse.* Philadelphia and New York.
Couto de Magalhães, J. V.
1940   *O Selvagem.* 4th ed. São Paulo and Rio. (First published in
          1876.)
Craydall, L. S.
1964   *The Management of Wild Animals in Captivity.* University
          of Chicago Press.
Curtin, J.
1912   *Myths of the Modocs.* Boston.
Curtin, J., and Hewitt, J. N. B.
1911   *Seneca Fiction, Legends, and Myths.* ARBAE, no. 34.
Curtis, E. S.
1907–30   *The North American Indian.* 20 vols. Norwood, Mass.
Cushing, F. H.
1887   *A Study of Pueblo Pottery as Illustrative of Zuñi Culture
          Growth.* ARBAE, no. 4.
1920   *Zuñi Breadstuff.* INM, no. 7.
Derbyshire, D.
1965   *Textos Hixkaryâna.* Belém-Para, Brazil.
Descola, Ph.
1984   *La Nature domestique: Techniques et symbolisme dans
          l'écologie des Achuar.* Paris. (Multigraph.)
Devereux, G.
1961   *Mohave Ethnopsychiatry and Suicide: The Psychiatric
          Knowledge and the Psychic Disturbances of an Indian
          Tribe.* BBAE, no. 175.
Dixon, R. B.
1908   "Achomavi and Atsugewi Tales." *JAFL,* vol. 21.
1912   *Maidu Texts.* PAES, no. 4. Leiden.

Dorsey, G. A.
1904   *Traditions of the Arikara.* Carnegie Institution of Washington Publications, no. 17.
1906   *The Pawnee. Mythology: Part I.* Id., no. 59.
Dorsey, G. A., and Kroeber, A. L.
1903   *Traditions of the Arapaho.* Field Museum Publications no. 81, Anthropology Series, vol. 5. Chicago.
Dorsey, J. O.
1888   "Abstracts of Omaha and Ponca Myths: Fairies." *JAFL,* vol. 1.
1890   *The Cegiha Language.* CNAE, vol. 6.
1895   *A Study of Siouan Cults.* ARBAE, no. 11.
DuBois, C. G.
1901   "The Mythology of the Diegueños." *JAFL,* vol. 14.
1904a   "Mythology of the Mission Indians." Id., vol. 17.
1904b   "The Story of the Chaup: A Myth of the Diegueños." Id.
1906   "Mythology of the Mission Indians." Id., vol. 19.
1908a   "Ceremonies and Traditions of the Diegueño Indians." Id., vol. 21.
1908b   *The Religion of the Luiseño of Southern California.* UCPAAE, vol. 8, no. 3.
Duviols, P.
1974–76 "Sumaq T'ika ou la dialectique de la dépendance." In G. Dumézil and P. Duviols, "Sumaq T'ika: La Princesse du village sans eau." *JSA,* vol. 63.
Edmonson, M. S.
1971   *The Book of Counsel: The Popol Vuh of the Quiche Maya of Guatemala.* New Orleans: Tulane University Press.
Ehrenreich, P.
1948   "Contribuições para a Etnologia do Brasil." Translated by Egon Schaden. *RMP,* n.s., vol. 2. São Paulo.
Enders, R. K.
1935   *Mammalian Life Histories from Barro Colorado Island, Panama.* Bulletin of the Museum of Comparative Zoology of Harvard University, vol. 78, no. 4.
1940   "Observations on Sloths in Captivity at Higher Altitudes in the Tropics and in Pennsylvania." *Journal of Mammalogy,* vol. 21.
Erikson, E. H.
1943   *Observations on the Yurok: Childhood and World Image.* UCPAAE, vol. 35, no. 10.

Ewers, J. C.
1945   "The Case for Blackfoot Pottery." *AA,* vol. 47, no. 2.

Farabee, W. C.
1922   *Indian Tribes of Eastern Peru.* Papers of the Peabody Museum of American Archaeology and Ethnology, Harvard University, vol. 10. Cambridge, Mass.

1967   *The Central Arawak.* Museum of the University of Pennsylvania, Anthropology Publications, no. 9.

Fenton, W. N.
1953   *The Iroquois Eagle Dance.* BBAE, no. 156.

1962   "This Island, the World on the Turtle's Back." *JAFL,* vol. 75.

Fewkes, J. W.
1919   *Designs on Prehistoric Hopi Pottery.* ARBAE, no. 33.

Fock, N.
1963   *Waiwai: Religion and Society of an Amazonian Tribe.* Nationalmuseets skrifter. Ethnografisk Roekke, no. 8. Copenhagen.

Fontana, Bernard L.; Robinson, William J.; Cormack, Charles W.; and Leavitt, Ernest E., Jr.
1962   *Papago Indian Pottery.* American Ethnological Society Monographs. Seattle.

Foster, G. M.
1955   "Contemporary Pottery Techniques in Southern and Central Mexico." Middle American Research Institute Publications, no. 22. New Orleans: Tulane University Press.

1965   "The Sociology of Pottery: Questions and Hypotheses Arising from Contemporary Mexican Work." In F. R. Matson, ed., *Ceramics and Man.* Viking Fund Publications in Anthropology, no. 41. New York.

Frate, D. A.
1984   "Last of the Earth Eaters." *The Sciences.* New York Academy of Sciences.

Freud, S.
1933   *New Introductory Lectures on Psycho-Analysis.* Translated by W. J. H. Sprott. New York: Norton.

1935   *A General Introduction to Psycho-Analysis.* Authorized English translation of the revised edition by Joan Rivière. New York: Liveright.

1948   *An Autobiographical Study.* Translated by James Strachey. London: Hogarth Press and the Institute for Psycho-Analysis.

1950   *The Question of Lay Analysis*. Translated by Nancy prater-Greg. New York: Norton.

1962   *Totem and Taboo*. Translated by James Strachey. New York: Norton.

1963   *Psychoanalysis and Faith: The Letters of Sigmund Freud and Oskar Pfister*. Edited by Heinrich Meng and Ernst L. Freud. Translated by Eric Mosbacher. London: Hogarth Press and the Institute for Psycho-Analysis.

1964   "The Acquisition and Control of Fire." Translated by James Strachey. Pp. 187–93 in *The Standard Edition of the Complete Psychological Works of Sigmund Freud*, vol. 22. London: Hogarth Press and the Institute for Psycho-Analysis.

Freud, S., and Jung, C. G.

1974   *The Freud-Jung Letters: The Correspondence between Sigmund Freud and C. G. Jung*. Edited by William McGuire. Translated by Ralph Manheim and R. F. C. Hull. Bollingen Series XCIV. Princeton: Princeton University Press.

Frikel, G. P.

1953   "Kamáni." *RMP*, n.s. 7. São Paulo.

Garcia, S.

1935–37   "Mitologia Machiguenga." *Misiones Dominicanas del Peru*, vols. 17–19. Lima.

1942   "Mitologia de los selvajes Machiguengas." *Actas y Trabajos Científicos del 27° Congreso Internacional de Americanistas* [1939]. Lima.

Garcia-Rendueles, M.

1978   "Version primera y segunda del mito de Nunkui en aguaruna y español." *Amazonia Peruana, Mitologia*, vol. 2. Lima.

Gatschet, A. S.

1888   "Fairies: Notes on Creek Dwarfs." *JAFL*, vol. 1.

1890   *The Klamath Indians of South Western Oregon*. CNAE, no. 2.

Gifford, E. W.

1928   *Pottery-making in the Southwest*. UCPAAE, vol. 23, no. 8.

Gillin, J.

1936   *The Barama River Carib of British Guiana*. Papers of the Peabody Museum, vol. 14, no. 2. Cambridge, Mass.

Gimbutas, M.

1981   "Vulvas, Breasts and Buttocks of the Goddess Creatress: Commentary on the Origin of Art." In G. Buccellati and

Ch. Speroni, eds., *The Shape of the Past: Studies in Honor of Franklin D. Murphy.* Berkeley and Los Angeles: University of California Press.

Goeje, C. H. de
1943   "Philosophy, Initiation and Myths of the Indian of Guiana and Adjacent Countries." *Internationales Archiv für Ethnographie,* vol. 44. Leiden.
1946   *Etudes linguistiques caribes.* VKNAW, Afd. Letterkunde, n.s. vol. 49, no. 2.

Goffart, M.
1971   *Function and Form in the Sloth.* Elmsford: Pergamon Press.

Goodwin, G.
1939   *Myths and Tales of the White Mountain Apache.* MAFLS, no. 33.

Grain, J. M.
1957   "Kashiri (historieta lunar)." *Misiones Dominicanas del Peru,* vol. 38. Lima.

Grassé, P. P.
1955   *Traité de zoologie.* Vol. 17, fasc. 2. Paris: Masson.

Greenberg, J.
1956   "A General Classification of Central and South American Languages." Paper Read at the 5th Congress of Anthropology and Ethnology. Philadelphia. (Multigraph.)

Grenand, P.
1980   *Introduction à l'étude de l'univers wayãpi: Ethnoécologie des Indiens du Haut Oyapock (Guyane française).* Paris: SELAF.

Grinnell, G. B.
1892   *Blackfoot Lodge Tales.* New York.

Gullart, J. M.
1958   "Mitos y legendas de los Aguarunas del alto Marañon." *Peru Indigena,* vol. 7, nos. 16–17. Lima.

Haeberlin, H. K.
1924   "Mythology of Puget Sound." *JAFL,* vol. 37.

Harner, M. J.
1962   "Jivaro Souls." *AA,* vol. 64, no. 2.
1977   *Les Jivaros.* Paris: Payot.

Hartt, Ch. F.
1952   *Os Mitos amazônicos da tartaruga.* Translated, with notes, by L. da Camara Cascudo. Recife.

Hearn, L.
1901   *Glimpses of Unfamiliar Japan.* 2 vols. Boston: Houghton Mifflin.

Héritier, F., and Izard, M.
1958   *Aspects humains de l'aménagement hydro-agricole de la vallée du Sourou.* Bordeaux: ISHA.

Hewitt, J. N. B.
1903   *Iroquoian Cosmology.* ARBAE, no. 21.
1928   *Iroquoian Cosmology II.* ARBAE, no. 43.

Hildebrand, E. R. von
1976   "La Manufactura del Budare entre la tribu Tanimuka (Amazonia, Colombia)." *Revista Colombiana de Antropologia,* vol. 20.

Hildebrand, M. von
1975   "Origen del Mundo segun los Ofaina." *Revista Colombiana de Antropologia,* vol. 18.
1979   *Cosmologie et mythologie tanimuka (Amazonie colombienne).* Thèse de 3ᵉ cycle, University of Paris VII. (Multigraph.)

Hissink, K., and Hahn, A.
1961   *Die Tacana. I: Erzählungsgut.* Stuttgart.

Hocart, A. M.
1929   *Lau Islands, Fiji.* Bernice P. Bishop Museum, Bulletin no. 62. Honolulu.

Howry, J. C.
1978   "Ethnographic Realities of Mayan Prehistory." In D. L. Browman, ed. *Cultural Continuity in Mesoamerica.* The Hague and Paris: Mouton.

Hugh Jones, St.
1979   *The Palm and the Pleiades: Initiation and Cosmology in Northwest Amazonia.* Cambridge, Eng.: Cambridge University Press.

Huxley, F.
1956   *Affable Savages.* London: Rupert Hart-Davis.

Ihering, R. von
1940   *Dicionário dos animais do Brasil.* São Paulo.

Jacobs, E. D.
1959   *Nehalem Tillamook Tales.* Eugene, Oregon.

Jacobs, M.
1945   *Kalapuya Texts.* University of Washington Publications in Anthropology, no 11. Seattle.

1959 *Clackamas Chinook Texts.* 2 vols. Publication of the International Journal of American Linguistics.

Jakobson, R., and Waugh, L.

1979 *The Sound Shape of Language.* Bloomington, Ind.: Indiana University Press.

Jesuits

1972 *Relations des* ——. 6 vols. Montreal: Editions du Jour.

Jones, W.

1915 *Kickapoo Tales . . . Translated by T. Michelson.* PAES, no. 9. Leiden and New York.

Josselin de Jong, J. P. B.

1914 *Blackfoot Texts.* VKAWA, Afd. Letterkunde, n.s. vol. 14, no. 4.

Karsten, R.

1923 *Blood Revenge, War, and Victory Feasts among the Jibaro Indians of Eastern Ecuador.* BBAE, no. 79.

1935 *The Head-Hunters of Western Amazonas.* Societas Scientiarum Fennica. Commentationes Humanarum Litterarum, vol. 7, no. 1. Helsingfors.

1967 *The Toba Indians of the Bolivian Gran Chaco.* Acta Academiae Aboensis, Humaniora, vol. 4. Oosterhout N.B.

Kensinger et al.

1975 *The Cashinahua of Eastern Peru.* Haffenreffer Museum of Anthropology, Brown University, Studies in Anthropology and Material Culture, no. 1.

Krieg, H.

1939 "Begegnungen mit Ameisenbären und Faultieren in freier Wildbahn." *Zeitschrift für Tierpsychologie,* vol. 2, no. 3.

1961 "Das Verhalten der Faultiere (Bradypodidae)." In vol. 8 of *Handbuch der Zoologie,* ed. Helmk, von Lengerken, and Stark.

Kroeber, A. L.

1901 "Ute Tales." *JAFL,* vol. 14.

1906 "Two Myths of the Mission Indians of California." Id., vol. 19.

1907 *Gros Ventre Myths and Tales.* APAMNH, vol. 1, no. 2.

1908a "Origin Tradition of the Chemehuevi Indians." *JAFL,* vol. 21.

1908b *Ethnography of the Cahuilla Indians.* UCPAAE, vol. 8, no. 2.

1925 *Handbook of the Indians of California.* BBAE, no. 78.

1948a   "Seven Mohave Myths." *Anthropological Records,* vol. 11, no. 1, Berkeley and Los Angeles: University of California Press.
1948b   *Anthropology.* Rev. ed. New York: Harcourt, Brace.
Kruse, A.
1946–49   "Erzählungen der Tapajoz-Mundurukú." *Anthropos,* vols. 41–44.
La Barre, W.
1980   *Culture in Context.* Durham, N.C.: Duke University Press.
Labiche, E.
1892–94   *Théâtre complet.* 10 vols. Paris: Calmann-Lévy.
1967   *The Italian Straw Hat.* Translated by Frederick Davies. New York: Theatre Arts Books.
Lacarrière, J.
1960   *Sophocle, dramaturge.* Paris: L'Arche.
Latcham, R. E.
1924   *La Organización social y las creencias religiosas de los antigos Araucanos.* Santiago, Chile.
Laughlin, R. M.
1977   *Of Cabbages and Kings: Tales from Zinacantán.* Smithsonian Contributions to Anthropology, no. 23. Washington D.C.
Léger, D.
1981   "L'Engoulevent oiseau-forgeron et oiseau-riziculteur dans le Centre-Vietnam." *Orients.* Paris and Toulouse: Sudestasie-Privat.
Lehmann-Nitsche, R.
1922   "Las Constelaciones del Orión y de las Híadas, etc." *RDMLP,* vol. 26. Buenos Aires.
1927   "El Caprimúlgido con quatro ojos." Id., vol. 30.
1928   "Las tres aves gritonas: Los mitos del Carau, del Crispin y del Urutaú o Cacuy y su origen indigena americano." *Revista de la Universidade de Buenos Aires,* 2d ser.
1930   "El Caprimúlgido y los dos grandes astros." *RDMLP,* vol. 32.
Léry, J. de
1975   *Histoire d'un voyage faict en la terre du Brésil.* Facsimile of 1580 edition. Geneva: Droz.
Lévi-Strauss, C.
1963a   *Structural Anthropology.* Translated by Claire Jacobson and Brooke G. Schoepf. New York: Basic Books.
1963b   *Totemism.* Boston: Beacon Press.

1966   *The Savage Mind.* Chicago: University of Chicago Press.
1969a   *The Elementary Structures of Kinship.* Translated by Rodney Needham. Boston: Beacon Press.
1969b   *The Raw and the Cooked.* Vol. 1 of *Introduction to a Science of Mythology.* [*Mythologiques.*] Translated by John and Doreen Weightman. Chicago: University of Chicago Press.
1973   *From Honey to Ashes.* Vol. 2 of *Introduction to a Science of Mythology.* [*Mythologiques.*] Translated by John and Doreen Weightman. Chicago: University of Chicago Press.
1978   *The Origin of Table Manners.* Vol. 3 of *Introduction to a Science of Mythology.* [*Mythologiques.*] Translated by John and Doreen Weightman. New York: Harper & Row.
1981   *The Naked Man.* Vol. 4 of *Introduction to a Science of Mythology.* [*Mythologiques.*] Translated by John and Doreen Weightman. New York: Harper & Row.
1982   *The Way of the Masks.* Translated by Sylvia Modelski. Seattle: University of Washington Press.
1984   *Paroles données.* Paris: Plon.
Linné, S.
1945   "The Ethnologist and the American Indian Potter." In F. M. Matson, ed., *Ceramics and Man.* Viking Fund Publications in Anthropology, no. 41. New York.
Lockwood, T. E.
1979   "The Ethnobotany of Brugmansia." *Journal of Ethnopharmacology,* vol. 1.
Lounsbury, F. G.
1978   "Iroquoian Languages." In *Handbook of North American Indians,* vol. 15. Washington, D.C.: Smithsonian Institution.
Lowie, R. H.
1909   *The Assiniboine.* APAMNH, no. 4, pt. 1. New York.
McDermott, L.
1901   "Folklore of the Flathead Indians of Idaho." *JAFL,* vol. 14.
McIlwraith, T. F.
1948   *The Bella Coola Indians.* 2 vols. Toronto.
MacNeish, R. S.
1978   "Late Pleistocene Adaptations: A New Look at Early Peopling of the New World as of 1976." *Journal of Anthropological Research,* vol. 34, no. 4.
1982   "A Late Commentary on an Early Subject." In J. Ericson et

al., eds. *Peopling of the New World.* Los Altos: Ballena Press.

Magaña, E.

1982a   "Note on Ethnoanthropological Notions of the Guiana Indians." *Anthropologica,* vol. 24.

1982b   "Hombres salvajes y Razas monstruosas de los Indios Kaliña de Surinam." *Journal of Latin American Lore,* vol 8, no. 1.

Mallery, G.

1887   *Pictographs of the North American Indians: A Preliminary Paper.* ARBAE, no. 4.

1894   *Picture-writing of the American Indians.* ARBAE, no. 10.

Maquet, J. J.

1961   *The Premise of Inequality in Ruanda.* London: Oxford University Press.

Medawar, P. B., and Medawar, J. S.

1983   *From Aristotle to Zoos: A Philosophical Dictionary of Biology.* Cambridge, Mass.: Harvard University Press.

Meggers, B.; Evans, C.; and Estrada, E.

1965   *The Early Formative Period of Coastal Ecuador: The Valdivia and Machalilla Phases.* Washington D.C.: The Smithsonian Institution.

Meggitt, M.

1962   *Desert People.* Sydney: Angus & Robertson.

Métraux, A.

1931   "Mitos y cuentos de los Indios Chiriguano." *RDMLP,* vol. 33. Buenos Aires.

1939   *Myths and Tales of the Matako Indians.* Ethnological Studies, no. 9. Göteborg.

1943   "The Social Organization and Religion of the Mojo and Manasi." *Primitive Man,* vol. 16, nos. 1–2.

1944   "South American Thunderbirds." *JAFL,* vol. 57.

1946a   *Myths of the Toba and Pilagá Indians of the Gran Chaco.* MAFLS, vol. 40. Philadelphia.

1946b   *Ethnography of the Chaco.* BBAE, no. 143.

Michelson, T.

1927   *Contributions to Fox Ethnology.* BBAE, no. 85.

Monod-Becquelin, A.

1975   *La Pratique linguistique des Indiens Trumai.* 2 vols. Paris: SELAF.

Montaigne, M. de

    Essais, bk. III, ch. XI.

Mooney, J.
1900   *Myths of the Cherokee.* ARBAE, no. 19.
Moratto, M. J.
1984   *California Archaeology.* Orlando: Academic Press.
Morley, S. G.
1946   *The Ancient Maya.* Stanford, Calif.: Stanford University Press.
Murphy, R. F.
1958   *Mundurucu Religion.* UCPAAE, vol. 49, no. 1.
Musters, G. Ch.
1872   "On the Races of Patagonia." *Journal of the Royal Anthropological Institute,* vol. 1.
Naranjo, P.
1979   "Hallucinogenic Plant Use and Related Indigenous Belief Systems in the Ecuadorian Amazon." *Journal of Ethnopharmacology,* vol. 1.
Neill, E. D.
1884   "Life among the Mandan and Gros Ventre Eighty Years Ago." *American Antiquarian and Oriental Journal,* vol. 6.
Nicklin, K.
1919   "The Location of Pottery Manufacture." *Man,* vol. 14, no. 3.
Nimuendaju, C.
1919–20   "Bruchstücke aus Religion und Überlieferung der Šipáia Indianer." *Anthropos,* vols. 14–15.
1946a   "The Tucuna." *Handbook of South American Indians.* 7 vols. BBAE, no. 143.
1946b   *The Eastern Timbira.* UCPAAE, no. 41.
1952   *The Tukuna.* UCPAAE, no. 45.
Nino, B. de
1912   *Etnografía chiriguana.* La Paz, Bolivia.
Nordenskiöld, E.
1920   *The Changes in the Material Culture of Two Indian Tribes under the Influence of New Surroundings.* Comparative Ethnographical Studies, no. 2. Göteborg.
1924   *Forschungen und Abenteuer in Südamerika.* Stuttgart: Strecker & Schröder.
Nunberg, H., and Federn, E., eds.
1962–74   *Minutes of the Vienna Psychoanalytic Society.* 4 vols. Translated by M. Nunberg. New York: International Universities Press.

Oosten, J. G.
1983   "The Incest of Sun and Moon." *Etudes Inuit,* vol. 7, no. 1,
            Quebec: Laval University Press.
Opler, M. E.
1940   *Myths and Legends of the Lipan Apache.* MAFLS, no. 36.
1941   *An Apache Life-Way.* Chicago: University of Chicago Press.
1946   "The Mountain Spirits of the Chiricahua Apache." *Master-
            key,* vol. 20.
Orbigny, A. d'
1935–37   *Voyage dans l' Amérique méridionale.* 9 vols. Paris.
Orico, O.
1929   *Os Mythos amerindios.* Rio de Janeiro and São Paulo: Edi-
            tora Ltda.
1937   *Vocabulario de Crendices Amazonicas.* São Paulo and
            Rio de Janeiro: Cⁱᵃ Editora Nacional.
Ortiz-Gomez, F.
1983   *Organisation sociale et mythologie des Indiens Cuiba et
            Sikuani (Guahíbo), Llanos de Colombie.* Thèse de 3ᵉ
            cycle, EHESS. (Multigraph.)
Parker, A. C.
1912a   *The Code of Handsome Lake, the Seneca Prophet.* New
            York State Museum Bulletin, no. 163. Albany.
1912b   "Certain Iroquois Tree Myths and Symbols." *AA,* vol. 14.
Parsons, E. C.
1916   "The Zuñi Łámana." *AA,* vol. 18.
Pellizzaro, S.
n.d.   *Etsa Defensor de los Shuar.* Mundo Shuar, Ser. F, no. 6.
            Sucua.
1978   *Nunkui.* Id., no. 8.
1980a   *Ayumpúm: Mitos de la Cabeça cortada.* Id., no. 5.
1980b   *Tsantsa: Celebracion de la Cabeça cortada.* Id., no. 9.
1982   *Etsa: El Modelo del hombre shuar.* Id., Mitologia shuar,
            no. 7.
Penteado Coelho, V.
1984   "Historias Waurá." *Publicações do Museu Municipal de
            Paulinia,* no. 27.
Pereira, F.
1942   "Legendas Machiguengas." *Revista del Museo Nacional,*
            vol. 11, no. 2. Lima.
Petrullo, V.
1939   *The Yaruros of the Capanaparo River, Venezuela.* Bureau

of American Ethnology, Anthropological Papers, no. 11.
Washington, D.C.

Phinney, A.
1934   *Nez Percé Texts.* CUCA, no. 25. New York.

Posener, G.
1959   *Dictionnaire de la civilisation égyptienne.* Paris: Hazan.

Posinsky, S. H.
1957   "The Problem of Yurok Anality." *American Imago,* vol. 14, no. 1.

Powell, J. W.
1881   "Sketch of the Mythology of the North American Indians." *ARBAE,* no. 1.

Preuss, K. Th.
1919–26   "Forschungsreise zu den Kagaba." *Anthropos,* vol. 14, no. 21.

Radcliffe-Brown, A. R.
1948   *The Andaman Islanders.* Glencoe, Ill.: Free Press. (First published, 1922.)

Rand, S. T.
1894   *Legends of the Micmacs.* New York and London.

Ratcliffe, F.
1963   *Flying Fox and Drifting Sand.* Sydney: Angus & Robertson.

Ray, V. F.
1963   *Primitive Pragmatists: The Modoc Indians of Northern California.* Seattle.

Recinos, A.
1950   *Popol Vuh: The Sacred Book of the Ancient Quiché Maya. English version by D. Goetz and S. G. Morley from the Translation of Adrián Recinos.* Norman: University of Oklahoma Press.

Reichard, G. A.
1947   *An Analysis of Coeur d' Alene Indian Myths.* MAFLS, no. 41.

Reichel-Dolmatoff, G.
1968   *Desana: Simbolismo de los Indios Tukano del Vaupés.* Bogotá: University of the Andes.
1978   "Desana Animal Categories, Food Restrictions, and the Concept of Color Energies." *Journal of Latin American Lore,* vol. 4, no. 2.

Riggs, S. R.
1890   *A Dakota-English Dictionary.* CNAE, no. 7.

Riley, C. L.
1952   "The Blowgun in the New World." *SWJA*, vol. 8, no. 3.
Ritchie Key, M.
1978a   "The History and Distribution of the Indigenous Languages of Bolivia." Paper presented at the American Anthropological Association, 77th Annual Meeting, Los Angeles. (Multigraph.)
1978b   "Araucanian Genetic Relationship." *International Journal of American Linguistics*, vol. 44, no. 4.
Ritchie Key, M., and Clairis, Chr.
1978c   "Fuegian and Central South American Language Relationships." *Actes du 42ᵉ Congrès International des Américanistes* (1976), vol. 4. Paris.
Rivet, P., and Rochereau, H. J.
1929   "Nociones sobre creencias, usos y costumbres de los Catios del Occidente de Antioquia." *JSA*, vol. 21.
Robbins, Ch. S.; Bruun, B.; and Zim, H. S.
1966   *A Guide to Field Identification: Birds of North America.* New York: Golden Press.
Rodrigues, J. Barbosa
1890   *Poranduba Amazonense.* Anais da Biblioteca Nacional de Rio de Janeiro, vol. 14 (1886–87), fasc. 2.
1899   *O Muyrakytã e os idolos symbolicos: Estudo da origem asiatica da civilização do Amazonas no tempos prehistoricos.* 2 vols. Rio de Janeiro.
Roheim, G.
1950   *Psychoanalysis and Anthropology.* New York: International Universities Press.
Roth, W. E.
1915   *An Inquiry into the Animism and Folklore of the Guiana Indians.* ARBAE, no. 30.
Rueda, M. V.
1983   *Setenta Mitos shuar recogidos por R. Tankamash.* Quito, Ecuador: Mundo Shuar.
Russell, F.
1908   *The Pima Indians.* ARBAE, no. 26.
Saake, W.
1958   "Die Juruparilegende bei den Baniwa des Rio Issana." *Proceedings of the 32nd Congress of Americanists (1956).* Copenhagen.

Sablott, J. A., and Rathje, W. L.
1975   "The Rise of a Maya Merchant Class." *Scientific American,*
         vol. 233, no. 4.
Sagard, G.
1636   *Histoire du Canada.* 4 vols. Paris.
Sahagun, B. de
1950–63 *Florentine Codex: General History of the Things of New
         Spain.* In 13 parts. Translated by A. J. O. Anderson and
         C. E. Dibble. Santa Fé, N.M.
Sales, A. de
1981   "La Relation forgeron-chaman chez les Yakoutes de Sibé-
         rie." *L'Homme,* vol. 21, no. 4.
Sapir, E.
1910   "Song Recitative in Paiute Mythology." *JAFL,* vol. 23.
1968   *Selected Writings of—in Language, Culture, and Person-
         ality.* Edited by D. G. Mandelbaum. Berkeley and Los An-
         geles: University of California Press.
Sapir, E., and Spier, L.
1903   *Wishram Ethnography.* University of Washington Publica-
         tions in Anthropology, no. 3. Seattle.
Sauer, C. O.
1950   "Cultivated Plants of South and Central America." *Hand-
         book of South American Indians.* 7 vols. BBAE, no. 143.
Schaden, E.
1963   "Caracteres especificos da cultura Mbüa-Guarani." *Re-
         vista de Antropologia,* vol. 2, nos. 1–2. São Paulo.
Schaeffer, C. E.
1950   "Bird Nomenclature and Principles of Avian Taxonomy of
         the Blackfeet Indians." *Journal of the Washington Acad-
         emy of Sciences,* vol. 40.
Schomburgk, R.
1922   *Travels in British Guiana, 1840–1844.* Translated and
         edited by W. E. Roth. 2 vols. Georgetown.
Schultz, H.
1964   "Informações etnográficas sôbre os Umutina (1943, 1944
         e 1945)." *RMP,* n.s. vol. 13.
Schultz, H., and Chiara, V.
1973   "Mais Lendas Waura." *JSA,* vol. 60.
Seeger, A.
1977   "Fixed Points on Arcs and Circles: The Temporal, Pro-
         cessual Aspect of Suyá Space and Society." *Actes du 42^e
         Congrès International des Américanistes,* vol. 2. Paris.

1981   *Nature and Society in Central Brazil: The Suyá Indians of Mato Grosso.* Cambridge, Mass.: Harvard University Press.

Seler, E.
1961   *Gesammelte Abhandlungen zur Amerikanischen Sprach- und Altertumskunde.* 5 vols. Graz: Akademische Druck und Verlagsanstalt.

Skinner, A.
1916   "Plains Cree Tales." *JAFL,* vol. 29.
1921   *Material Culture of the Menomini.* INM.

Skinner, A., and Satterlee, J. V.
1915   *Folklore of the Menomini Indians.* APAMNH, vol. 13, no. 3.

Smith, E. A.
1884   *Myths of the Iroquois.* ARBAE, no. 2.

Sophocles
1959   *Oedipus Rex.* Translated by David Grene. In *The Complete Greek Tragedies,* edited by David Grene and Richmond Lattimore, vol. 2. Chicago: University of Chicago Press.

Soustelle, J.
1979   *L'Univers des Aztèques.* Paris: Hermann.
1982   *Les Maya.* Paris: Flammarion.

Sparkman, Ph. S.
1908   *The Culture of the Luiseño Indians.* UCPAAE, vol. 8, no. 4.

Speck, F. G.
1921   "Bird-Lore of the Northern Indians." *Public Lectures of the University of Pennsylvania,* vol. 7.
1928   *Native Tribes and Dialects of Connecticut: A Mohegan-Pequot Diary.* ARBAE, no. 43.
1935   "Penobscot Tales and Religious Beliefs." *JAFL,* vol. 48.
1938   "The Cane Blowgun in Catawba and Southeastern Ethnology." *AA,* vol. 40.
1946   "Bird Nomenclature and Song Interpretation of the Canadian Delaware: An Essay in Ethno-Ornithology." *Journal of the Washington Academy of Sciences,* vol. 36, no. 8.

Spier, L.
1923   "Southern Diegueño Customs." UCPAAE, no. 20.

Spruce, R.
1908   *Notes of a Botanist on the Amazon and Andes.* 2 vols. London.

Stephen, A. M.
1936   *Hopi Journal.* Edited by E. C. Parsons. 2 vols. CUCA, no. 23.
Stevenson, M. C.
1905   *The Zuñi Indians: Their Mythology, Esoteric Fraternities, and Ceremonies.* ARBAE, no. 23.
Stirling, M. W.
1938   *Historical and Ethnographical Material on the Jivaro Indians.* BBAE, no. 17.
Stradelli, E.
1890   "L'Uaupés e gli Uaupés. Leggenda dell'Jurupary." *Bolletino della Società geografica Italiana,* no. 3. Rome.
Strong, W. D.
1929   *Aboriginal Society in Southern California.* UCPAAE, no. 26.
Suárez, J. A.
1973   "Macro-Pano-Tacanan." *International Journal of American Linguistics,* vol. 39, no. 3.
Swanton, J. R.
1905–9   *Contributions to the Ethnology of the Haida.* Jesup North Pacific Expedition. MAMNH, vol. 5, no. 1.
1929   *Myths and Tales of the Southeastern Indians.* BBAE, no. 88.
1938   "John Napoleon Brinton Hewitt." *AA,* vol. 40.
Tastevin, C.
1925   "La Légende de Bóyusú en Amazonie." *Revue d'Ethnographie et des traditions populaires,* vol. 6, no. 22.
1926   "Le Haut Tarauacá." *La Géographie,* vol. 45.
Teale, E. Way
1965   "'Sleeping One' of the Hopis." *Natural History,* vol. 74, no. 10.
Teit, J. A.
1930   *The Salishan Tribes of the Western Plateaus.* ARBAE, no. 45.
Teschauer, C.
1925   *Avifauna e flora nos costumes, superstições e lendas brasileiras e americanas.* 3d ed. Porto Alegre.
Thévet, A.
1568   *The New Found VVorlde, or Antarctike, wherin is contained wöderful and strange things. . . .* London.
Thompson, J. E.
n.d.   *La Semilla del Mundo: Legendas de los Indios Maquiritares en el Amazonas Venezolano.* (Multigraph.)

Thompson, J. Eric S.
1970   *Maya History and Religion.* Norman, Okla.
Thompson, L. C., and Thompson, M. T.
1972   "Language Universals, Nasals, and the Northwest Coast."
          In *Studies in Linguistics in Honor of G. L. Trager.* The
          Hague.
Thompson, S.
1929   *Tales of the North American Indians.* Cambridge, Mass.:
          Harvard University Press.
Ulloa, Don A., and Juan, Don J.
1748   *Relación historica del viaje a la America.* Madrid.
Van Tyne, J.
1929   "Notes on the Habits of *Cyclopes dorsalis.*" *Journal of
          Mammalogy,* vol. 10, no. 4.
Vega, G. de la
1737   *Histoire des Yncas rois du Pérou.* Amsterdam.
Verissimo, J.
1886   *Scenas da vida amazonica.* Lisbon.
Vernant, J.-P., and Vidal-Naquet, P.
1981   *Tragedy and Myth in Ancient Greece.* Translated by Janet
          Lloydd. Atlantic Highlands, N.J.: Humanities Press.
Viertler, R. B.
1979   "A Noção de pessoa entre os Bororo." *Boletim do Museu
          Nacional, Antropologia,* no. 32. Rio de Janeiro.
Vogt, C.
1884   *Les Mammifères.* Paris: Masson.
Voltaire
1764   *Commentaires sur Corneille: Remarques concernant
          "Horace" (Acte III, scène I).* In *Œuvres complètes,* vol. 31.
          Paris: Garnier, 1880.
Wagley, Ch.
1940   "World View of the Tapirapé Indians." *JAFL,* vol. 53.
Wagley, Ch., and Galvão, E.
1949   *The Tenetehara Indians of Brazil.* CUCA, no. 35.
Wagner, C. P.
1967   *Defeat of the Bird God.* Grand Rapids, Mich.: Zondervan.
Walker, J. R.
1917   *The Sun Dance and Other Ceremonies of the Oglala Divi-
          sion of the Teton Dakota.* APAMNH, vol. 16, no. 2.
Wallace, A. R.
1889   *A Narrative of Travels on the Amazon and Rio Negro.*
          London.

Wallis, W. D.
1923   "Beliefs and Tales of the Canadian Dakota." *JAFL*, vol. 36.
Waterman, T. T.
1909   "Analysis of the Mission Indians Creation Story." *AA*, vol. 11.
Wavrin, marquis de
1937   *Moeurs et coutumes des Indiens sauvages de l' Amérique du Sud.* Paris: Payot.
Weiss, G.
1972   "Campa Cosmology." *Ethnology*, vol. 11.
1975   *Campa Cosmology: The World of a Forest Tribe in South America.* APAMNH, vol. 52, no. 5.
Whiffen, Th.
1915   *The North-West Amazons.* London.
White, R. C.
1957   "The Luiseño Theory of Knowledge." *AA*, vol. 59.
Wilbert, J.
1962   "Erzählgut der Yupa-Indianer." *Anthropos*, vol. 57, nos. 3–6.
1963   *Indios de la Region Orinoco Ventuari.* Fundacion La Salle de Ciencias Naturales, Monograph no. 8. Caracas, Venezuela.
1970   *Folk Literature of the Warao Indians.* Latin American Studies, no. 15. Los Angeles: University of California Latin American Center.
1974   *Yupa Folktales.* Los Angeles: University of California Latin American Center.
1984   *Folk Literature of the Tehuelche Indians.* Latin American Studies, no. 59. Los Angeles: University of California Latin American Center.
Wissler, C., and Duvall, D. C.
1908   *Mythology of the Blackfoot Indians.* APAMNH, vol. 2.
Witthoft, J.
1946   "Bird Lore of the Eastern Cherokee." *Journal of the Washington Academy of Sciences,* vol. 36.
Witthoft, J., and Hadlock, W. S.
1946   "Cherokee-Iroquois Little People." *JAFL*, vol. 59.

Acknowledgments

*

My thanks go to Sonia Schmerl, Peter Kupfer, James Tucker, and Gerald Root for their help in editing this translation. I wish above all to thank Claude Lévi-Strauss for his unfailing patience in answering my queries and for reviewing the manuscript.

BÉNEDICTE CHORIER
December 1987